TELEVISED REDEMPTION

Muhammad Speaks, December 1964. "This here is one of our best ministers. . . . You shouldn't throw away truth. If no one will buy it, just take it back home and give it away." Elijah Muhammad discussing the value of the Nation of Islam newspaper (quoted in "The Messenger of Allah Speaks on the Importance of the Muhammad Speaks Newspaper," *Nation of Islam's Women Committed to Preserving the Truth*, www.noiwc.org).

Televised Redemption

Black Religious Media and Racial Empowerment

Carolyn Moxley Rouse,
John L. Jackson, Jr., *and*
Marla F. Frederick

NEW YORK UNIVERSITY PRESS

New York

NEW YORK UNIVERSITY PRESS
New York
www.nyupress.org

References to Internet websites (URLs) were accurate at the time of writing. Neither the author nor New York University Press is responsible for URLs that may have expired or changed since the manuscript was prepared.

Library of Congress Cataloging-in-Publication Data
Names: Rouse, Carolyn Moxley, 1965– author.
Title: Televised redemption : Black religious media and racial empowerment /
Carolyn Moxley Rouse, John L. Jackson, Jr., and Marla F. Frederick.
Description: New York : NYU Press, 2016. | Includes bibliographical references and index.
Identifiers: LCCN 2016023929| ISBN 978-1-4798-7603-7 (cl : alk. paper) |
ISBN 978-1-4798-1817-4 (pb : alk. paper)
Subjects: LCSH: African Americans—Religion. | Religion on television. |
Television broadcasting—Religious aspects. |
Television in religion—United States.
Classification: LCC BR563.N4 R68 2016 | DDC 200.89/96—dc23
LC record available at https://lccn.loc.gov/2016023929

New York University Press books are printed on acid-free paper, and their binding materials are chosen for strength and durability. We strive to use environmentally responsible suppliers and materials to the greatest extent possible in publishing our books.

Manufactured in the United States of America

10 9 8 7 6 5 4 3 2 1

Also available as an ebook

CONTENTS

ACKNOWLEDGMENTS

This book would have been impossible without the incredible generosity of the many interlocutors with whom the three of us have worked over the years. Thanks to all the people who have graciously and courageously allowed us to examine their spiritual/religious beliefs and practices in our attempt to understand Africana religio-political possibility. Thank you for your time, meals, rides, and spare rooms. You were our teachers. Thank you, Jennifer Hammer at New York University Press for being willing to work with us on this project—and for always providing us with valuable feedback and encouragement. Thank you, Constance Grady and Alexia Traganas for your stewardship bringing the book to press. And thanks to the anonymous readers who helped us revise and clarify some of our claims. Diana Burnett, Carleigh Beriont, and Jasmine Reid helped us to prepare the final draft of this manuscript for submission. Thank you for your meticulous efforts. Finally, we want to thank our families, colleagues, and friends, whose counsel, company, and feedback have been critical throughout.

Introduction

In *Plessy v. Ferguson*, the 1896 Supreme Court case affirming the legality of racial segregation in the United States, Justice Henry Billings Brown made a most extraordinary claim in his draft of the majority opinion. His legal argument was predicated on the belief that racism is natural and, therefore, not something the courts can effectively adjudicate:

> Legislation is powerless to eradicate racial instincts or to abolish distinctions based upon physical differences, and the attempt to do so can only result in accentuating the difficulties of the present situation. If the civil and political rights of both races be equal, one cannot be inferior to the other civilly or politically. If one race be inferior to the other socially, the Constitution of the United States cannot put them upon the same plane.[1]

In the long, drawn-out march toward full citizenship, African Americans have had to push back against what Brown called "racial instincts."[2] Defined by strong dispositions and taboos marking black and white bodies as fundamentally discrete and antagonistic, beliefs about racial inferiority and superiority have proven difficult to unlearn. In this respect, Justice Brown was right: political and civil rights are not necessarily transferable to social rights. African Americans have known, since the first slaves learned to speak the master's language and worship by way of the master's religion, that the battle for equality had to take place on at least two fronts—that of the law and the popular imagination. To be seen as fully human, and therefore deserving of equal legal protections and rights, African Americans had to repurpose the master's rhetorical tools to prove that blacks were endowed by God with the same gifts of reason, goodness, and free will that whites boasted. As the last three hundred years have shown, this has been no easy task, but African Americans have excelled at understanding the political, existential, and intellectual machinery often intended to marginalize and oppress. Well before Emancipation, Negroes had already translated a white supremacist reading of Christianity into a gospel of unabashed freedom and transcendence. As an early nineteenth-century white clergyman noted, somewhat painfully, in the Baptist periodical the *Religious Herald*, "Many of the blacks look upon white people as merely taught by the Book; they consider themselves instructed by the inspiration of the Spirit."[3]

Humanization necessitated struggles over representation and recognition. Blacks had to find a way to write their own stories, define their own identities, and rearticulate concepts of justice in light of human difference.[4] And they did. Taking control of black representation has been a central feature of black transformative praxis from antislavery and anticolonial movements to Black Lives Matter. Citizenship for blacks was forged out of what Cornel West describes as collective insurgency articulated through art and discourse.[5] Legislative and legal reforms were critical, but the cultural work of changing hearts and minds required a different approach. Disrupting learned racial instincts has meant the purposeful mobilization of theater, fiction, music, poetry, visual arts, dance, film, television, and now digital social media, targeted to the largest possible audiences. What these aesthetic renderings of alternative truths have done is reassemble racial, ethical, religious, historical, and cultural narratives in ways that denaturalize white supremacist commonsense. What emerges in these mediated spaces are challenges to dehistoricized notions of race and difference that, as Stuart Hall notes, move "us into a new kind of cultural positionality, a different logic of difference."[6]

Slavery, Jim Crow, convict leasing, and mass incarceration were all predicated on the idea that blacks were less intelligent, less moral, and less capable of pro-social behavior despite overwhelming evidence to the contrary. Notably, *commonsenseness*, a term capturing how we see our cultural beliefs as natural and irrefutable facts, continues to be the way by which black inferiority is made real. In hindsight, Justice Brown's argument that racism is *instinctually just* seems outrageous—at least it should. As a cultural process, race-making remains, for most, hidden in plain sight. As a result, race as a category of difference is naturalized and dehistoricized, with the construction of whiteness representing a vivid case in point.[7] When we forget where feelings about race come from, they shape institutional outcomes even without active intention and create "racism without racists," as sociologist Eduardo Bonilla-Silva has labeled it.[8] If we trace education, health, wealth, and incarceration disparities to these unmarked norms, we can recognize how assumptions about biological and cultural difference impact the ways in which people are treated and defined.

The dehumanization and reclassification of blacks as fundamentally different and/or inferior did not end with the Supreme Court's 1954 *Brown v. the Board of Education* desegregation ruling. Some writers continue to argue that genes and behavior mark clear borders between races, while others use "culture of poverty" arguments to explain contemporary racial inequalities of outcome and possibility.[9] Many of these same writers are housed in elite think tanks and academic institutions, and often contribute to newspaper op-eds and television news talk shows. Notably, racial commonsense has continued to animate political discourse well into the twenty-first century, even though the majority of social scientists understand race to be a product of history as opposed to biology or cultural pathology. Regardless of how many Americans consider "the race question" settled in the United States, for the religious communities considered in this book, the project of redeeming the race through media has continued to be an urgent priority.

The purpose of this book is to demonstrate the powerful role black religious media has had since the eighteenth century in not only marking unmarked racial norms, but in altering racial instinct. Black religious media continues to challenge the taken-for-granted notions of white and European superiority not from a position of science and reason, but from a position of morality and justice. It has been central in humanizing African Americans, such that by the twenty-first century, around 40 percent of white voters chose a black president. We certainly do not argue that the election of a black president has marked an end point in the trajectory toward a "post-racial" America. Instead this book focuses on what black religious media has done to open a space for reconsidering what race means and for promoting racial justice.

Most historical representations of the struggles for racial justice avoid discussions of the critical subjective work required to change minds. Our goal as anthropologists in this book has been to unearth the motivations for the radical attitudinal changes toward race and racial identity in the last three hundred years. These subjective dispositions are often lost to history, but we aimed to recover them by working backward. For us this meant methodologically starting with our conversations in the field and then moving in reverse to recover the texts, images, and sounds that led to the three traditions we focus on in this book: Christian prosperity ministry, African American Islamic consciousness, and black Hebrew Israelite reframings of race and belonging. By juxtaposing three different religious outlooks and their histories, we show that black identity, in part defined by identification with the past, has never been one thing. We selected Christianity, Islam, and Judaism because they represent the three Abrahamic faiths and the dominant religions among African Americans in the United States. We set out to describe what religious media was doing to viewers or listeners to change how they felt about themselves and the world. [10]

In this book, we employ anthropological theory and ethnographic methods to understand how African Americans continue to try to break free of what Edward P. Jones, in his Pulitzer Prize–winning novel, describes as *The Known World*.[11] For centuries African Americans have had to develop, for lack of a better term, a code, or language, for understanding and articulating the ineffable. Oppression and its sources have not always been obvious, and therefore it is through stories, icons, tropes, and signifiers that African Americans have found a way to mediate their experiences with racism. But African Americans continue to challenge "the known world" of common sense. The racial instincts Justice Brown wrote about were so powerful that for many whites, taking a child to a lynching was considered a valuable education. In anthropology we write about the role of disgust and notions of filth in the development of concepts of the self. We also study taboos delineating that which is human from that which is animal; that which is clean versus that which is dirty. We are interested in dirt or matter out of place because it helps us to think about how societies map the distance between, in the words of Mary Douglas, "purity and danger."[12] Given what we know about cultural notions of purity and danger, the Civil Rights Act of 1964 should not be understood simply as a moment when white people came to their senses. Taboos regarding race are powerful, particularly those imprinted in childhood, and are as difficult to let go of as taboos against eating certain foods or proscriptions around caste and first cousin marriage.

We started with the assumption that a belief about racial inferiority is often as powerful as a sense of disgust. Thus, the emotional and cognitive work necessary to change minds about race rarely comes from a place of cold rational logic. The idea that slavery or racism was wrong required, for some, a complete reframing of that aforementioned known world. Whites had to have a "come to Jesus" moment. This moment could be proceeded by the simple recognition that the black nanny who fed and loved you had to be one of God's children, or that the black child you played with, who learned everything as well as you did, could not possibly be intellectually inferior. While the role intimacy plays in challenging racism is important, in this book we focus on the mass-mediated images, words, and sounds that ultimately compelled a "come to Jesus" moment for blacks as well as whites.

For this book, the media on which we chose to focus had the power to effect radical dispositional changes in the consumer. We determined this power through interviews with our interlocutors and observations at our field-sites. We then traced media that inspired an epiphany in our interlocutors to historical touchstones marking the development of the concepts framing contemporary media. For the historical analysis we had to do our best to assess the affective impact of the media. Often that required being attentive not only to what was explicitly articulated in religious media, but to the nonverbal as well, including the multiple explanation points and capital letters in David Walker's 1829 *Appeal*, an impassioned articulation of the rights of black people to physically defend themselves in the face of oppression, and the depictions in advertisements and cartoons in *Muhammad Speaks*, the official journal of the Nation of Islam.[13] Ultimately, our goal has been to make visible the extraordinary labor and conceptual brilliance that has gone into trying to articulate a postcolonial blackness that effectively counters racism. In addition to locating the emergence of a common consciousness, the study of black religious media also exposes the schisms and ruptures within what outsiders often denote as "*the* black community." American history textbooks often begin African American history at the point at which black bodies were unloaded on docks and placed on auction blocks, and then bracket that history with Martin Luther King, Jr., who, with Lyndon B. Johnson's extraordinary leadership and compassion, is believed to have put all this racist nonsense to rest. Missing from much of these histories are narratives of blacks as subjects rather than objects of history—as victims *and* perpetrators shaping social realities rather than merely victims of social forces beyond their control.

This book focuses on the struggles—undeniably contentious—over how to represent blackness. Throughout African American history, religious leaders, intellectuals, and business leaders have been at odds about the meaning of blackness, and more critically about precisely *which* representation of blackness would most likely compel the state to provide equal rights and protections. And the disputes were often ugly. Some black leaders believed, and still believe, that poor and morally loose blacks were the cause of continued black oppression. Others believed in colonialism as a redemptive project and traveled to West Africa and the Congo to save savages and reap financial rewards. In the late twentieth century, some black religious leaders turned their back on Martin Luther King, Jr., when he began to focus on poverty, and others failed to preach against mass incarceration or note the staggering spread of HIV/AIDS in the black community. The moral ambiguity of the victims—the poor, the convicted, and the diseased—threatened the redemptive narrative they were trying to tell. Historically, creating a politically viable representation of blackness that has the power to redeem the race and effect real social change has been met by more failure than success.

What we find in the early media is success in capturing the imagination of some but not enough people, or enough people but at a time when the structures were not in place for large-scale change to take place. And often the effectiveness of a message promoted by a particular group was unrelated to the number of people professing the faith. For example, membership in the Nation of Islam, at its peak in the 1960s, was dwarfed by the number of African American Sunni Muslims in the 1990s. Yet the impact of the Nation of Islam's rhetoric and social praxis far exceeds the impact of African American Sunni Islam. Regardless of momentary effectiveness or ineffectiveness, throughout the longue durée of African American history, black religious media has been central to ongoing efforts to open up a space for black citizenship.

Over the last three hundred years religious media has successfully humanized folks such that the concept of black inferiority has gone from being acceptable to being taboo; from being used as a rationale by the highest court in the land to being associated with racist trolls on social media. This volume makes visible the labor that has gone into dismantling the master's house from the perspective of those often marked merely as hapless victims. Far from being passive in the struggle for black citizenship, African American media producers have performed the arduous semiotic and discursive work necessary to make civil rights happen long before the famous March on Washington in 1963. And the work continues today as black folks continue to try to disrupt commonsense.

The fact that in 2015 the killing of nine African American Christians in Charleston, South Carolina, led to the symbolic end of the American Civil War through the decision to finally remove the Confederate flag from state grounds was no accident.[14] The victims could have been eulogized as a group unlucky to be at the wrong place at the wrong time, thus allowing the South to once again leave discussions about the Confederate flag for another day. Instead, the victims were identified as descendents of a long line of black Christians sacrificed in order for the United States to fulfill its providential role as the land of equality. Their martyrdom was comprehensible because black religion has mediated the relationship between whites and blacks for centuries. Not only has it worked to reverse the narrative of white supremacy, but it also translates black experience in ways that make it intelligible to others. As a result, the massacre of a Bible study group and media reaction to that tragedy did the work that hundreds of political speeches could not. To be clear, black religious media includes not only media produced by black religious groups but also media produced by others about the black religious experience. And the stakes of this media are high.

As an example of the power of black religious media, we can consider Al Qaeda's use of the iconic imagery and rhetoric of Malcolm X to justify their anti-Obama stance. Their appropriation of this Nation of Islam leader's speech demonstrates the global impact African American religious media has had on what might be called "georacial" formations and contemporary postcolonial politics.[15] Fifteen days after the election of Barack Obama as the first black president of the United States, Al Qaeda's news organization released a video, a missive to the incoming president-elect, characterizing him as little more than a "house negro." This derogatory term—akin, in many ways, to the pejorative "Uncle

Figure I.1 Al Qaeda leader Ayman Al-Zawahiri commenting on the 2008 election of United States President Barack Obama, whom he casts as a dishonorable black man in contradistinction to Malcolm X.

Tom"—has been used to differentiate traditional "race men" within the African American community from would-be race traitors and sell-outs. House slaves and field slaves had a different relationship to slavery, the argument goes, and that difference pivots on their investment in the "peculiar institution."[16] The video depicts Malcolm X proclaiming:

> There were two kinds of Negroes. There was that old house Negro and the field Negro. And the house Negro always looked after his master. When the field Negro got too much out of line, he held him back in check. He put him back on the plantation. The house Negro could afford to do that because he lived better than the field Negro. He ate better, he dressed better, and he lived in a better house . . . And he loved his master more than his master loved himself. But then you had the field Negroes who lived in huts, had nothing to lose. They wore the worst kind of clothes, they ate the worst food, and they caught hell. They felt the sting of the lash. They hated their master . . . And today you still have house Negroes and field Negroes. I'm a field Negro.[17]

The use of Malcolm X's house versus field Negro dichotomy provides a partial clue about whom Al Qaeda was trying to reach. The visuals they used tell even more of the story. A triptych dominates their eleven-minute video. The panel on the left contains an image of Obama wearing a yarmulke at the Wailing Wall in Jerusalem. The two Jews on either side of him in the image are meant to prove that Obama has no loyalty to the religion of his father. The middle panel contains a photo of Al Qaeda's then number two leader, Ayman Al-Zawahiri, dressed in white and seated in front of a bookcase containing numerous volumes of hadith and secondary Qur'anic texts. The books, white turban, and prayer bump, or zabiba, all signifying his commitment to prayer, represent Al-Zawahiri as a pious scholar of the faith. The right-hand panel contains the iconic image of Malcolm X in Mecca on his knees in prayer. The house Negro/field Negro distinction is rendered in stark relief on opposite sides of that triptych, with Al-Zawahiri personifying the dispassionate arbiter and literal mediator of this seemingly simple truth.

The video was less an effort to insult Obama than an audacious attempt to undercut his potential influence in the Muslim world. Obama's nomination disrupted some of the rhetoric that justified Al Qaeda's violence. The easy binaries that had been used by the network to recruit new members—good/bad, subjugated other/Western imperialist, brown/white, Muslim/infidel—were now complicated by the election of an African American man born to a Muslim Kenyan. In order to reignite hatred for the West, now embodied in a black man, Al Qaeda mobilized Malcolm X's image and speech as rhetorical evidence for the claim that Obama served the interests of powerful Western masters. Obama, the video warns, is an old-school imperialist who will protect the interests of Israel and the West over those of the world's weak and oppressed. At the global level, black Western imperialists were rebranded as house Negroes writ large. Mimicking the projects of Malcolm X (who also went by the name Malik al-Shabazz) and the Nation of Islam in the 1960s, Al Qaeda used media to make a point about appropriate racial sincerity.[18] As Zawahiri's voice over notes, "You represent the direct opposite of honorable black Americans like Malik al-Shabazz, or Malcolm X (may Allah have mercy on him)."[19]

While it may not be surprising that Al Qaeda tried to make a case about Obama being a lapdog for others' interests, it is instructive that they chose to appropriate the words and images of Malcolm X in order to energize that claim. Indeed, the fugitive producers of this anti-America video seemed to believe that they knew Barack Obama (and/or "black America" and/or black America's appreciation for figures like Barack Obama and Malcolm X). And they came to this understanding through the mass-mediated iconography of black religious media from the 1960s. The idea that one can know "the other" through mass-mediated consumption is fascinating, and it grounds one of the central concerns of this book.

The question of how African Americans have defined themselves, defined others, and been defined through electronic and digital mass mediation is at the center of our analysis. Racism is often characterized as a form of misrecognition, and religious media attempts to make blacks recognizable not only to others, but to themselves as well. Working against racist forms of misrecognition, religious media has been used to write blacks into moral narratives in which God bestows salvation on African Americans re-enlightened as to God's true will. Separating agency from essence, the Abrahamic traditions have been used to argue that consciousness, intention, and action trump the physical body, which is indeed, but not in deed, black. In this redemptive media, race is treated as an artifact, not the essence of one's being, thereby allowing free will to be the necessary precursor for full membership into humanity. This book focuses specifically on black religious media because it has transformed black subjectivity both by providing black Americans with new conceptual and practical tools for how to be in the world and by changing how black people are made intelligible and recognizable as moral citizens. Religious media has challenged some of the very ways in which race has historically been articulated, producing political possibilities that have yet to be fully replicated by "secular" movements. In this book, we examine how religious media deploys new forms of racialized thinking to interrupt particular genealogies of race-based exclusion and derogation.

Like language, mass media reconciles us to the social and natural world and can literally mediate our every waking hour. We are trained to interpet mass media in ways that can sometimes be strikingly similar to the ways in which we are taught to speak and read. Stories are replaced by iconography or terminology that then acts as a self-evident kind of shorthand. Media signifiers condense narratives about value, meaning, history, and the future into symbols and words that can easily be deployed and redeployed in mediascapes. These signs are meant to speak for themselves, and over time, these same visual/mass-mediated signifiers begin to stand in for history itself, often in decidedly ahistorical ways, just as the terms "house Negro" and "field Negro" were used by Malcolm X and then resurrected by Al Qaeda to stand in for a complex national history in which political subjectivity was *not* neatly determined by a slave's fit within such easy binaries.[20]

Regardless of what these media signifiers lack in historical depth, Barack Obama would have been incomprehensible to the American public were it not for the discursive work on race that has taken place in mediascapes, such as "I have a dream . . . ," Selma, the Little Rock Nine, the Watts Riots, James Cone, Muhammad Ali, *Roots*, Rodney King, and the Million Man March. Each of these signifiers names not just a time or an event, but also an iconic moment when the way people felt and talked about race was altered. The public was waiting to see if Obama was ideologically more like Martin Luther King, Jr., or James Cone. Was he charming like Muhammad Ali or frightening like Louis Farrakhan? Was his family's story like Alex Haley's, one of working hard and overcoming, or was he simply a spoiled "affirmative action baby"?[21] And as the "birthers"[22] never let Americans forget, his relatively exotic form of blackness and foreignness actually provided space for decoupling him from America's historic leaders, including native-born race men like W. E. B. DuBois.

Of course, these signifiers of slavery, civil rights, race, and religion are by no means determinate and fixed, but they do constitute elements of America's cultural literacy and, therefore, provide a foundation for the kinds of knowing that have radically changed the status of blacks from terrorized slaves and freemen to citizens (although theirs is a citizenship complicated by mass incarceration and continuing forms of exclusion).[23] The American public did not read Barack Obama as if he emerged from a blank slate upon which he wrote his own destiny. Instead, his codeshifting and measured attempts to associate himself with icons, from President Lincoln to Jay-Z, are what made him legible at all. What the Al Qaeda video reminds us is that these rich symbols and canonized historical narratives that African Americans have used to make sense of themselves also circulate internationally and have been taken up by others around the world to gloss Americanness in its various forms and manifestations.

This book describes the ways in which black religious media has been at the forefront of attempts to shape and reshape black subjectivity, often in competing attempts to categorize black bodies into submission or to liberate them from conceptual and even physical bondage. We characterize the media production of these different groups as "redemptive" because they express the will to liberate blacks from abjection and subjugation, from oppression and exploitation. The power of this media lies in its attempt to alter the emotional dispositions, ideologies, and behaviors of believers and others, potentially helping people to imagine new ways of being in the world.

In the process of providing blacks with tools for changing their social dispositions, this media also changes how those outside "the community" think about race and belonging. It informs them about who the members are, what they believe, and what one can expect from them by way of work ethic, political commitments, family organization, and gender roles. The media productions of black Christians and Muslims have forever altered, and perhaps overdetermined, how blacks are seen by others and how they see themselves. Moreover, the media production of black Jews demonstrates how difficult it is to step away from entrenched notions of race and identity or deeply held preconceptions about racial and religious possibility.

Redemptive Media-Scapes

In *Formations of the Secular*, anthropologist Talal Asad asserts that the Civil Rights movement was cast by Martin Luther King, Jr., as a means for white redemption.[24] The images that circulated on television, in magazines like *Ebony*, and in newspapers around the country graphically depicted the forms of violence that protected institutionalized bigotry in America. Images of blacks being sprayed with water hoses and pummeled by police batons were juxtaposed with their steadfast religious commitments to nonviolent activism. "To be redeemed," Asad writes, "and to redeem others was to restore an inheritance—the Judeo-Christian heritage in general and the American expression of it in particular. In this way the prophetic language of the Old Testament was fused with the Salvationist language of the New."[25] Asad argues that King offered white America deliverance from its history of moral debasement.

What Asad fails to thematize, however, is the degree to which such commitments to secular political reform, by way of moral and religious arguments, were not simply a way to make whites feel good about their racial achievements. Black Americans were as committed to redeeming their race as they were to redeeming the nation. The efforts of Civil Rights leaders were in keeping with over two hundred years of discourse dedicated to exploring ethical, legal, and religious justifications for a more robust form of racial inclusiveness. It was more than just narrowly strategic in that it cast its sights beyond the immediacy of short-term political gain. What these leaders had learned from the past was that violent resistance to slavery and Jim Crow had only reinforced the racist logics used to legitimate segregation, disfranchisement, violence, and murder. What the leaders of the Civil Rights movement recognized was that after winning a series of battles, the real war over the future of American society would be fought over precepts and principles able to sway hearts and minds. During the Civil Rights movement, not only did blacks have to author their own salvation, but they also had to beat back long-held assumptions about white racial superiority. Asad is right that the Civil Rights movement redeemed whites and the very principles of America's constitutional democracy, but it also simultaneously redeemed and humanized blacks.[26]

The Civil Rights movement was neither the first nor the last quasi-religious or religious movement that tried to redeem African descendants from the slings and arrows of white supremacy. In *Black Redemption*, Randall Burkett describes how Marcus Garvey's Universal Negro Improvement Association and African Communities League (UNIA) embodied a call for existential salvation through everyday acts of resistance to white supremacy.[27] It was imagined that by knowing their historical relevance as sons and daughters of ancient civilizations, blacks would embrace the fact that they were equal to whites in moral capacity and intellect. At the same time, they recognized that the belief that, against all odds, blacks could fight their own subjugation through faith was largely fanciful. Like Malcolm X's father, the Reverend Earl

Little, who was an organizer for the UNIA, those who resisted white supremacy often died at the hands of white racists. Being a leader in the UNIA meant that belief had to be matched by action, which could lead to violence. But for many, once these redemptive narratives of salvation through the embodiment of new understandings of origins, racial essences, and religious goodness took hold, there was often no going back.

As anthropologist St. Clair Drake notes, Africa "was revitalized in the twentieth century by Marcus Garvey, who seemed to want to make the uplifting and redemption of that continent and its peoples a concrete political objective of the UNIA—without denying the continent's more traditional role as a symbol of the eschatological goal toward which all of history was leading. It was precisely in holding these two dimensions of the 'redemption of Africa' together that Garvey achieved that religious synthesis of ethos and worldview that was so essential an ingredient in his power."[28] Beyond the UNIA, black religious movements, as Burkett and Drake describe, have rarely been marked by a monastic turn inward to quiet engagement with ancient texts. Black religious movements encouraged orthopraxy, or practice informed by ideology, and remained strident, bold, and full of political purpose.[29] Making a bold and impassioned case for the social, economic, and legal enfranchisement of black folks characterizes exactly what has always been at stake in the media productions of black Muslims, Christians, and Jews.

Audiences and Constraints

Black religions might be said to sit somewhat precariously between empowering and constraining their adherents. Empowerment comes from interpretations of faith and politics that provide new ways of seeing and acting in the world. Constraints emerge when a community of believers sets rules for how to think and behave in order for the redemptive narratives to persuade outsiders that blacks are the moral and intellectual equals of whites. Even without the added emphases of religious belief, there is a history of blacks chastising other segments of the black community for making the race "look bad." As far back as the nineteenth century, blacks have lashed out at other blacks for keeping the race down. W. E. B. DuBois focused on the positive by articulating the notion of a talented tenth, a demographic of blacks who actually served the race proud in mixed company.[30] But what about the other 90 percent? In 2007, for example, using Pew data, Juan Williams articulated a thesis that "now" there are two black Americas: one includes hard-working middle-class blacks, and the other includes people whose culture keeps them locked in cycles of poverty.[31] Similarly, wealthy black comedian Bill Cosby lashed out at poor blacks at the NAACP's fiftieth anniversary of *Brown v. Board of Education*. Importantly, the legal and economic empowerment of the individual is thought to reside in the collective performances of all blacks, which explains Cosby's rant. To be clear, these public figures did not create the "culture of poverty" argument. Anthropologists did. But long before Oscar Lewis coined the phrase, black religionists were critiquing other blacks for causing their own social and spiritual self-destruction.[32]

Since blacks began using mass media as a means to fight against slavery and institutional racism, two dominant tropes have been in play: the victim, objectified and pitiable; and the perpetrator, wanton and beyond the rule of law. The use of this victim/perpetrator dichotomy—Chris Rock's blacks versus niggers, Juan Williams' two black Americas, Bill Cosby's Shaniqua, Taliqua, and Mohammed versus upstanding blacks—has rendered more nuanced public debates nearly impossible. Legal scholar Michelle Alexander, in *The New Jim Crow*, and political scientist Cathy Cohen, in *The Boundaries of Blackness*, argue that the strategy to disavow black abjection through the deployment of the virtuous and unblemished black martyr has paralyzed black leaders from stepping forward to support the most vulnerable: substance abusers caught in a racist criminal justice system, or those suffering from HIV/AIDS.[33] The fear was that fighting for the rights of the morally impure would simply slow down the already sluggish march toward full democratic participation.

Countering some of this narrative that there exists a segment of black society that is almost irredeemable, the Nation of Islam remonstrated against the black bourgeoisie, blaming them for continued black disfranchisement. In their reading of history, which can be traced back to Malcolm X's house slave/field slave dichotomy, the "field Negro" was responsible for most of the political progress actually made through the 1970s. But the message of the Nation was at odds with that of many black leaders who felt that anyone representing the black community had to be morally beyond reproach—meaning educated, free of vices, devout, and employed. Black leaders feared that by addressing what some might describe as self-inflicted suffering, they would nourish negative stereotypes that had the power to produce real effects. Red-lining, the academic achievement gap, racial health disparities, unemployment, and wealth and income inequality are just some of the exclusions produced and reproduced by beliefs about the intellectual and moral inferiority of blacks. The fact that black religious communities still struggle to strike a balance between redemptive narratives meant to prove to others that African Americans are whites' moral equals, on the one hand, and to chastise complicated and fallible members of their own communities, on the other, speaks to the fact that blacks in America are still insecure about their status as full citizens. As we show, benefits of religious intervention with regard to issues of citizenship have been uneven. Their impact is explored ethnographically in the chapters that follow.

Resignification, or the discursive practice of destabilizing one symbolic system in order to imagine it anew, attends to both the needs of the faithful *to heal* and desires for legitimacy in the eyes of those outside the faith community. This politics of recognition is at the heart of religious media given that it attempts to make the particularities of a religious community intelligible to outsiders while simultaneously attempting to guide or even alter the dispositions of believers themselves. Black religious media seeks not only to make coherent the belief system of the media producers but also to demand deliverance from oppressive and discriminatory politics and policies often bolstered by racist logics. At the same time that black religions offer a particular exegetical reading of scripture, they also attend to race relations and identity politics. They do so presupposing that the two seemingly distinct spheres, the so-called secular and religious, are not just mutually constitutive but inextricably linked when it comes to the politics of race-based exclusion.

Embedded in black religion is a self-conscious awareness of audience. The sense that outsiders are eavesdropping—or that the state is generating intelligence on the machinations of black radicals emboldened by religious fervor—plays a significant role in how black religious media is framed. This recognition that the audience may include people as far away as the caves of Afghanistan produces a kind of white noise that producers of religious media sometimes attend to and other times ignore. Audience—in this case, the imagined other—is often perceived as a threat or an enemy with the power to subjugate. There is no more striking demonstration of the disruptive potential of a hostile audience than in the 2008 public airing of sermons preached by Reverend Jeremiah Wright, the former pastor of President Barack Obama. Reverend Wright was caught on camera preaching a sermon that critiqued American foreign policy, racism, and economic exploitation of black and brown communities. With the help of the media, he was subsequently denounced as anti-American despite his years of distinguished military and community service. Discussions in the media rarely mentioned that Wright was one of only a few black pastors in a predominantly white denomination, that he received invitations to the White House during the Clinton administration, or that his church had made historic efforts in the areas of education, the remediation of HIV/AIDS, support of Pan African freedom, and care of the elderly. Instead, Reverend Wright and the United Church of Christ, the church he pastored, were eviscerated in a media-driven analysis that sought to typecast him as an anti-American black radical. Over thirty-years of Wright's ministry was summed up in a two-minute clip of one sermon, and the sound-bite threatened to derail Barack Obama's presidential candidacy. Reverend Wright and Barack Obama in many respects were irrelevant. Instead, the response of the white audience had been primed by centuries of suspicion about the radical nature of the black church. The visual and verbal signifiers tapped into cultural narratives and genealogies that are as entangled in the image of Malcolm X holding a rifle as he looks outside his window as they are in Martin Luther King, Jr., sermonizing during the height of the Civil Rights movement.

The Reverend Wright incident highlights the power of media to distort, as well as the tremendous work required to make an unedited clip from Wright's sermon legible to average white Americans. The rebuffing of Wright by media-pundits led to Obama's gradual move away from him. In many ways this event presaged Obama's continuing struggle to avoid associating himself with religion and race politics at the risk of being cast as the president for *black* Americans and not *all* Americans.

Obama's refusal to be cast in the role of a Reverend Jesse Jackson, Reverend Al Sharpton, Rev. Martin Luther King, Jr., or, to the chagrin of Al Qaeda, Malcolm X, speaks to the power of religiously mediated racial tropes. These tropes can facilitate communication, but they can also lock people into prescribed social performances. Obama's political strategy of disassociation became necessary because iconic renderings of black moral character do not support individuality or the types of hybridity that Obama's self-narratives have attempted to foster: his mixed-raced and bicultural parentage, his transnational upbringing, and his refusal to let his own identification as a black man limit his inclusivist moral imagination. And it is this hybridity that most Americans, even black Americans, find incomprehensible.[34] Scholar Cornel West's and media personality Tavis Smiley's casting of the president as a kind of race traitor in the press was a function of the fact that Obama broke free of traditional redemptive narratives and did not enact political blackness as they thought it should be enacted.[35] But there was precedent. Both Martin Luther King, Jr., and Malcolm X tried to connect the struggle of blacks and whites toward the end of their lives, and they both read the other as embodying the wrong kind of racialized politics. Black religious media shapes racial identities, demands particular racial performances, and has the power to unseat racist stereotypes. It also has the power to scold and further marginalize the already marginal.

The Medium and Resignification

Why does this book focus on religion and media? There are, after all, political discourses that attempt to redeem the race and other forms of grassroots activism that press key social concerns. What makes mass-mediated religious discourses particularly interesting is that they not only articulate what it means to be, as Lewis Gordon might put it, existentially black, but they also provide totalizing instructions for how people should act and feel.[36] The fact that religious media has the ability to shape people's dispositions, what Pierre Bourdieu calls *habitus*, makes it powerful and compelling as a research object.[37]

On their own, religion and media each share many fundamental characteristics. Most notably, religion and media mediate our experiences in the world with a promise of inescapable ubiquity. Although often vague and indeterminate, religious texts sketch out necessary forms of doctrine-based practice informed by sacred texts. While there is much disagreement among different churches, masjids, and Israelite communities, to be part of a faith community often requires submission, albeit of a contested and negotiated kind. Media shares this pretension to totality and includes implicit interpretive strategies (specific genre-based syntax and short-cuts) deployed as symbolic shorthand (editing, angles, composition, film speed, focus, soundtrack) and used to generate emotions (much like the emotional potency of traditional black homiletics and registers).

These ideological, discursive, and aesthetic short-cuts—rhetorical forms—rely on symbols laden with meaning that presume a shared cultural literacy. Ultimately, however, this media is read and misread, interpreted and misinterpreted, regardless of shared literacy.[38] Media names a reality through the constant signification and resignification of signs, and these tropes that script our moral universe mediate our experiences at the level of the everyday. Together, religion and media have the power to alter what we know about ourselves and the world, and they are increasingly fused in a world of what might be called religious mediatization. We see religion's relationship to media most distinctly in the case of renaming.

Within black religions renaming oneself has been one of the most important tools of resignification. This renaming, a form of embodiment-by-proxy, works against forms of misrecognition that make blacks vulnerable to racism and its attendant disenfranchisements: red-lining, mass incarceration, reduced access to healthcare, and differential treatment by educators.[39] These signifiers are meant to help free blacks from feelings of abjection, as well as to communicate new social identities. Converts to Islam, for example, often change their names. Within the Nation of Islam in the 1950s and 1960s, new members would often replace their last name with an X. The rejection of one's "slave name" was a signifier of a deeper rejection of white supremacy. For Sunni Muslims, adopting an Arabic name is not so much a turning away from the past as an embrace of the culture and wisdom of the Prophet Muhammad.

For Hebrew Israelites and various black Jews, adopting Hebrew names often signaled the fullest embrace of a new identity. Naming continues to be such a powerful signifier that to be called "black" instead of "African" or to confuse African Americans with Canaanites or Babylonians is associated with a whole host of conceptual traps that lead to self-hatred and self-destruction. Members of the Nation of Islam, for example, were not Negroes; they were Asiatics. Black Hebrew Israelites are decidedly not Jews. Some are not even African. Black Christians, on the other hand, adamantly rebuke white denominations that use the same history and text, with many emphasizing that Jesus was born with "wooly hair." A great deal is at stake in renaming. Summarizing the origin myth of the Nation of Islam, historian Claude Andrew Clegg highlights the importance of revisionist logics that begin with the donning of new names:

> The black people, the first and sole human residents of the planet, were organized into thirteen tribes, which formed a Nation united by skin color (black), religion (Islam), and natural disposition (righteousness). . . . Ruling the earth from the sprawling continent of Asia, the black people prided themselves on being the original "Asiatic blackman, the maker, the owner, the cream of the planet earth, God of the universe."[40]

The history of Asiatic blackmen, as narrated by the Nation of Islam, is replete with instances of brilliance, triumph, and goodness. It is prophetic and profound. In contrast, the often-told stories of Negroes in North America describe instances of subjugation and powerlessness, debasement and denigration. This history of failure, as narrated in high school classrooms throughout the United States, opens up spaces for questions about whether blacks have the ability to lead themselves. Racial categories get linked to canonized histories in ways that imprison blacks in tropes of racial inferiority and make naming one's own story nearly impossible—yet absolutely necessary.

Media and Struggles for Citizenship

In his now-classic argument, summed up in the phrase "the medium is the message," Marshall McLuhan argues that if one wants to understand the message of media one must study both the medium—film, journalism, books, radio—and the content. In this book, we examine the role religious media has played in and through several different media sources, focusing primarily on the relationships between politicized religious rhetoric and electronic media (mostly visual) productions.[41] While we try to escape what might be called McLuhan's "technological determinism," we also recognize that written, aural, and/or visual mediums impact viewers differently. Though we reject the idea that technology determines how the audience interprets a message, we also recognize that black Muslims, Christians, and Jews use media in ways that link to how religious authority is understood. Contemporary African American Muslims, for example, tend to deploy media that is open and accessible: blogs, online forums, and journals.[42] This is related in part to the way in which Qur'anic exegesis is a required practice of all (literate) Muslims. In addition, Muslims are encouraged to lead one another in daily prayers, and anyone who claims deep knowledge of the faith can lead a congregation. This dynamic differs markedly from Christian televangelism, in which a charismatic minister, often not the holder of a degree from a seminary, has singular authority to speak for the faith and is often seen as being touched by God or chosen to lead the faithful. Like Muslims, Christians also use websites and online forums, but the centers of gravity for Christian media have largely been profit oriented ventures on cable television. Finally, the use of radio by black Hebrew Israelites reflects a particular ethic around language and renaming that makes aural communication an important part of knowledge production. The relationship between technologies and interpretive practice has not necessarily been essential to the faiths themselves but rather to the ways in which religious authority and authenticity are reckoned in the early twenty-first century. Equally important are funding, revenue, and distribution issues, where Christian media dominates given its larger audience size.

Rather than attempt to pool and categorize vast amounts of religious media, we have chosen in this book to focus on explicit and implicit discourses about citizenship vis-à-vis three religio-racial communities. Why citizenship? The struggle for citizenship and a sense of belonging is at the heart of black religious media. The Nation of Islam placed this mandate front and center. They wanted reparations from the United States in the form of two states, in which a second would be created out of the first and be a place where blacks could rule themselves. By the 1950s and 1960s, in the midst of postcolonial struggles around the world, many African Americans felt that they needed to look beyond the United States for membership in a community that would be more just, hopeful, and inclusive. Rather than desiring American legal citizenship, the contemporary religious projects of the Muslims and African Hebrew Israelites, in particular, demonstrate a desire for a cultural citizenship that transcends certain forms of nativism. With the transition from Nation of Islam to Sunni Islam, African American Muslims began to fight for recognition as members of the *ummah*, an international community linked by faith and the imagination, and African Hebrew Israelites chose to migrate to Dimona, Israel, where they struggled for decades, renouncing their American citizenship as a symbolic and literal show of faith. Only in the early twenty-first century did the Israeli government award members of the Dimona community permanent residential status, a step that the community imagined as the penultimate one before inevitable citizenship and one that allowed community members to work legally for the first time. Finally, since slavery, black Christians have been at the forefront of demanding the recognition of blacks as the moral equals of white co-religionists. While African American Christians identify most strongly with beliefs about American exceptionalism, Christian televangelism since the Civil Rights era has globalized black Christian spirituality and more and more Christians now feel a sense of unity with Christians from all corners of the globe.

To capture black struggles for belonging and citizenship rights, we present experiences of the faithful from Sharjah to Dimona, from Sanaa to South Carolina. Methodologically, this book draws on both historical analysis and ethnographic fieldwork with members of each of the religious communities. These groups have produced and distributed media meant to humanize the race, and our aim was to understand the impact these "televised" messages about black humanity and moral citizenship have had on the practices of the faithful. While all of our interlocutors, observed in churches, temples, and mosques, do not necessarily identify as black or African American, they all have African American heritage (though some Hebrew Israelite camps would dispute even that), and a good many were born in the United States. We first offer a historical look at the fight for equal protection and rights in the United States and the contribution of black religious media toward achieving this goal. We then draw on our ethnographic engagement with these communities, moving to broaden our gaze to include the international relationships desired by our interlocutors and their efforts to gain membership by establishing their religious authority via media.

Representing oneself in religious mediascapes is a gesture of social intimacy, a call to engage in conversations about the most complex aspects of what it means to be human. Therefore, just as we, as hosts and hostesses, may control which rooms in our houses we allow our guests to visit, black religious media regulates the story of black subjectivity not only through what it represents, but also through what it chooses not to represent. For the black community, representations are created with every expectation that the art piece, documentary, TV show, feature film, book, blog, and so on, will stand in for the whole, in a kind of racial synecdoche. What is at stake in any misreading of the black community is the production of fraught generalizations—stereotypes—that have the potential to diminish rights to full citizenship.

The culture of poverty theory is a case in point. Since the 1960s, this theory has been used to argue that black health, educational, economic, and incarceration disparities are the end result of black social dysfunction, weak moral character, and/or intellectual inferiority. President Ronald Reagan, who caricatured recipients of aid as Cadillac-driving (black) welfare queens and who associated politically with notorious racists, built his national social and economic agenda on culture of poverty theories. The idea that poor (black) people lack the character and capacity to take advantage of a free market justified the dismantling of much of the social safety net. In addition to busting unions and deindustrializing cities, Reagan encouraged the bleeding of programs, like education, designed to equalize opportunities. It is no coincidence that his agenda disproportionately impacted African Americans.

The us-versus-them discourses framing culture of poverty theories articulate a relationship between citizenship and deservedness that organizes people according to who is and who is not worthy of state support and legal protections. By legitimating reasons for exclusion, culture of poverty theories have, in the late twentieth and early twenty-first century, indirectly led to the systematic disfranchisement of voters, from ex-felon "civil death," to gerrymandering, to the infusion of cash into electoral politics following the Supreme Court's 2010 Citizens United decision, a ruling asserting that large campaign contributions by rich donors constitute acts of free speech. What should be clear is that racialized politics does not only disfranchise black people. It starts by treating the black body and black culture as unique, but then quickly marks individuals of any race who exhibit "black" characteristics as raced, as in the case of white sickle cell disease patients in the early twentieth century, who were reclassified as black because it was thought that anyone with the disease had to be black.[43] A Marxian would argue that this classification of us and them is useful for maintaining economic and social inequality.

Given this book's goal of showing how three very different faiths deploy new notions of black subjectivity and citizenship through mass-mediated practices/productions, it is fair to ask how we have organized this endeavor. From the point of view of all three authors, this has been one of the most (if not the most) difficult research projects we have undertaken. New media is generated quickly and is plentiful. We have chosen, therefore, to focus on a few case studies rather than trying to capture black religious media in all of its discursive and material fullness. Instead of casting our net widely, we chose to explore, historically and ethnographically, a handful of works by a subset of engaging and somewhat representative producers and consumers. Of particular interest is the question of what these media producers are trying to represent, why they are making the choices they do, and how these representations are received by others. We also trouble the contours of these questions, especially given the fact that our interlocutors dispute some of what other African Americans consider as the constitutive center of the black community—a dispute about who, in fact, has the authority to represent the race and who can legitimately call themselves the faithful.

Chapters

This book is organized into two sections. As noted, the first section focuses on the historical antecedents used to authorize each religio-racial faith tradition and their particular redemptive narratives as instantiated in their responses to—and mobilizations of—mass media in the battle to define national belonging and existential worth in the context of ubiquitous assumptions about black depravity and primitivity. Through the juxtaposition of these three different (though also overlapping) histories, we can see that black identity has never been depicted as one thing. The histories that have mattered and continue to matter to African American Muslims, Jews/Israelites, and Christians—with their different emphases and interpretations—speak to the use of history as a signifying practice. In this case what is signified is a black subjectivity fully humanized. The second section presents ethnographies of black religious media told from diverse corners of the world. These ethnographies demonstrate the continued importance of the corporeal, or the raced body, in the age of digital media and global communications.

Chapter 1 begins our exploration of the specific facets of each faith community with a focus on African American Christianity. The chapter delves into the development of African American Christian broadcasting over the past thirty years. Fused with mainstream media, black Christian televangelism looks distinctly different from the messages of redemption mapped out by black Muslims and black Hebrew Israelites. While the mid-century history of black Protestant religion on television was dominated by images of dark-hued Southerners advocating for the civil rights of African Americans by praying, singing, and nonviolently protesting in the streets, African American Christian media in the past thirty years has taken a decidedly individualist approach to redemption. Contemporary narratives of personal empowerment, salvation, and prosperity broadcast by black televangelists around the world map disjointedly onto histories of collective struggle for the redemption of the entire race. Biblical injunctions mandating social and political critique fade in light of audience-centered messages of individual change and personal empowerment. This more personalized tone in more recent African American Christian media reflects not only a change in sociopolitical climate since the 1960s, but also a shift in Christian media broadcasting, a shift driven as much by global neoliberal market demands as by religious inspiration.

Chapter 2 focuses on the Nation of Islam. Given state-sponsored and state-endorsed violence against blacks, the Nation of Islam encouraged followers to develop a religious disposition that intertwined ideas about faith with ideas about the rights and duties of citizenship. The chapter looks particularly at the NOI's assertion about the right of self-defense as part of its effort to characterize blacks as worthy of respect. It begins with an analysis of David Walker's *Appeal* (1829), published in the first African American newspaper, *Freedom's Journal.*[44] *The Appeal* was one of the first instances in which media was used to justify a right of self-defense against the United States. One hundred years later the Nation of Islam echoed Walker's thesis, developing it further into a faith disposition. In the 1960s NOI leaders Elijah Muhammad's and Malcolm X's justification for self-defense came to define the Nation of Islam in American media. In response, much of the redemptive work in the media produced by the Nation was an attempt to validate blacks' entitlement to protecting themselves physically and psychologically from white supremacy. Rather than leading to the growth of a hate movement, the dispositions encouraged by the Nation of Islam actually inspired the opposite. This chapter explores why.

Chapter 3 focuses on black Hebrew Israelites. Relating a compelling origin story for black Judaism/Hebrewism/Israelite-ism in the United States requires that the storyteller discuss how Africans in the Americas—from the colonial period to the twenty-first century—have long confounded conventional assumptions about the links between race and religion. It entails conjuring tales of how the earliest African captives claimed Jewish descent from the corners of their Bostonian slave cells; recounting the complicatedly "colored" Christianities of early postbellum America, Christianities that were as quick to racialize Jesus (and the early Jews) as to genuflect to portraits of some European-featured God; recasting slave revolts—and the vaingloriously suicidal proclivities of those who lead them—in their fullest philo-Israelitic zeal; and requiring that the tale, especially if spun by an anthropological narrator, be brought up to a present moment of urban sidewalk spaces saturated with gnostic beliefs that are more prevalent in the lives of many black Americans than some religious experts seem willing to publicly acknowledge—beliefs such as Nuwabianism and Five Percenterism, which are completely incomprehensible without recognition of their historical and ongoing ties to various forms of black Israelite practices/beliefs. This chapter articulates portions of this history—and maps out a few of these important contemporary connections across denominations and larger religious traditions within black America, connections that mark a concerted effort to rethink prominent parameters of national and global citizenship in the twenty-first century.

In this book's second half, the ethnography section, Chapter 4 considers the efficacy of African American Christian personal redemption narratives, which are intended primarily to disrupt psychic as opposed to social limitations on progress. Drawing on ethnographic research with black Christian women in the United States, the chapter argues that televangelists speak to women's personal concerns about economic sus-

tainability in a way that black protest narratives of the previous generation, committed primarily to racial uplift, ignored. Prosperity gospels, it
turns out, advance in the hands of women. Far from simply promising
wealth without work, the much-maligned gospel introduces languages
of possibility that disrupt economic and social limitations placed on
black women. By the latter half of the twentieth century, black televangelists had stumbled upon the realization that there is little redemption
of the race without the redemption of its women. Framing prosperity
as possible and inherent to the believer regardless of social markers like
race, class, or *gender* meant that women writ large instantly transcended
the dictates of social norms or religious expectations. As with other in-
stantiations of black redemption over the twentieth century, such as Father Divine's Peace Mission Movement and Marcus Garvey's Universal
Negro Improvement Association, black women's redemption in particular provides the litmus test for interpreting the pulse of a movement.
The wild success of T. D. Jakes' "Woman Thou Art Loosed" ministry
has redefined what it means to address black women's concerns over not
only sexuality, but also economic possibility. And addressing these concerns helps us to think about how any discussion about the implications
of race and religiosity for questions of citizenship is incomplete without
some discussion of the gendered coefficients of any citizenry.

Chapter 5 explores how the postracial aspirations of African American Muslims play out both on the Internet and on the ground. In many
instances, race still determines who is given authority to speak for the
faith. Therefore, while African American Muslim media producers
continue to aspire to postracialism—or a society free of racial discrimination and race-based identification—they acknowledge forms of exclusion and marginalization that make it difficult to develop an audience of
Muslims who are not African American. The chapter highlights several
instances of racially and ethnically inflected misrecognition, including
the story of an expat journalist who finds forms of fellowship and citizenship in the United Arab Emirates—forms unavailable to her in the
United States. The story returns us to the history of the Nation of Islam
and its efforts to achieve rights of full citizenship for blacks either in
the United States or in a territory handed over to them by the U.S. government. While in the twenty-first century the legitimacy of the U.S.
government is taken for granted, the question of African American citi-

zenship remains less settled. Lingering concerns about what the United States has to offer African Americans, given that blacks continue to be disproportionately marginalized, are in part why many black Muslims seek recognition within the *ummah*, or world community of Muslims. This chapter describes how digital media in particular has been coopted into newer redemptive projects regarding race and citizenship.

Chapter 6 draws on research at an independent radio station in Philadelphia, WURD 900AM, owned by a family with complex and nuanced ties to the African Hebrew Israelites of Jerusalem (AHIJ), the transnational spiritual community of African American expats that has been based in southern Israel for over forty years. The chapter takes an ethnographic look at one weekly show on WURD, *The Green Hour*, which is produced and hosted by two "saints" from the AHIJ community, and it explores how that show demonstrates an attempt to place specific claims about racial injustices in critical conversation with seemingly distinctive and separable domains such as environmentalism and health literacy. *The Green Hour* uses airtime to highlight new and innovative products that are environmentally safe and/or vegan-inspired, which the show's producers help to sell wholesale and retail throughout the country in line with the AHIJ's rigorous reconceptualization of the human body's cellular capacities and its championing of specific techniques for keeping human bodies healthy and whole—for hundreds of years (maybe even forever). This immortalist reconceptualization of the body's physical capacities is based on the AHIJ's purposeful reading of contemporary medical science and their fascinating rereading of the Holy Bible, especially the Old Testament (Torah). Using their radio show as an example of how this Hebrew Israelite group interfaces with a larger African American community in the United States and abroad, the chapter provides an ethnographic and analytic window into how the "Kingdom" gets its message (to use the station's tag-line) "on the air, online, and in the community." Moreover, with its focus on radio (often ignored in modern fetishizations of "new media"), the chapter also seeks to make a case for the continued relevance of seemingly outmoded concepts (such as the "televised" of this book's title, *Televised Redemption*), concepts that aren't so much antiquated as reanimated in our "convergent media" moment. As these Hebrew Israelite radio hosts argue for the physical and spiritual value of veganism and make a weekly case for God's requirement that his chosen people serve as stewards for the entire planet, they are also conjuring new ways of understanding citizenship in varied local, national, and international manifestations.

In all, this book illuminates how black religious media has been and continues to be part and parcel of the long struggle for equal protection and social inclusion in American society. By representing the moral capacities of African Americans, this media continues to play a role in insuring that legal rights transfer to social rights. Importantly, mass incarceration, marked by the disproportionate prosecution and sentencing of blacks, began soon after the adoption of civil rights legislation. And residential and educational segregation grew worse, not better, after initial efforts at racial desegregation in the early 1970s. A generalized sense of black inferiority has replaced more explicit beliefs about white supremacy, but in the end the effects are largely the same. The legal rights of blacks are whittled away as new discourses of black inferiority legitimate new forms of exclusion. To counter this racial recursion, black religious media continues to impact—at the level of social dispositions—how blacks perceive themselves and are perceived by others. Without this mediated discursive work, it is doubtful that the United States would have come as far as it has in addressing the race question. But as this book makes clear, the work of redeeming the race continues. And black Christians, Muslims, and Jews/Israelites have taken on this challenge by proclaiming, in numerous and varied televised forms, that blacks are equally the sons and daughters of God.

PART I

Redemptive Media Histories

1

Black Christian Redemption

Contested Possibilities

"Black religion," whether conceptualized variously by whites
and blacks as an amorphous spirituality, primitive religion,
emotionalism, or actual black churches under the rubric of
"the Negro Church," groaned under the burden of a multiplicity of interpreters' demands ranging from uplift of the
race to bringing an ambiguous quality of "spiritual softness"
to a materialistic and racist white culture.
Curtis Evans, *The Burden of Black Religion*

The central and most enduring feature of Black Religion is its
sustained and radical opposition to racial oppression. At bottom, Black Religion is an instrument of holy protest against
white supremacy and its material and psychological effects.
Sherman Jackson, *Islam and the Blackamerican*

"A young Negro boy" seated "on a stoop in front of a vermin-infested
apartment house in Harlem," "a young Negro girl" seated "on the stoop
of a rickety wooden one-family house in Birmingham"—their present is
marked by poverty; their future is enveloped by muted possibility. [1] It
was the summer of 1963. Paucity smothered hope. Martin Luther King,
Jr., evoked their lives in the opening of *Why We Can't Wait* to tell the
larger story of the civil rights struggles that engulfed Alabama. The book
is a crystalized assessment of faith at work in the process of redeeming
black lives. A chastisement of white religion not far from King's lips,
the irony of black life trapped in the clutches of a poverty outlined and
sanctioned by white Christian supremacy was only too striking. Both
the former captor and the formerly captured, landlord and sharecropper,
"Miss Ann" and maid, fervently entreated the same God.

Arguably more so than their black Hebrew and black Muslim counterparts, black Christians in the United States shared a God with their
white masters in many pre-emancipation settings, sometimes even
worshiping in the very same sanctuary as their oppressors. In the early
1960s, in the context of violent and state-sanctioned white supremacy,
Martin Luther King, Jr., weary of the suggestion from white clergy that
civil rights leaders be patient, took pen to pad and drafted a letter to his
white ministerial colleagues explaining why one hundred years after the
Emancipation Proclamation, the admonition for blacks to "wait" even
longer rang so hollow. His "Letter from a Birmingham Jail" waged a
searing critique of white Christianity's complicity in black oppression
and undeniable abandonment of God's mandate for universal justice:

> In the midst of blatant injustices inflicted upon the Negro, I have watched
> white churchmen stand on the sideline and mouth pious irrelevancies
> and sanctimonious trivialities. In the midst of a mighty struggle to rid
> our nation of racial and economic injustice, I have heard many ministers
> say: "Those are social issues, with which the gospel has no real concern."
> And I have watched many churches commit themselves to a completely
> otherworldly religion which makes a strange, un-Biblical distinction be-
> tween body and soul, between the sacred and the secular.[2]

To his consternation, biblical injunctions like "Let justice roll on like a
river; righteousness, like a never-failing stream" were seemingly long-
erased from the bibles of Southern whites, or interpreted in ways that
stopped just along the borders of racial community.[3] Black and white
Christians all too often embraced divergent interpretations of the same
texts. For King and other civil rights protesters, justice was not only
about voting rights and integrated lunch counters, but ultimately about
economic possibility and political agency.

Black redemption in the context of American history has thus consistently been inflected with the need to address both race and class, the
two tied together through the long history of black economic exploitation under slavery, sharecropping, and Jim Crow. The latter, which
came only to a slow and dawdling halt in the early 1970s, lived insidi-
ously on in what Michelle Alexander has called "the new Jim Crow"
of institutionalized prison-industrial complicity proffered in seemingly

race-neutral terms.[4] The black church's response to these challenges varied widely, with different ministries reading the black struggle for freedom against different interpretations of Christian eschatology and then, based on those readings, determining how to respond as good Christians in the service of God and the nation.

Developing a sense of one's commitment to the nation also meant developing a sense of one's commitment to the economy. Institutional racism excluded most blacks from participation in the free market, given everything from laws forbidding ownership of land to banks refusing loans to qualified blacks. As a result, blacks struggled to understand these exclusions not only at a pragmatic level in order to navigate them but also at a theological level with respect to the question of whether Christian ideals of social justice are even compatible with what Max Weber described as rational bourgeois capitalism.[5] Scholars like C. Eric Lincoln and Lawrence Mamiya characterized the rubric of black church spiritual and civic responses to dialectical tensions between polarities like "accommodation" and "resistance," "priestly" and "prophetic," or "otherworldly" and "this worldly."[6] Building on this dialectical framing, scholars like Hans Baer and Mayer Singer went further, categorizing black churches in terms of their articulated relationship to capitalism. Mainstream religious communities, for example, encouraged congregants to participate in traditional forms of schooling, believing that through disciplined self-regulation one earns one's place within a capitalist economy. For magico-religious spiritualist sects, which waited on salvation in the afterlife, "pie in the sky" wealth was the reward of true faith; for thaumaturgic sects, a believer was thought to attain wealth in this life via supernatural means;[7] and for messianic or nationalist sects like the Nation of Islam, it was necessary to reject corporate capitalism for its racism and imperialism, yet possible to embrace capitalism with a little "c." Notably, many of these sects promoted black-owned businesses, often helping with financing and training for member-owned establishments.

Pushing back against some of these more binary and rigid mappings of the religious, sociologist Omar McRoberts posits the notion that where church parishioners live—locality and proxemics—is a better indicator of their commitments to urban renewal than an exact reading of scripture or denominational affiliation. For parishioners in the churches that McRoberts studied, whether or not one lives, shops, eats, and goes to school in a community determines how and whether one gets involved in its transformation. Such attention to the lived reality of people's lives complicates professed ideological commitments. Thus, one's relationship to *the street*, that is, to particular local streets and neighborhoods, more accurately reflects one's commitment to social uplift work in poor urban areas than the strict rubrics of theological or denominational orientation articulated by Lincoln and Mamiya or Baer and Singer.[8] Each of these neatly crafted frameworks inevitably abut piercing questions about the *possibility* of black redemption in America. Regardless of how black church communities respond, the question always lingers whether or not black Americans can achieve economic and social parity in a system built upon the very idea of the economic exploitation of black and brown bodies. For leaders and participants in the Civil Rights movement, such social and economic realities demanded a response, and not one of despair. King's admonitions to create the beloved community represent deep faith in the possibility of black redemption in America. Importantly, such black protest religion has not died. It resides in movements like the Moral Mondays campaign, which admonishes North Carolina legislators to advocate for the needs of the poor and marginalized and see their budgets as "moral" documents, not simply economic plans, and elements of the Black Lives Matter campaign, which began as a movement against violence toward black people.

This chapter explores changes over time in redemption narratives within black Christian communities. How have they understood themselves and their faith in the context of over three centuries of institutionalized racism? Using so-called new and old media as a focal point for such narratives, this chapter pays particular attention to how changes in media formats, platforms, institutions, and distribution channels—from print to radio to television to the Internet—illuminate how redemption is crafted and understood. More specifically and pointedly, how did the most high-profile forms of black religiosity move from political protest to prosperity gospels? What role did electronic mass media play in this development? And how might we understand media's role in prosperity faith becoming the most popular and seemingly hegemonic form of institutionalized black religion at the millennium?

The transformation from calls for abolition and equal protections, to civil rights and social justice, to prosperity and free market salvation mark dramatic turns in how the narrative of black redemption has been cast. In the nineteenth and early twentieth century, not only were newspaper and journal editors using their platform to address Americans, but writers like Ida B. Wells-Barnett also traveled abroad to showcase black suffering before largely sympathetic audiences in Europe and Africa. With the introduction of radio and television, sounds and images could do the traveling and impassion people in their living rooms through visceral appeals for social justice predicated on aural and visual evidence. And for much of the twentieth century, civil rights was articulated as the need to fundamentally transform the conditions of black life.

Following the Civil Rights and Voting Rights Acts, attempts at social and economic integration, and changes in Federal Communication Commission regulations, the redemptive narratives began to change. Black religious programming began to advance a more individualized message of self-help and redemption, most noticeably through the distribution of prosperity gospels. Such gospels have been propelled from once quaint, seemingly heretical teachings on wealth and Christianity into transnational proclamations of God's intention of creating prosperity for every believer—from those of King's Alabama ghettos to contemporary Brazilian favelas and South Africa's infamous shantytowns. The ascendancy of this prosperity gospel teaching, as a now transnational model of economic uplift, is a story best grasped through an understanding of the contestations taking place within American economic and social history.

Redemption through Protest

The history of mediated messages of redemption rendered by black Christians extends far beyond the civil rights movement. Since its founding in the United States, African American religion, tied as it has been to white Christian ideals and the "American Dream," has had to orchestrate a counternarrative of what redemption might look and feel like for Africans in America. "Black" Christianity was thus nurtured as a critique of the status quo, a referendum on American Christianity proper. Black leaders from the earliest days of the republic—women like Jarena Lee, Zilpha Elaw, and Maria Stewart, as well as men like Frederick Douglass, Martin Delany, and David Walker—took pen and pencil in hand to mark on paper their profound disappointment with Christianity's role as handmaiden of torture, and with America's failure to live up to its founding promise.

Such communications find their earliest expressions in the production of slave narratives and abolitionist newspapers. Scholars have emphasized the value of the autobiographies, pamphlets, and sermons that exposed the brutality of slavery in such piercing terms as to help fuel the antislavery movement. From the oldest slave narrative ever penned, Olaudah Equiano's *The Interesting Narrative of the Life of Olaudah Equiano, or Gustavus Vassa, the African Written by Himself* (circa 1745–1797) to Harriet Jacobs's *Incidents in the Life of a Slave Girl*, to Frederick Douglass's *Narrative of the Life of Frederick Douglass, an American Slave Written by Himself*, we have received tales lamenting both the callousness of chattel slavery and the arduous struggle for post-chattel liberty.[9] The appendix to Douglass's narrative crafts, in the most striking way, both the redemptive possibility of "the Christianity of Christ" as well as the oppressive nature of the "Christianity of this land." The distortion of Christianity made by white Americans through their support of race-based slavery rendered American Christianity not only invalid, but also relatively useless, without profound recalibration, to the project of political and existential redemption for African Americans. White Christianity in its crudest form was, after all, a state-sanctioned and state-deployed tool for oppression.[10] It was the peculiarity of white Christianity that made America's "peculiar institution" of racial slavery possible in the first place. Douglass's addendum thus explains both black affinity to and aversion from Christianity:

> What I have said respecting and against religion, I mean strictly to apply to the *slaveholding religion* of this land, and with no possible reference to Christianity proper; for, between the Christianity of this land, and the Christianity of Christ, I recognize the widest possible difference—so wide, that to receive the one as good, pure, and holy, is of necessity to reject the other as bad, corrupt, and wicked. To be the friend of the one, is of necessity to be the enemy of the other. I love the pure, peaceable, and impartial Christianity of Christ: I therefore hate the corrupt, slaveholding, women-whipping, cradle-plundering, partial and hypocritical Christianity of this land.

Indeed, I can see no reason, but the most deceitful one, for calling the religion of this land Christianity. I look upon it as the climax of all misnomers, the boldest of all frauds, and the grossest of all libels. . . . We have men-stealers for ministers, women-whippers for missionaries, and cradle-plunderers for church members. The man who wields the blood-clotted cowskin during the week fills the pulpit on Sunday, and claims to be a minister of the meek and lowly Jesus. The man who robs me of my earnings at the end of each week meets me as a class-leader on Sunday morning, to show me the way of life, and the path of salvation. He who sells my sister, for purposes of prostitution, stands forth as the pious advocate of purity. He who proclaims it a religious duty to read the Bible denies me the right of learning to read the name of the God who made me. . . . The warm defender of the sacredness of the family relation is the same that scatters whole families,—sundering husbands and wives, parents and children, sisters and brothers,—leaving the hut vacant, and the hearth desolate.

We see the thief preaching against theft, and the adulterer against adultery. We have men sold to build churches, women sold to support the gospel, and babes sold to purchase Bibles for the *poor heathen! all for the glory of God and the good of souls!* The slave auctioneer's bell and the church-going bell chime in with each other, and the bitter cries of the heart-broken slave are drowned in the religious shouts of his pious master . . . The dealers in the bodies and souls of men erect their stand in the presence of the pulpit, and they mutually help each other. The dealer gives his blood-stained gold to support the pulpit, and the pulpit, in return, covers his infernal business with the garb of Christianity. Here we have religion and robbery the allies of each other—devils dressed in angels' robes, and hell presenting the semblance of paradise.

White Christianity's racist slaveholding logics were thus always in tension with the possibility of black Christian redemption. This disjuncture marked, for many, the tenuous relationship between black Americans and Christianity, which has placed in question, most acutely among black Muslims, black Hebrews, and black humanists, the true possibility for redemption meted out through the Bible and its Jesus. Despite the influence of white Christian abolitionists in the struggle for liberation, the overwhelming acquiescence of white Christianity to black oppression made Christianity suspect. The redemptive possibility of Christianity, however, lay in its very power to critique the slaveholding Christianity of this land and to offer blacks a vision of existential possibility commensurate with their humanity. Redemption was thus, first and foremost, found in protest. Subsequent expressions of black religion as righteous protestation represented a renunciation of white (oppressive) Christianity. It was this sense of protest and possibility that inspired black versions of Christianity committed to the liberation, education, and uplift of black people and politicized versions of Christianity that circulated through newspapers, magazines, journals, and other media.

The founding of *Freedom's Journal* (later renamed *Rights of All*) on March 16, 1827, by John B. Russwurm and Reverend Samuel E. Cornish marked the first newspaper publication by African Americans. Established to counter the white press's negative portrayal of blacks as lazy, subhuman and degenerate, *Freedom's Journal* not only articulated the beauty and substance of black life, but it also advocated for black freedom and educational access. The announcement for the inaugural issue of the paper stated:

> Daily slandered, we think that there ought to be some channel of communication between us and the public, through which a single voice may be heard, in defense of five hundred thousand free people of colour. Too often has injustice been heaped upon us, when our only defense was an appeal to the Almighty, but we believe that the time has now arrived, when the calumnies of our enemies should be refuted by forcible arguments . . . [and to espouse the cause of the slaves who] are our kindred by all the ties of nature.[11]

Subsequent to the founding of *Freedom's Journal* and given the white press's unwillingness to discuss the conditions of African Americans in other than racist registers, several other black newspapers were formed to address these same concerns and made explicit appeals for public recognition of the deplorable social conditions to which blacks were subjected in the United States. These newspapers, which were founded between the mid-1830s and mid-1840s, included the *National Reformer*, the *Colored American*, the *Mirror of Liberty*, the *Mystery*, the *Genius of Freedom*, the *Ram's Horn*, and the *North Star*.[12] And, as their names suggest, the papers were committed to the emancipation of slaves and the advancement of black life. Men like Frederick Douglass and Reverend Alexander Crummel regularly contributed columns to such papers, framing and disseminating a self-conscious case for blacks' humanity. Of course, emerging articulations of racial redemption were mediated not only through written texts. Crossing into slave states, women like Harriet Tubman and Sojourner Truth used "slave telegraphs" as word of mouth communications to usher people to freedom through organized and clandestine institutions such as the Underground Railroad.[13]

Wrestling with America—its promises of hope amid its betrayal of those promises—all the while singing songs to a God of hope and deliverance, black religionists during the eighteenth and nineteenth centuries made concessions with the land of their ancestors' birth. Black Christians worked with one another and alongside white Northern abolitionists and missionaries to create a world in which blacks could potentially thrive—or even just survive. From the founding of the first black Baptist church in the United States in the 1740s to the establishment of the first formally black denomination, the African Methodist Episcopal church, in 1816 (out of the Free African Society of 1787), black Christians reconciled their "two warring ideals in one dark body," African *and* American, and resolved to find redemption in America.[14] With its three primary commitments to salvation, emancipation, and education, the mission of the African Methodist Episcopal Church reflected the ways in which black Christian possibility/identity could not only be embraced, but also celebrated. Notably, the *AME Church Review* was established in 1841, the oldest periodical published by an African American church body and one of the oldest church newsletters to champion emancipation outside of Quaker journals. The content of the *Review* reflects the ongoing concerns of faith in service of liberation.[15] The written mediated word held the power both to interpret the experiences of blacks and to sway the opinions of black compatriots and potential white allies. In addition to establishing periodicals, black religionists across denominational lines pooled their resources together to found black primary and secondary schools, colleges and universities, fraternal organizations, hospitals, burial societies, and a host of other institutions suited to redeem black life. In effect, they established organizations that proffered from cradle to grave an ideal of American hope and possibility. The building of such a magnificent infrastructure was central to the development of an educated and middle-class community. Collective action rendered individual sacrifice transformative. The "nation within a nation" that became the black church not only harnessed the pain and suffering of blacks but also bolstered the hopes, ambitions, and possibilities of black creativity, courage, and entrepreneurship. The mass-mediated word was central to this project.

The creation and publication of journals committed to the redemption of black people, however, often occurred under duress and amidst constant threats of physical violence. The very production of the medium was for black freedom fighters a defiant act of liberation, while for others, an act of treason against a white supremacist state. As early newspaper publications, slave narratives, and religious journals advocated for freedom, the real prospect of emancipation brought with it questions pertaining to the possibility of thriving in the post-bellum era. Immediately following emancipation in 1865, newspapers like the *New Orleans Tribune* published harrowing accounts of blacks mutilated and murdered. "To see the Negroes mutilated and literally beaten to death as they sought to escape, was one of the most horrid pictures it has ever been our ill-fortune to witness," opined the *Tribune*.[16] Standing up against Black Codes and the emerging Ku Klux Klan, these presses were under constant threat of bankruptcy and physical destruction. Near the turn of the century, editorials by T. Thomas Fortune and W. E. B. DuBois attracted both blacks and whites and advocated for full citizenship and equal protection under the law for African Americans. Anti-lynching advocate and writer Ida B. Wells-Barnett brought the truth of Southern aggression to light in papers like the *Living Way* and the *Gate City Press*. In 1889 she assumed control over the *Free Speech and Headlight*, a paper ultimately destroyed by a white mob in protest over Well's articles defending black womanhood and black men, while outlining the debauchery of white Southerners.[17] The truth that Wells wanted to highlight was that more often than not black victims of lynching were those who merely stood up for their rights or owned businesses that made whites feel that they were acting "uppity."

Turn-of-the-century concerns about the safety of black people and the possibilities of black redemption in the segregated South reverberated only more loudly in the twentieth century with the development of the phonograph, the sale of "race records," and urban migration. However, given ongoing threats of violence and the urgency of black freedom, race leaders made little room for superfluous entertainment. According to historian Lerone Martin, for those in churches and religious organizations who were fighting for the liberation of black people, the development of race records introduced a challenge to the work of protest and social uplift.[18] "Established black faith communities believed that race records promoted immoral forms of amusement and recreation that hindered black morality and racial advancement. Guided by racial uplift ideologies, these churches framed their concerns for race records in terms of cultural politics."[19] Race records, with their emphasis on entertainment, encouraged forms of "amusement" like minstrelsy and blues music believed by some to work in opposition to the respectability narratives proffered by black religious leaders. Respectability politics, after all, were designed to ward off both violent and nonviolent white attacks on the black community and to promote the idea that blacks, because of their dignified behavior, deserved respect and the full rights of citizenship. Women activists in organizations like the Woman's Convention Auxiliary of the National Baptist Convention (WC), the largest black denomination in the country at the time, and the National Association of Colored Women (NACW), saw in race records, as well as the success of indiscreet entertainers like Ma Rainey, a clear derailment of their diligent efforts toward the advancement of black women.[20]

As much as one might like to imagine that protest politics infused all black religious expression and that commercialization of religious messages is a contemporary phenomenon, Martin's work demonstrates that the introduction of the phonograph shifted both the substance and the aesthetic of popular black religion. Competing with race records, black ministers began to produce commercially successful sermons, which were sold by the thousands through white owned distribution houses like Paramount and Columbia Records. Financial success became the litmus test of white industries that ventured to record and distribute black voices, not racial uplift. Central to a preacher's signing with a recording house was his ability to attract audiences and sell records. Calvin P. Dixon, who was one of the first to deploy the phonograph in the distribution of his messages, was known as the "Black Billy Sunday," preaching against moral decay as blacks entered the clutches of urban life in the course of the Great Migration. Black preachers' deployment of recorded sermons as a means of reaching the masses through evangelistic messages meant that they intended to "sanctify the phonograph and race records for church work"; ultimately, they set the trend and established "the practice of selling to the souls of black folk."[21]

Whether or not these recordings promoted the work of social uplift and protest is a debatable point. As Martin explains, while some scholars have insisted that the "phonograph sermons offered resistance to (black) middle-class hegemony by stylistically authenticating and voicing the experiences of the working class," others contend otherwise.[22] Instead, they believe that "record executives had no interest in recording formally schooled clerics proclaiming a social gospel, but rather purposely signed clergy who agreed to avoid sermons that openly challenged 'widely accepted cultural conceptions of race, class, and gender stratification.'"[23]

What is clear from the advancement of technology to audible recordings is that concerns with race, class, and gender discrimination continued into the mid-century as black religionists steadfastly looked toward tools of mediation to challenge, inspire, and organize the masses. The very intersection of race, class, and gender concerns led to the development of the Civil Rights movement. Although Martin Luther King, Jr., and other popular male figures have often been the central figures around whom such narratives are told, women's working in the 1940s southern rural communities to guard against sexual violation from white men is what prompted the massive organizing efforts. The place of women's bodies on the front lines of the Civil Rights movement was indeed an extension of the work carried out by Wells-Barnett in her publication efforts. Despite the claims of the threat of "black brutes" to white women's virtue, as films like *The Birth of a Nation* (1915) suggested, those who were truly vulnerable, as Wells-Barnett had argued, were black women. Legally viewed as "unrape-able," they were in constant danger of forcible, unprosecuted rape—their many-hued descendants over the decades telling the story through their very bodies. Danielle McGuire's "new history of the civil rights movement" places the concerns of women at the forefront.[24] In the NAACP's 1944 campaign to secure justice for Recy Taylor, a black woman brutally raped by six white men while she was walking home from church, women like Rosa Parks took Taylor's story not only to the communities through word of mouth, but also to newspaper publications and northern radio stations, to advocate justice for Taylor and her family. This intersection of race, class, and gender in the interpretation of civil rights history highlights the ways in which shame served to keep some people silent and prevented a broadcasting of the troubles faced by blacks for fear of ongoing reprisals. Black women, having noted redemptive possibilities through both radical politics and the politics of respectability, found in broadcast media a place to tell their stories, while always aware that not all media outlets presented a fair and/or apologetic posture toward black suffering. As historian Barbara Savage explains, black efforts toward "broadcasting freedom" were always challenged by politics of distribution, with both federally funded and privately funded outlets hesitant to talk about race issues.[25] Black-owned outlets, like the *Chicago Defender*, were by far the most expedient means of communicating complete, detailed stories without the censorship and biased editorializing of the white press.[26] The 1955 funeral of fourteen-year-old Emmett Till, murdered for allegedly flirting with a white woman, became another lightning rod of the movement. Till's mother insisted that the world see how badly white Mississippi racists had tortured her son and mutilated his body. Images of Emmett's body were printed in the *Chicago Defender* and *Jet* magazine, both pivotal black periodicals of the time. According to Sasha Torres,

> Mamie Till Mobley, Till's mother, brilliantly insisted on iconizing the abused body of her son, demanding an open casket past which mourners in Chicago streamed for four days, and allowing *Jet* to use an image of Till's battered face, bloated and misshapen from river water, on its cover. It would not be going too far to say that Mobley thus invented the strategy that later became the SCLC's [Southern Christian Leadership Conference's] signature gesture: literally *illustrating* southern atrocity with graphic images of black physical suffering, and disseminating those images nationally.[27]

With the advance of the full blown Civil Rights movement, the struggle would play out in the press, particularly in the burgeoning medium of television. While newsreels rolled, Christianity itself was on trial, as white Christians in the South—like their forebears during Frederick Douglass's time and in Ida B. Wells's era—antagonized blacks or sat idly by on the sidelines. Historian Charles Marsh in *God's Long Summer* recalls how competing claims to and demands of Christianity were made during the height of the Civil Rights movement in the summer of 1964, as God had to contend with a multiplicity of petitioners' demands.[28] At the same time that Fannie Lou Hamer, who along with the Student Nonviolent Coordinating Committee (SNCC) helped organize Mississippi's Freedom Summer, was praying that her Christian God would bring deliverance to black people, Sam H. Bowers, Jr., imperial wizard of the Ku Klux Klan of Mississippi, was praying that his Christian God would reaffirm white supremacy. Adding to this list of demands, William Douglas Hudgins, white pastor of a prominent Southern Baptist church in Jackson, prayed that his Christian God would maintain the status quo and keep his congregants' business, social, and religious interests in order, and Edwin King, a white Methodist minister who challenged the segregation practices in Mississippi, prayed that God would intervene on the side of justice. If nothing else, God was busy during the summer of 1964. Despite sharing a faith with white supremacists, black civil rights workers continued to believe in the redemptive power of their religious commitments. To compel people to take their side, to see Christianity as fundamentally antiracist, leaders made use of newspapers, radio, and the increasingly important medium of television.

Images in the media of white brutality and stubborn resistance to racial equality seemed to aid in the movement's growth, particularly outside of the South. Television captured in black and white and later in colored images a visceral hatred for blacks that manifested in a willingness to sic attack dogs and aim powerful water hoses at peaceful protesters. Central to the strategy of civil rights leaders was to "contrast the racial terrorism of the South with national ideals and democratic discourses."[29] Martin Luther King, Jr. "understood the impact that the assaults on peaceful protesters had on a wider U.S. population. He therefore incorporated the presence of the cameras within the organization's protesting strategy."[30] Known to cancel marches if the news media would not attend, organizers tried to strategically orchestrate events in such a way that white sympathizers might put pressure on their legislators and the U.S. president to intervene.[31]

Believing in the ideals of freedom, democracy, and justice, black Christians marched, prayed, sang, and went to jail to demand equal protections under the law in a nation long since abandoned by other black free-thinking religionists. Thus, members of the Nation of Islam argued that whites were beyond redemption and thus rejected integration as a worthy goal. For them the fight was psychological. Black redemption required recognition that blacks did not need whites to legitimate their own history, to build their own societies, or, put simply, to humanize them. They strove to build their own "Nation" within a nation. Black Hebrew Israelites, likewise, abandoned America's racist "heathens" and reached out across the Atlantic to map out a redemption plan rooted in Israel, the "true" motherland, they believe, of black people.

These longings for an ideal, non-American, homeland were not new. In the early 1900s Marcus Garvey led the largest black mass movement in history, based on his ambitious "Back to Africa" vision. By purchasing ships and selling tickets, the project was intended to transport the marginalized masses back to the place of their collective birth/capture. Before Garvey, black Christians had set sail across the Atlantic with the aid and encouragement of the American Colonization Society to establish Liberia as a homeland for black Americans, this having been both a solution to the race problem in America and a part of their larger plan of redemption for black people.[32] How Africa, postcolonialism, and globalization are understood with respect to race issues in the United States in many respects explains the different religio-political orientations of black Christians, Muslims, and Jews. Black Christians typically view themselves as American and therefore see their struggles as uniquely American. Black Muslims, on the other hand, tended to link religiously to majority Muslim countries and other brown people outside the United States, often equating their struggles with postcolonial struggles around the world, regardless of race. Alternatively, black Hebrew Israelites identified geographically with a place that they have argued fundamentally differentiates their concerns from the concerns of people in sub-Saharan Africa, Asia, and Latin America. For all groups, this need to articulate a geography of belonging is tied in no small way to a desire for cultural citizenship and acceptance.

We see this desire reflected in the narratives of African American migrants. In the final declarative act of washing of his hands of America, W. E. B. DuBois relinquished hope of black redemption in America, a place that would recognize the full and equal humanity of black people.

After studying the challenges facing black folks in the United States, helping to found the NAACP, and penning hundreds of books and articles in national press outlets opining America's betrayal of its darker-hued brethren, DuBois, at the age of ninety-three, packed up and left. The hope of redemption diminishing in his frail body, he and his wife, Shirley Graham DuBois, set sail for Ghana to live out his last days on a continent he could call home.

The day after DuBois's death on August 27, 1963, during the March on Washington, Martin Luther King, Jr., would ascend the podium and, prompted by Mahalia Jackson, tell the nation about his bold dream. Black religious leaders like King situated black ethereal and existential longing in the context of American history, reminding believers of the challenges and possibilities of America. And yet, reconciling with the ideal of America meant reconciling with both the nation and its economic system, capitalism—and the exorbitant profits that came from the exploited bodies of black laborers. Murdered before he could complete his Poor People's Campaign, King had turned his attention not only to the cancer of American racism and the atrocities of the Vietnam War but also to the turpitudes of capitalism.

Learning to Prosper

The triumph of protest religion through the passage of *Brown v. the Board of Education* in 1954, the Civil Rights Act of 1964, and the Voting Rights Act of 1965 ended the long history of state-sanctioned legalized oppression. In no small way, the media proved essential to the advancement of black freedom in America. Central to the effort by the 1960s was the medium of television. Ironically, the height and subsequent decline of civil rights advocacy occurred just as the foundations of religious television broadcasting were expanding to include more conservative voices. While King's voice was muted by an assassin's bullet, the most popular religious voices heard on television would eventually come from religious broadcasters, their narratives of redemption modulated by their theological orientations and the mechanics of market-driven religious broadcasting. In the 1960s, aside from Martin Luther King, Jr., Billy Graham was the best known preacher of the day. The two, however, held opposing politics on the role of civil rights advocacy.

Graham was a conservative, born of the school of gradualism. Although he integrated his services long before doing so was popular, Graham still held tremendous reservation about direct action and civil rights protest, believing instead, along with many white ministers and some black ministers, that blacks should wait until the hearts and minds of whites changed for society to shift course. And yet, as Carolyn Dupont explains in a study of the history of evangelicals in Mississippi, "Contrary to evangelicals' assertions, the conversion of every Mississippian in the state would never correct the sufferings caused by an exclusionary political system, a deficient educational system, a discriminatory economic system, and an unfair judicial system. Yet this individualistic notion of social change allowed Mississippians," among other southern evangelicals, "to decry government initiatives as ineffective and unwarranted intrusions."[33] For Dupont, "white supremacy flourished, in part, *because* of evangelical religion's strength and not in spite of it."[34] With this cosmology "white supremacy cultivated its central myth: that blacks' difficulties arose from their own failings, and whites bore neither guilt nor responsibility for them."[35]

It was this nagging admonition to "wait," to trust in the eventual transformation of individual hearts, that had inspired King's "Letter from a Birmingham Jail."[36] And, yet, it was precisely this type of religious/social conservatism that made it to religious airways. King's rabble rousers, more connected to the social gospel and the type of work meted out by members of the Federal Council of Churches, did not take to religious television to broadcast their justice-oriented understanding of faith and were additionally not welcomed in the evolving, genteel, predominantly white and male oriented world of religious broadcasting.

The history of the dominating influence of conservative religion on religious television goes back to the launching of religious television broadcasting on Easter Sunday, 1940. While the vast majority of producers and distributors of religious broadcasting messages were originally from mainline Protestant, Catholic, and Jewish communities, by the 1970s the majority of religious broadcasters would come from more theologically and socially conservative traditions. Enjoying the lion's share of free airtime, in the early days of religious broadcasting, mainliners excluded evangelicals and charismatics from the power centers that dominated broadcasting, while offering the FCC's designated free air time to their colleagues. Feeling locked out, a group of evangelicals organized the National Religious Broadcasters Association in 1944, on the heels of the founding of the National Association of Evangelicals in 1940, and pledged their commitment to biblical authority over what they saw as the more liberal leanings of mainline churches associated with the Federal Council of Churches. According to conservatives, these churches had stretched the limits of the gospel beyond sin and repentance, and espoused a social gospel committed to radical social change, including civil rights advocacy and support for women's liberation through the ERA and later abortion rights. They believed such advocacy not only disrupted social life, but diverted Christian attention toward individual soul salvation and the gradual social change presumed to follow. From its inception, this group drew clear lines between itself and the liberal Federal Council of Churches with a resolution sent to radio and television broadcasters throughout the country in 1946.

> One misconception is that American Protestantism is one unified religious group, whereas in fact there are two distinct kinds of Protestants in America today. Each adheres to a particular form of teaching—the one the antithesis of the other. One group believes the Bible to be the infallible rule for belief and conduct whereas the other does not.[37]

And yet evangelicals' emphasis on "biblical faith" also included an allegiance to free-market capitalism and conservative social ideologies. The Soviet threat of "godless Communism" led many religious conservatives to close ranks around capitalism, hailing it in many regards as a hallmark of a Christian nation. Whatever their differences, religious conservatives rallied against three "evil forces that threatened the country: communism, secularism, and moral degeneracy."[38] This commitment coalesced in an alignment of religious conservatives with the pro-business, pro-capitalist focus of the Republican Party, despite various liberal Protestant critiques of capitalism and its abuses. The effective realignment between evangelical Christians and the free-market sensibilities of the Republican Party took place between the 1940s and 1960s. "Conservative Christians . . . resonated not only with the Republicans' moral traditionalism but also with their willingness to protect foreign mission fields from communism and their defense of limited government at home, against welfare programs and commercial regulation."[39] Advancing their theology, religious conservatives took to the airwaves.

The presence of evangelicals in the television broadcasting industry grew only slowly until 1960, when the Federal Communications Commission decided to end their distinction between "paid-time" and "sustaining-time" programming. For years, the FCC had ruled that "sustaining-time" programming rendered a public service to the local audience through the distribution of free religious service broadcasting. By contrast, the new ruling effectively stated that the public interest could be served through paid-time, profit-driven, programming. This decision resulted in a decline in mainline denominations on television and ushered in the era of market-driven religious broadcasting. The "paid-time" model of ministry benefited mostly those who could package, sell, and distribute their materials most rapidly. In the fast-paced world of American broadcasting, evangelicals and charismatics won out.

Aside from evangelical preachers like Billy Graham, more charismatic figures like Oral Roberts, Kenneth Copeland, and later Kenneth Hagin enjoyed a significant share of religious broadcast time. Although these figures tended to be less explicitly political in their statements, their conservative religious and social politics often left them silent supporters of the status quo concerning race and racism. After all, it was largely the progressive racial and gender politics of Jimmy Carter that lost him the support of Southern Baptists and evangelicals, groups that initially enthusiastically supported his election during a season national magazines hailed as "The Year of the Evangelical." Jerry Falwell's assistance in the dismantling of Carter's presidency with his Moral Majority movement, along with Pat Robertson's Christian Coalition, signaled the rise of the religious right in the United States.

While white televangelists dominated the air in the robust early days of paid-time programming, the first and most popular nationally broadcast African American televangelist was Reverend Frederick Eikerenkoetter. As ethicist Jonathan Walton explains, "Rev. Ike stands in the history of African American religious broadcasting as a connectional figure. He links the converging religio-cultural practices of the first half of the twentieth century with the social and technological advances utilized by African Americans in the post–civil rights era. . . . Rev. Ike is not only a connectional figure but a pivotal figure."[40] Eikerenkoetter's

flamboyant style and dress rebuffed civil rights leaders with their de-
mure black suits. And, yet, it was precisely the emphasis upon financial gain that Eikerenkoetter believed civil rights advocates missed. He
envisioned training black people to imagine their limitless possibility,
by placing mind over matter and thinking right. According to Eikerenkoetter, "I'd begin my radio broadcast saying 'You can be what you want
to be; you can do what you want to do; you can have what you want to
have, if you believe in the God in you.'"[41] Eikerenkoetter's mind science
lessons, built upon a combination of new thought, word of faith, and
charismatic inflections, operated to turn black people's attention inward
instead of outward.

The emergence of religious broadcasting, and particular forms of
black religious broadcasting, thus coincided not only with the decline
in civil rights activism but also with the rise in conservative religious
broadcasting and the entrenchment of neoliberal economic policies. As
a result, the strategy for redeeming black life has been radically altered
by the emergence in the past thirty years of a different type of black
religious ethos, one marked by hyper-individualism and a radical commitment to capitalist possibility. The attempts at redemption in this regard are articulated as a desire to transform black economic possibility
through the psychosocial redemption of black Americans. No longer
focused on eliminating government sanctioned hindrances to black economic, social, political uplift (such as low minimum wage, tax breaks to
the wealthy, withdrawal of affirmative action programs, mass incarceration, residential tax based education), popular black religious mediated
messages posit black possibility as stifled primarily and almost exclusively by the religious and psychological limitations of individuals. Such
conclusions place black individuals at the center of their own deliverance, rendering the state largely inculpable.

A number of scholars have traced this trend in black religious
media.[42] In *Watch This!*, for example, Walton examines how three leading black televangelists, T. D. Jakes, Creflo Dollar, and Eddie Long, each
of whom is from a different denominational background, all espouse
elements of the prosperity gospel made famous by early proponents like
Oral Roberts and Kenneth Hagin. Although different, each ministry,
Walton contends, thrives because it promotes ideals that work in mainstream discourses pertaining to "economic advancement, the minimiz-

ing of race, and Victorian ideals of the family."[43] The universalist pull of religious broadcasting almost requires that market share preempt concerns about speaking to a local audience. The message must be global, able to meet the concerns of the larger audience of believers. In this way contestations over raced, classed, and gendered inequities are minimized in order to put forth a universal and unified faith in God.

Currently, the astounding proliferation of prosperity gospels is decidedly American, as well as being transcontinental in scope. In some ways it is the most American of gospels. Celebrating abundance, individualism, and the blessings of prosperity, it prides itself on possibility. The prosperity gospel and its excesses are quintessentially rooted in American free market capitalism, the type outlined in agreements between Europe and America in the 1970s. Many pioneering prosperity preachers in other parts of the world, like Africa and Asia were, predictably, trained in the United States or mentored by U.S. pastors. Believers in the prosperity gospel believe ultimately in the possibilities of America. Though some other religionists have long since abandoned America, these religionists are true believers. Prosperity—rooted in the salvation work of Jesus, honed at times through the discipline of work, sealed always by the practice of giving, materialized by faith—is redemption.

Conclusion

For all of its appeals to Jesus, "the blood," holiness, salvation, and heaven, black Christianity, as a dominant strand of black religious life in the United States, registers no higher calling from society than the redemption of the race. If indeed it succeeds in rapturing black folks to heaven, yet fails to transform the social and economic conditions that lay bare the quotidian nature of black life in urban and rural settings alike to the eyes of politicians, social critics, and the public, it fails. Existential concerns trump ethereal ones. The uncertainty of the latter renders dependency on the former. Heaven is, after all, "a blessed Hope." Redemption under these circumstances mocks the "dry as dust religion" chided by Martin Luther King and necessitates a cure. Redemption, earthly redemption, is its social mandate.

To the extent that mass-distributed, mass-consumed televised faith responds to individual crisis and eschews the collective angst, it affirms the functional reasonableness of America and its social and economic systems. In the past thirty years, since the civil rights era, the most popular religious voices on paid-time television networks such as Trinity Broadcasting Network, the Inspiration Network, and Daystar overwhelmingly emphasized that not protest, but faith—faith in God *and* faith in America (and admittedly American capitalism)—is central to redemption. The first may historically be rendered a given; the second is a faith that is always "already," but "not yet." For the past several centuries black religion has marked redemptive possibilities through belief *and* protest and yet contemporary calls for protest and collective action through Black Lives Matter and Moral Mondays signal a renewed sense of urgency among many black Americans and their allies for addressing structural hindrances to black redemption.

2

Racial Redemption

Language in Muslim Media

We wish to plead our own cause. Too long have others spoken for us.
Masthead of *Freedom's Journal* (1827–1829)

Dedicated to freedom, justice and equality for the so-called
Negro. The Earth belongs to Allah.
Masthead of *Muhammad Speaks* (1960–1975)

Bismillah ir-Rahman ir-Rahim: Bringing humanity together
in moral excellence with Truth and Understanding.
Masthead of *Muslim Journal* (1981–present)

The Nation of Islam began in the 1930s in Detroit, Michigan, where W.
D. Fard, a door-to-door salesman most likely of South Asian descent,
converted the then Elijah Poole to a faith that combined elements of
Islam with prescriptions for black empowerment. After Fard disappeared, his pupil, by then known as Elijah Muhammad, went on to
convert many disaffected blacks by proclaiming Fard to be Allah and
himself to be his final messenger. While that was clearly a radically
unorthodox teaching, the Nation of Islam began adopting orthodox Sunni Muslim practices and beliefs as early as the 1950s when it
introduced Arabic into its Chicago Muhammad University of Islam
elementary and high school curriculum. The introduction of Arabic
followed deepening engagements with Muslims from the Middle East
and South Asia. But well before the Nation of Islam began to build
relationships with brown and black anticolonial leaders from abroad,
the FBI had listed the organization as a dangerous cult and put it
under surveillance.

Figure 2.1 The cover of the first *Muhammad Speaks*. The Nation of Islam's ideology of separation and belief about the existential threat posed by those who reject their claims stand in stark contrast with the spiritual, political, racial, and economic goals of the Christian-led Civil Rights movements of the 1950s and 1960s.

Figure 2.2 This cartoon is meant to depict the power of the Nation of Islam to radically alter black dispositions. The Nation felt that by refusing to challenge fundamental beliefs about the state, the race, and the body, the church was simply reproducing black disfranchisement.

As a result of this surveillance, the first of a number of FBI raids against the Chicago temple occurred in 1942. From this raid, the only charges that could be successfully lodged against Elijah Muhammad and thirty-seven other defendants was draft evasion. These men chose jail over fighting for a country that enslaved their ancestors and continued to endorse institutional racism at home and imperialism abroad.[1] African American converts to the Nation of Islam in the mid-twentieth century loudly rejected the authority and legitimacy of the United States government, eventually casting it in *Muhammad Speaks* as beyond redemption. *Muhammad Speaks*, the Nation of Islam's newspaper, sold in major cities across the United States from 1961 to 1975 and articulated a political ideology that members adopted for themselves. As represented in the pages of the paper, the rejection of the state's authority by the Nation of Islam posed an even greater threat to the U.S. government than the well-organized, nonviolent civil rights activists who were inspired by Christian faith and who desired a seat at the table. It was one thing for a state to try to hold at bay a population who, though despised, believed in the legitimacy of the state and the tenets undergirding state structures. It was another to be confronted by people, also despised and disenfranchised, who rejected the legitimacy of the state, including its monopoly on violence. The Nation of Islam was decidedly not going to wait for the state to recognize the humanity of their brethren (figure 2.3). Instead, its followers turned their back on a corrupt state that, they argued, could not possibly offer them the type of salvation they needed and wanted in their lifetimes.

As a result of the Nation of Islam's refusal to accept the legitimacy of the United States government, it became one of the most reviled African American organizations of the twentieth century.[2] Because of its unorthodox version of Islam and refusal to embrace the pacifist ethic of the Civil Rights movement, journalists often characterized it as a dangerous cult. In truth the threat the Nation posed to those outside the organization has been profoundly overstated. The leadership never supported communism, which might have aligned the NOI with powerful anti-American movements, and members were allowed to act violently only in self-defense.[3] Moreover, their social and economic agendas were in many ways quite conservative.[4] Yet from the 1940s to the early 1970s FBI director J. Edgar Hoover demanded that the Nation be treated as a threat to the very foundation of American society.

But it was not only white Americans who were afraid of the organization. Many black leaders, including future Supreme Court Justice Thurgood Marshall, publicly denounced the leaders as reprobates. Marshall had his own personal reasons. He was frequently ridiculed by Elijah Muhammad and Malcolm X for his integrationist goals and conviction that by working within the law blacks could achieve racial equality. By 1960 even Martin Luther King, Jr., had embraced the need for extralegal activism in order to free people from the "myths and half-truths" of racism.[5] Ultimately, the Nation and Marshall opposed each other publicly through colorful name-calling. Marshall averred that the Nation of Islam was run by recently released thugs and "handkerchief-head Negroes." He also called Malcolm X a lowlife and a pimp and suggested that

Figure 2.3 April 1962. Promises made by whites regarding integration are represented as merely a game. In many ways this cartoon echoes the ruling decision in *Plessey vs. Ferguson* in which Judge Brown notes that legal rights do not necessarily translate to social rights.

the organization was financed by Arabs like Egypt's President Gamal Abdel Nasser.[6] For their part, Elijah Muhammad and Malcolm X called Marshall a tool of white folks, a fool, and "a half-white nigger."[7] While the barbs amounted, in many respects, to a family spat played out in the media, their professed ideological differences spoke directly to the question of why Islam.

The tensions between Marshall and the Nation colorfully represent some of what Islam provided African Americans that Christianity did not.[8] Black Muslims did not simply reject the authority of the state. They challenged mainstream understandings of world history and white supremacy, the very foundations upon which American exceptionalism and white entitlement were built (figure 2.4). In that respect J. Edgar Hoover was right, but for the wrong reasons. The Nation of Islam was not a threat to the United States because it espoused self-defense. It was a threat because it challenged the integrity of myths endorsing state-

Figure 2.4 April 1962. In this cartoon Thurgood Marshall is represented as a weak child easily manipulated by the U.S. government, embodied in the form of a giant President J. F. Kennedy. Kennedy is schooling Marshall about why blacks should not worry about economic and land reparations and why professions of equality are enough.

sponsored violence and institutional racism. The members attended to different truths, meaning that they were beyond the control of discourses that legitimated state interests. For black Muslims, submitting to such concepts and histories amounted to participating in their own disenfranchisement. While there were certainly many problematic aspects of the Nation of Islam, its approach to rethinking race, truth, and citizenship remains a critical feature of not just African American Islam, but American Islam today.[9]

This chapter analyzes the stakes in the Nation of Islam's approach to what Ida B. Wells-Barnett in 1910 described as "the Negro question." In her article entitled "How Enfranchisement Stops Lynching," Wells-Barnett describes how without equal protections, violence fills the space of law.[10]

> The Negro question has been present with the American people in one form or another since the landing of the Dutch Slave Ship in Jamestown, Virginia, in 1619. . . . The flower of the nineteenth century civilization for the American people was the abolition of slavery, and the enfranchisement of all manhood. Here at last was a squaring of practice with precept, with true democracy, with the Declaration of Independence and with the Golden Rule.[11]

After describing how slave labor wrested a living from the "bowels of the earth" and thus saved British pioneers from their "miserable failures," Wells-Barnett goes on to note that the drafting of the Declaration of Independence, the Bill of Rights, and the Constitution were hopeful moments of enlightenment only to be ignored by much of the white South:

> Although the Constitution specifically says, no state shall do so, they *do* deprive persons of life, liberty, and property without due process of law, and do deny equal protection of the laws to persons of Negro descent. . . . Having swept aside the constitutional safeguards to the ballot, it is the smallest of small matters for the South to sweep aside its own safeguards to human life. . . . The mob says: "This people has no vote with which to punish us or the consenting officers of the law, therefore we indulge our

brutal instincts, give free rein to race prejudice and lynch, hang, burn them when we please." She [South Carolina] has led in all the secession movements for the nullification of the constitution and for the abrogation of the 14th and 15th amendment[s]. She has led in all the butcheries on the helpless Negro which makes the United States appear a more cruel government than Russia, for her deeds are not done under the guise of democracy and in the name of liberty.[12]

Importantly, the connections Wells-Barnett draws among law, violence, and enfranchisement are echoed in the politico-religious discourses of the Nation of Islam and the Sunni Muslim community.

By focusing on the central language ideologies at play in Muslim media, specifically around violence, race, and citizenship, we can see the Nation of Islam's unique approach to redeeming the race. The Nation took taken-for-granted assumptions about the United States, race, and the supposed value of integration and flipped these narratives through resignification. We see this quite clearly in *Muhammad Speaks* cartoons that disrupt commonly held views by juxtaposing pregnant signifiers in an effort to render an alternative truth (figure 2.5).

Theories of language link identity, belief, and even aesthetics to how we use language and to what we talk about.[13] Theories of language mirror theories of media in the sense that both language and media are constellations of signifiers attempting to communicate something, although that something is open to interpretation by the listener and viewer and is thus indeterminate. Like George Bernard Shaw's Eliza Doolittle, who is able to pass as British high society after Henry Higgins schools her in upper-class phonetics and acceptable topics of conversation, we are shaped by language ideologies, which ultimately affect what we can and cannot do.[14]

At the same time that our linguistic competencies limit our agency, we do have some control. We can adjust how we talk, adapting our speech to fit each social context. Notably, switching linguistic registers (varieties of speech) and codes (words) is one of President Obama's skills. His speech performances have been seen as an expression of his sensitivity toward others, as well as indications of his competence, legitimacy, and humility, and they have been part and parcel of his political success.[15] In addition to switching registers and codes, speakers can playfully re-

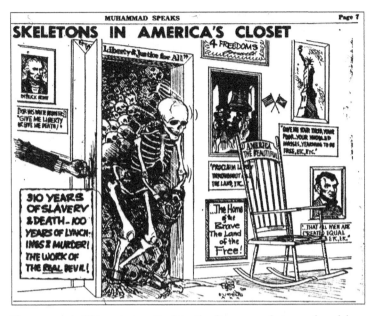

Figure 2.5 1962. This cartoon articulates the discrepancy between the celebration of the United States as the fulfillment of the American Enlightenment project of equality for all and the actual racist practices the government supported directly or through state surrogates—most notably black lynchings.

assemble signifiers in an effort to alter prevailing ideologies. In the political arena this resignification is best exemplified by the changing of the term "estate tax" to "death tax." Through simple word substitution, taxing a small percentage of the richest Americans came to be viewed as government overreach. "Death tax" impassioned the electorate by effectively casting the state as a heartless necrophiliac, lusting after the hard-earned wealth of the newly dead. This resignification was countered in direct and indirect ways by "Occupy Wall Street," and "I am the 99%," which redirected attention toward the controllers of capital and structural inequality. And the playful deployment of concentrated signifiers and countersignifiers continues.

As "systems of representation," language ideologies are the product of complex social and political histories.[16] They matter because the power to persuade depends on how well a media producer is able to work within a language ideology to convince. The values and meanings embedded in the signifiers at play, therefore, provide a window to the values and dispositions of the viewers as well.

The ideologies on which this chapter focuses include the right of blacks to self-defense and the meaning of whiteness. Both were subject to ongoing debates and resignification within the Nation of Islam and represent the Nation's contribution to new ways of thinking about race and citizenship. The chapter explores key debates linked to African American Muslim identity as reflected in African American Muslim media to show that the Nation of Islam and later African American Sunni Islam were shaped by engagement with a set of critical questions at particular historical moments. This chapter includes many cartoon images from the Nation's newspaper, *Muhammad Speaks*, which graphically represent the Nation's ideology and political rhetoric. African American Islam has become mainstream since the death of its longtime leader Elijah Muhammad, and with that shift have come changes in Muslim media. What remains, however, is a continued unsettling of (racial) identity, (historical and religious) truth claims, and (rights and duties of) citizenship.

In Defense of Self-Defense

The most significant contribution made by the Nation of Islam toward racial redemption was its articulation of the many reasons why blacks had a right to defend themselves (figure 2.6). But the Nation was not the first to articulate the right of black people to fight against the state and state surrogates. Frederick Douglass, Ida B. Wells-Barnett, and W. E. B. Dubois, among others, authored articles claiming the right of self-defense in the face of judicial and extra-judicial killings. The authorization of violence was significant because it not only put the fear of God in some whites, it also asserted in unequivocal terms black equality and agency, which whites had worked so hard to suppress.

It is important to recall that the stakes of a pro-self-defense ideology hinged on the failure of the United States to fulfill its promise of equality. This failure became particularly pronounced in the twentieth century as blacks, some of whom had fought in World War I, continued to be denied equal protection under the law. The Progressive Era of the late nineteenth and early twentieth century, a time when the social compact

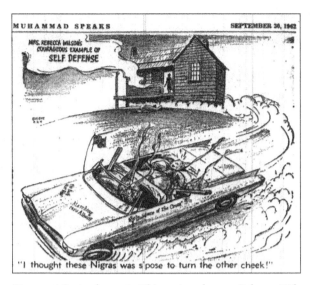

Figure 2.6 September 1962. This cartoon honors Rebecca Wilson, a twenty-one-year-old who used a .22-caliber revolver to protect herself and her family against seven armed and masked white supremacists. She shot five times through the door, killing Leroy Parks immediately and wounding another man. The white men were charged with violating an anti-masking ordinance (an ordinance aimed at diminishing white hate crimes) and with attempted murder. For the Nation of Islam, the story of Wilson encapsulates why blacks needed to practice self-defense. *Source*: Strain, Pure Fire: Self-Defense as Activism in the Civil Rights Era, 75–77.

was revitalized, failed to benefit the majority of African Americans, who instead had to stand on the sidelines as working-class whites received enhanced worker protections and expanded social benefits. In the first Great Migration of the early twentieth century, black Americans traveled north in search of relief from the Jim Crow South only to find racism in different institutional forms in the North.[17]

The response to this disfranchisement, visible in African American Muslim media, was an effort to assert rights of citizenship based upon a different set of moral claims. Giving up on the idea that law precedes justice, the Nation of Islam (and to a lesser extent the Sunni Muslims

Figure 2.7 December 1961. This cartoon demonstrates the ontological claims made regarding Islam as the authentic faith of slaves brought from Africa. Christianity is represented as the faith used by whites to brainwash and oppress slaves.

who followed) authored new discourses about racial possibility through ontological claims of racial origin and religious authenticity.

The story of Elijah Muhammad, a self-proclaimed prophet, and his encounter with the divine reveal less about the then Elijah Poole's existential motivations than about the urban economy before most Americans had television or the Internet. Muhammad's modern-day Trinitarian Jesus came in the form of a door-to-door salesman, W. D. Fard, whom he met in Detroit in 1931. Fard had been giving speeches, and word spread quickly about a savior who had come to help the black man reclaim his religious heritage. After Fard disappeared, Elijah Muhammad identified the mysterious South Asian preacher first as a prophet in his newspaper the *Final Call to Islam* (1934) and later as the embodiment of Allah.[18] Muhammad's divine providence, he told his growing congregation, was to guide the so-called Negroes out of the wilderness by teaching them their true history, faith, and capacity for moral goodness (figure 2.7).

At its best, the Nation of Islam promoted African American businesses, leadership, education, and political engagement. Its focus on the material results of action, or the rewards of discipline and solidarity, is what made the organization formidable. A passionate sense of common purpose was built, in large part, by identifying whites as a common enemy, a tactic that rankled many white Americans who imagined de jure segregation and extrajudicial violence the exception rather than the rule in the 1950s and 1960s. But for blacks, disenfranchisement and the threat of violence were the rule. As the Nation of Islam gained membership and political influence during this time, people were drawn to it not primarily on account of its charismatic leader, but on account of the embedding of difficult racial truths within the faith. Importantly, the Nation was not a cult in which members endowed a venerated individual with the power to name arbitrary truths and enact arbitrary rules. The ideology espoused by Elijah Muhammad was deeply rooted in black political protest dating back to the eighteenth century. And with the exception of its origin myth, the organization always tried to ground its ideological claims in empiricism, albeit in a cherry-picked variety. We see this in the media produced by or about the Nation in the 1950s and 1960s.

The Nation's media production worked to quietly celebrate the good works of members and to translate its message to skeptics, both black and white. Rather than shaming whites, Muhammad flipped the power dynamic by putting whites and the so-called black bourgeoisie on the defensive (figure 2.8). He argued that throughout history, whites had failed to prove their capacity for moral goodness and therefore must

Figure 2.8 January 1967. In this cartoon we see a black minister working with Uncle Sam to keep a black man from converting to Islam. The black minister's role in supporting Christianized white supremacy for his own economic gain is contrasted with a movement built on freedom, justice, equality, and economic self-sufficiency.

be considered an inferior race of "blue-eyed devils." Though the claim that "whites are devils" was delivered as a metaphor, it was interpreted by those outside of the Nation as a statement of racial essentialism and reverse racism. But members treated the descriptor as an analogy. The statement did not describe racial essence (it was not a reversal of white supremacy in that respect) but was a descriptor of action and deeds. Whites acted like devils. Indeed, the Nation of Islam attacked blacks, like Thurgood Marshall, by identifying them as white.

White or whiteness defined an ideology and worldview that endorsed unwarranted oppression of groups of people. And so why would the Nation of Islam reverse the moral binary? Blacks were terrorized by daily forms of violence, from humiliation to state-sanctioned murder. They were also cowed by discourses that cast blacks as morally and intellectually inferior. As simple as this analogy was, "blue-eyed devils" had the ability to reshape the dispositions of not only converts, but also blacks in the inner-city who sympathized with the Nation's mission of self-empowerment (figures 2.2 and 2.9).

In order to understand the power of this redemptive signifier, it is necessary to describe the quality of black abjection. In a documentary entitled *City of Muslims*, former minister of NOI Temple 27, Abdul Kareem, later Sulayman Beyah, depicts it beautifully when discussing Elijah Muhammad and the transition from Nation of Islam to Sunni Islam:

> He showed us how to have our own markets, he showed us how to have our own businesses. We know everybody had to pass [die], and he always taught us that someone was going to come after him and teach the religion because what he taught was to lift us up out of the mud so that we could become citizens; decent people, loving human beings. See he just made a man out of us. . . . Like Jesus when he gave the sight to the blind man. They asked the blind man who was he? The blind man said he didn't know who he was. He didn't care who he was all he knew was he was blind but now he could see. I know that I was in the mud. I know that I didn't have much going for me in the sense of character and he gave me a life.[19]

In this equating of himself with mud, dirt, or filth, Beyah's rendering fits perfectly with Julia Kristeva's notion of abjection, which she defines

Figure 2.9 August 1965. This cartoon series succinctly articulates the type of reeducation the Nation hoped to accomplish. In addition to expressing the beliefs of the Nation, the cartoon represents a particular form of black masculinity and sociality thought necessary to lead a new nation.

as the internalization of a sense of one's own moral inferiority, or "subjectified sin."[20] Religious notions of purity and defilement provide rich metaphors that continue to prove useful for white supremacists. Racism and sexism are, if nothing else, a product of languages that cast the other as dirty and sinful. The object of this scorn comes to identify as debased or "in the mud." But while language contributes to our sense of our own abjection, it is also through language that we remake ourselves.[21] In the documentary, Beyah casts himself as a debased uncivilized product of nature until Elijah Muhammad civilizes him through education, protocols for behaviors, opportunities for leadership, and reminders of his self-worth.[22] And this religious orthopraxy, which freed Sulayman Beyah from feelings of powerlessness and worthlessness, had a history.

Importantly the Nation of Islam's praxis, crystalized in the graphic imagery and cartoons in *Muhammad Speaks*, had roots in the eighteenth century when blacks preached against white supremacy.[23] But the ability to disseminate those teachings widely did not happen until the early nineteenth century, when technological innovations made cheap mass printing possible. Henceforth, groups from the Cherokees to labor organizations to religious institutions would disseminate tracts promoting various social agendas.[24] So the message of the Nation of Islam did not emerge in the 1930s with the arrival of Fard in Detroit, Michigan, or in 1913 with the founding of Noble Drew Ali's Moorish Science Temple of America in Newark, New Jersey, which similarly drew on the Islamic faith to shape a black (or Moorish) nationalist project. The ways in which the Nation of Islam framed issues of race, truth, and citizenship were the product of over three centuries of work honing a *black* political consciousness and a sense of *black* common cause, mediated through mass-distributed images, sounds, and texts. To be part of the black Muslim community required understanding the terms of these debates, but then deciding that the best response to white supremacy was economic and political separation (figure 2.1).

For many African Americans the concept of an independent black state, or the suggestion that blacks had a right to protect themselves from the state, was too radical. Many black Christians were turned off by the thorough rejection of the United States as a place of possibility for African Americans. But for the often disgruntled (former) Christians who joined the Nation, they were simply tired of attempting to play by the rules of Caesar. Two media events help us to understand the rationales for self-defense. The first is the publication of David Walker's *Appeal* of 1829.[25] The second is the publication of representations of a 1962 police shooting of Muslims in Los Angeles.[26]

Opening Salvo: The *Appeal*

David Walker's *Appeal* was published in *Freedom's Journal* (1827–1829), the first African American newspaper in the United States.[27] The publishers, Cornish and Russwurm, understood the potential of the printing press to disseminate information widely in order to develop a black political consciousness.[28] Before that, poor communication among states and even counties meant that a black community, with a shared set of values, discourses, and political objectives, remained in its infancy.[29] In the 1820s, the experiences of disparate groups of blacks— mostly enslaved, others not, some educated, and many of mixed-race descent—had yet to be summed up in compelling narratives that had the power to shape social dispositions and authorize political action.

The publisher's goal was to reach the half million free blacks believed to reside in the nation, many of whom could read. At its height, *Freedom's Journal* was read by eight hundred subscribers, but reached far more illiterate blacks through oral transmission. Geographically, the paper reached people as far north as Boston and as far south as Louisiana. There were also agents, donors, and others who organized collections for the paper in Haiti, England, and Canada. The agents included many leaders of African American churches as well as some white philanthropists who were avowedly antislavery.[30] Despite the reach of the paper, the revenues from advertising and the three-dollar per year subscription were not enough to sustain it. Moreover, many, such as Samuel Miller, a white professor at the Princeton Seminary, ended his subscription when the publishers took an open stance against state-sponsored colonization. Miller then used his bully pulpit to renounce the paper. White readership declined in lockstep.

Importantly, the publishers of *Freedom's Journal* were on a short leash. The paper was too radical for most whites, and when Russwurm wrote an editorial supporting the American Colonization Society, it became too conservative for most blacks.[31] On the front page of every *Freedom's Journal* was a statement about the importance of black self-representation as well as the words "Righteousness Exalteth a Nation," taken from Proverbs 14:34, and a quotation from President John Adams, who opposed slavery. Cornish and Russwurm also reminded readers that their paper was "Devoted to the Improvement of the Coloured Population."

Published in four installments, Walker's *Appeal* makes a passionate case for the rights of black people to physically defend themselves given the realities of slavery. At the time, David Walker was a member of the Massachusetts General Colored Association, a position that enhanced his credibility. His appeal was directed at colored people but he knew that white Americans, some sympathetic and some not, would be eavesdropping on this internal debate among black Americans:

> *My dearly beloved Brethren and Fellow Citizens*, Having travelled over a considerable portion of these United States . . . the result of my observa-

tions has warranted the full and unshaken conviction, that we, (coloured people of these United States,) are the most degraded, wretched, and abject set of beings that ever lived since the world began.[32]

Knowing that many educated blacks had faith that equality, as enshrined in the Constitution, would eventually become the law of the land, Walker reminded his readers that the framers of the Constitution actually believed that blacks were subhuman. This meant that the statement about the equality of all men applied only to those considered to be men.[33] After dismissing the Constitution as a possible tool for ending slavery, Walker assessed the value of Christianity to promote social change. While many blacks felt that by appealing to Christian ethics— the sort of "What would Jesus do?" approach to naming and shaming— they could change people's attitudes, Walker dismissed the power of Christianity to end slavery given that white preachers were often complicit in promoting the institution of slavery.[34]

Identifying himself as a true believer, as opposed to Christians who supported slavery, Walker nevertheless understood that casting himself as a better interpreter of the Bible left plenty of room for doubt. Racist Christians could easily dismiss his exegesis as wrong. Given this indeterminacy, Walker concluded that if appeals to the Constitution or Christianity failed, the only recourse available to blacks was violence. This call to arms he justified by returning to the Declaration of Independence, not in order to persuade, but in order to shame. In a dramatic shift, he speaks directly to white readers; his "we" becomes a sustained "you," as he reminds them that they had dishonored the principles upon which the country was founded:

See your Declaration Americans!!! Do you understand your own language? Hear your languages, proclaimed to the world, July 4th, 1776— "We hold these truths to be self evident—that ALL MEN ARE CREATED EQUAL!! that they *are endowed by their Creator with certain unalienable rights*; that among these are life, *liberty*, and the pursuit of happiness!!" Compare your own language above, extracted from your Declaration of Independence, with your cruelties and murders inflicted by your cruel and unmerciful fathers and yourselves on our fathers and on us—men who have never given your fathers or you the least provocation!!!!!![35]

The moral righteousness of the founding fathers is clearly embedded in the Constitution, but whether it was worse to be called a hypocrite than a violent racist overlord was an open question. African Americans living in post-revolutionary America were well aware that the words "all men are created equal" were neither an anticipated future nor a mistake. Drafters of the original documents, like Thomas Jefferson, did not accept the full humanity of blacks and believed that the poor and women lacked the full capacities of reason. The loftiness of their ideals was necessary in order to insure that the founders themselves would not become the victims of arbitrary legal exclusions. In other words, the statement of equality was a pragmatic necessity. Abolitionist William Lloyd Garrison even called the Constitution "an agreement with hell" and a "covenant with death" that should be annulled.[36] Natural law for the founders of the Constitution was a philosophy built on presentism, or the idea that the way the world is is the way "God" ordained the world to be, in a religious equivalent of sociobiology. Therefore, if blacks were slaves then that meant that God ordained for blacks to be slaves not men.

Regardless of whether or not racists could be shamed out of their beliefs, Walker's *Appeal* tapped into the dialectical potential of the founding documents. As Constitutional scholar Jack Balkin argues in *Constitutional Redemption: Political Faith in an Unjust World*,

> Constitutions are monuments both to liberty and license, equality and exploitation, hope and hypocrisy. The question is whether such a compromise, such a Constitution, can eventually be redeemed over time. . . . To answer that the Constitution can be redeemed is to have faith in a transgenerational project of politics. This faith is essential to the Constitution's legitimacy. It can be argued for, but it cannot be proven. It is a leap of faith.[37]

Balkin makes clear that with respect to law what constitutes reasonableness is always shifting. The one thing that matters for America's ongoing political project is for people to find ways to make a case for why they deserve equal protection, and for the law to be receptive to those concerns.

Ultimately, it took more than two hundred years of intellectuals and activists negotiating within this dialectical space of law and redemption for blacks to win equal citizenship. African Americans could have chosen to become "terrorists," like the American colonists, violently resisting a state that they believed gave them no other option. And some did, Denmark Vesey and Nat Turner being the most iconic leaders of slave rebellions. But to be clear, in part this book is written to de-politicize the word terrorism or terrorist. Definitionally "terrorism" refers to the use of violence for political ends but in no way refers to whether that act was just or not. Therefore, the term should never foreclose further discussion. To define an act as terrorism demands a follow up question, for what purpose? States use terror against citizens. Right wing and left wing organizations use terror. Terror is used against violent oppressive states as well as liberal progressive states. To label an act of terrorism with no explanation about context is itself a political act; rhetorical rather than analytical. Vesey and Turner's rebellions against chattel slavery were just. The KKK's terror against freed African Americans was not.

One of the key interests of this book is the question of why overwhelmingly African Americans did not resort to violence to achieve political ends. The United States became the country it is precisely because of how African Americans peacefully adjudicated each successive assault on their rights. Rather than take up the proverbial sword, blacks have relied on Americans' deep-seated sense of moral righteousness as a tool for shaming, primarily through religiously inflected speech. Slavery, racist violence, Jim Crow, and now mass incarceration and economic disfranchisement have all been met with words and signifiers and remarkably little violence. The fabric of American democracy is strong precisely because these discourses have found their way into Constitutional amendments, making it harder for exclusionary discourses to prevail. Every word of "all men are created equal" has been subject to arbitration, and therefore what we mean by *all* (Thirteenth Amendment) and *men* (Nineteenth Amendment) and *are* (Fifteenth Amendment) and *created* (the Declaration of Independence) and *equal* (the Bill of Rights) are now part of case law. Rather than exacting an eye for an eye, and despite never fully experiencing the promise of law, blacks held onto their faith in the Constitution.

What came to distinguish black religious and activist organizations from one another was not their commitment to cultivating moral character. They all considered it necessary for blacks to be beyond reproach or risk validating white supremacy. What ultimately distinguished African American Muslim political ideology from African American Christian political ideology was its degree of faith in the Constitution to open a legal space for blacks.

Walker recognized that citizens could reject the authority of the state and thus open up the possibility for resistance. Even under slavery, elected leaders understood that the state was under threat of delegitimization. As historian Eugene Genovese describes in his monumental text on slavery, "The law must discipline the ruling class and guide and educate the masses. To accomplish these tasks it must manifest a degree of evenhandedness sufficient to compel social conformity; it must, that is, validate itself ethically in the eyes of several classes, not just the ruling class."[38] Wealthy whites knew that maintaining this balance between law as repressive and law as equalizing was extremely tricky given the grotesqueness of slavery.[39] At any moment blacks could have chosen to break from the social contract. Walker suggested in his text that if blacks stopped believing in the Constitution's proposition of equality and justice, then the legitimacy of the state might be tested in battle.

One hundred years later, Walker's rejection of the authority of the state was taken up by the Nation of Islam and Marcus Garvey's Universal Negro Improvement Association ("One God! One Aim! One Destiny!").[40] Why did it take so long for the core of Walker's argument to find new audiences? In part it had to do with the incremental changes that occurred before and after the Civil War. Abolitionists had been slowly reforming the system such that African Americans began to reinvest hope in the law. But then came post-Reconstruction and the failure of the state to protect blacks from violence and institutional racism.

Walker's *Appeal* was perhaps the most important and popular series ever published by *Freedom's Journal*. But questioning under what conditions it is justifiable to use violence to overthrow a system like slavery was by all measures far too radical. The paper had to appeal to people with money, and white abolitionists seemed like an appropriate target audience. But white antislavery sentiment should not have been confused with pro-black or anticolonial sentiment. In many ways, it is no surprise that the publishers of the first African American newspaper had no idea who their audience was or how their readers would respond.

Nevertheless, the fact that the journal collapsed after only two years was in no way an indicator of the level of support for black radicalism.

By the twentieth century, many blacks, tired of waiting, had grown disaffected by what they perceived as ineffectual, almost apologetic, challenges to white supremacy by black Christian leaders. In response, in the early 1900s, radical new religions arose, espousing everything from racial return to Africa (Marcus Garvey's United Negro Improvement Association) to racial integration and abstinence (Father Divine's International Peace Mission movement).[41] While all had some level of success, the Nation of Islam stands out for its outsized role in the public imagination during the civil rights era. Being cast as the antithesis of the Christian-led pacifist protest movement, the Nation of Islam gained new members as it articulated a case for economic and social independence from whites. In the process of trying to make itself legible to outsiders, the organization made itself more legible to itself. In the end, what emerged from debates over the meaning of citizenship, race, and the larger question of God's mercy and purpose was a Sunni Muslim community dedicated to social justice and global citizenship. In the changing language ideology of the community, a conscious awareness that words and concepts emerge out of particular social contexts and therefore must be understood accordingly is notable.

Language Ideologies at Work: From Nation to Sunni

MALCOLM X: But as you know the Bible is written in symbols, parables and the serpent or snake is the symbol that is used to hide the real identity.

LOUIS LOMAX [AFRICAN AMERICAN JOURNALIST]: Well who was it?

MALCOLM X: The white man. . . . By nature he is evil.

LOUIS LOMAX: He cannot do good?

MALCOLM X: We don't have any historic example where we have found that they collectively [as a] people have done good.

Interview from *The Hate that Hate Produced* (documentary, 1959)

1. We want freedom.
2. We want justice. Equal justice under the law.
3. We want equality of opportunity. We want equal membership in society.
4. We want our people whose parents are descendants from slaves, to be allowed to establish a separate territory of their own. Since we cannot get along with them [whites] in peace and equality after giving them 400 years of our sweat and blood, we believe our contributions to this land and the suffering forced upon us by white America, justifies our demand for complete separation in a state of our own.

"What the Muslims Want," regular column, *Muhammad Speaks* (1960–1975)

W. D. MOHAMMED [ELIJAH MUHAMMAD'S SON]: The most profound change that was made was the change in the belief that God is black or manifest in black flesh and that the devil is white or manifest in Caucasian flesh. . . . But it has been in accord with the direction if not with the teachings of the Honorable Elijah Muhammad . . . because he gradually influenced the thinking of the membership in that direction. . . . And it is definitely in accord with the Qur'an, the book that the Honorable Elijah Muhammad established in the Nation of Islam as the supreme guide for the organization.

REPORTER: What is the attitude now toward whites and other races?

W. D. MOHAMMED: The attitude in the past as you know was one of suspicion and fear. Suspicion suspecting that the Caucasian would abuse the trust if they were trusted and a fear that the community wouldn't be able to grow with a Caucasian presence. The Honorable Elijah Muhammad felt that his work was one of healing; healing the minds and the spirit of the Bilalian or the black people. And he saw himself as a doctor of the mind and he was

digging deep secrets out of the minds and souls of the Bilalian people. And he felt that that could best be done in
privacy.
W. D. Mohammed, Press Conference (1976)

[This brother] said, "He's the baddest blackman ever walk
the shores of North America."
Imam Haroon Abdullah on Elijah Muhammad, *City of
Muslims*

In *Malcolm X: A Life of Reinvention*, Manning Marable describes the
broadcasting of the documentary *The Hate that Hate Produced* as a
pivotal moment in the Nation of Islam. [42] In the film, producer Mike
Wallace, who is white, and interviewer Louis Lomax, who is black, try to
make the case that the Nation of Islam was promoting a black supremacist agenda. In the opening exposition, Wallace cuts to footage of a
packed hall in which the Nation of Islam's morality play *The Trial* is
being performed. Wallace shows only a small portion of the end of the
play when the white race, embodied in a single man, is found guilty of
crimes ranging from lying and drunkenness to robbery. His punishment
is death.

In the documentary, interviews with Malcolm X and Elijah Muhammad, which come on the heels of Wallace's provocative opening,
establish that the Nation of Islam is a separatist organization. But the
documentary is not only about the Nation of Islam. The larger point the
producers attempt to make is that racism against whites is widespread.
In one exchange, Lomax baits Hulan Jack, the African American bor-
ough president of Manhattan, by asking him why he welcomed Elijah
Muhammad to New York City.

> JACK: I greeted him as Borough President of Manhattan.
> LOMAX: Should this be taken to mean that you agree with his religious,
> political, and economic philosophy?
> JACK: I know nothing about Muhammadanism. I have never sought to
> know anything about it . . .
> LOMAX: If I understand you properly, you have said to me that you
> issued these plaques, that you attend these meetings because as Bor-

ough President of Manhattan you have to recognize the existence of these groups. Is that correct?

JACK: Yes.

LOMAX: Now sir, with no harm meant, if the White Citizens Council has a meeting, would you give them a plaque; would you attend their meeting to speak?

JACK: Well, the White Citizens Council is not in existence in Manhattan, and certainly should have no reason for existence.

The Nation of Islam's assertion of the need for black self-defense was often compared to racists groups like the Ku Klux Klan. This accusation, articulated in the very title of the documentary "The Hate that Hate Produced," marks a recurring strategy of proclaiming black empowerment activism to be reverse racism. This was the case just after Reconstruction, when oppressive and violent white citizen groups organized to defend themselves against imagined racialized threats, most notably from free black men who were supposedly on the prowl to rape white women. Accusations of reverse racism appear again in anti–Affirmative Action discourses, in which the imagined threat is that of unqualified blacks taking jobs from qualified whites. The charge appeared again with the Black Lives Matter movement, which was accused of proclaiming that other lives do not. Equating efforts to dismantle racism *to* racism is an example of false equivalence or a logical fallacy. The Nation of Islam created a language for articulating their experiences with racism, not for creating structures to oppress whites.

At some level the producers of the documentary knew this so in an attempt to create some balance, the documentary provides an analysis, buried in the middle, of the role white supremacy and institutional racism played in producing hate.

> Hubert Humphrey told the NAACP 50th anniversary convention today that the Negro people are to be congratulated for returning love for hate, but here we are seeing tragic evidence, frightening evidence, that some Negroes are returning hate for hate. The white community must accept a good deal of the blame for the indignities the Negroes have suffered. The white community must admit its share of the blame and take corrective action.[43]

Until the airing of Wallace's documentary, whether or not the Nation of Islam practiced reverse racism mattered little to most Americans. Other than the FBI and urban blacks living in Detroit, New York, Chicago, and other cities where the Nation had a significant presence, most people had never heard of them. The film changed that. The rhetorical flourishes of the film were compelling to both whites and blacks and placed the Nation in the forefront of discussions already underway about the future of race relations in the United States. These discussions were generative, but not in a productive way. Rather than invite curiosity and a rethinking of structural inequality, the documentary forced people to pick sides. The nuances of the sort of private, not ready for primetime, therapeutic community-healing that Elijah Muhammad led for over two decades were suddenly lost. The metaphoric language used to pull people from the "mud" through revelations about the "blue-eyed devil" was suddenly transformed into a national language best articulated by Bakhtin:

> We are taking language not as a system of abstract grammatical categories, but rather language conceived as ideologically saturated, language as a worldview, even as a concrete opinion, insuring a maximum of mutual understanding in all spheres of ideological life . . . which develop in vital connection with the processes of sociopolitical and cultural centralization.[44]

Linguist Michael Silverstein in "The Uses and Utility of Ideology" argues that language offers us a short hand for expressing complex cultural values. [45] Therefore, condensing ideology in language is alone neither repressive nor empowering. As philosopher Michel Foucault theorized, state-sponsored discourses are useful for repression or for encouraging citizens to embody dispositions that facilitate state power including beliefs about justice, history, and the body.[46] On the other hand, discourses can be used to challenge state power through resignification. For example, white supremacy is built on the concept of racial essentialism, or the idea that different races are biologically and culturally distinct with whites being the most advanced. Rather than reject racial essentialism, the Nation of Islam resignified and redeployed it in their political rhetoric; blacks were now the most advanced. The refusal to complicate political rhetoric by acknowledging race as a cultural construct can be an effective political strategy.[47] Strategic essentialism has worked for many immigrant groups in order to position themselves socially, politically, and legally in the United States. [48] But while language can bring people together to fight for positive social change, there is no denying that it can also be used to incite racist mobs.[49]

The language used by the Nation was not meant to incite mobs; it was meant to heal victims of racism so that they could take control of their lives. Unlike the KKK or the White Citizen's Council, the group to which Louis Lomax refers, the Nation did not use violence to systematically terrorize people outside the organization as a strategy to gain political power. By pitting Martin Luther King's and the NAACP's pacifism against Elijah Muhammad's militancy, the film made the latter seem like the antithesis of the former when in fact there had already been a long history of conversations about the legitimate use of violence to resist institutionalized white supremacy. By decontextualizing the language practices and ideologies of the Nation, *The Hate that Hate Produced* transmuted the Nation's healing narratives into what Bakhtin calls publicistic discourse. This polemicized discourse ridicules rather than reveals, and ruptures the connections between experience and language.

> The importance of another's speech as a subject in rhetoric is so great that the word frequently begins to cover over and substitute itself for reality; when this happens the word itself is diminished and becomes shallow. Rhetoric is often limited to purely verbal victories over the word; when this happens, rhetoric degenerates into a formalistic verbal play. But, we repeat, when discourse is torn from reality, it is fatal for the word itself as well; words grow sickly, lose semantic depth and flexibility, the capacity to expand and renew their meanings in new living contexts.[50]

The charge of reverse racism was difficult to manage. On the one hand, the Nation of Islam wanted to be taken seriously for its trenchant social analysis, and the charge damaged its credibility. On the other hand, "blue-eye devils" neatly summed up the experiences of members in the Nation and therefore continued to organize people's understanding of race. With increased media attention, it became difficult for the organization to attend to member experience without alienating the public and vice-versa. And as the Nation honed its rhetoric for the media, questions about what the organization was grew. Was the Nation what members said it was in public, or in private and away from the attention of the media? The ideological struggles mirrored challenges with poor leadership at various temples and growing tensions between Elijah Muhammad and Malcolm X.

With its reputation damaged in the black community and divisions created within its own organization, the Nation realized that it had to restore what Bakhtin terms "semantic depth." Toward that end, *Muhammad Speaks* was founded in 1960 and was in publication until 1975, when Elijah Muhammad's son and successor, W. Deen Mohammed, changed the name to *Bilalian News* and later *Muslim Journal*. Throughout the 1960s, *Muhammad Speaks* read less and less like a religious screed and more like a mainstream black newspaper, less like UNIA's *Negro World* (1918) and more like the *Crisis* (1910), *Amsterdam News* (founded 1909), or *Chicago Defender* (founded 1905).[51] The newspaper featured reports on the Nation's economic and educational programs, ethnographic accounts of member's lives, world news, and sociological analysis. Tacking back and forth between factual news and religious ideology created a sense for the reader of a seamlessness between the two. The integration of Elijah Muhammad's religious message with mainstream journalism graphically represented the Nation's holistic approach to racial empowerment. Linking written text with visual images—photos, cartoons, meaning-laden symbols—the newspaper was a piece of visual and textual rhetoric that restored some semantic depth.

This depth moderated the public face of the organization in the 1960s, but that did not mean that within the Nation attitudes about racism and the establishment had changed. In the early 1960s, members were witnessing the same images of lunch-counter sit-ins, attacks on Freedom Riders, and attempts at school desegregation as the rest of the world. For black Muslims these stories and images were evidence that trying to work with whites was not only a waste of time; it was dangerous. What happened in Los Angeles on April 22, 1962, only further validated the Nation's nonintegrationist agenda (figure 2.10).

According to the *Los Angeles Times*, "One policeman was shot and two savagely beaten in a blazing gunfight during a riot at the anti-white Muslims headquarters early today. One black-suited Muslim cultist was

MUHAMMAD CALLS FOR UNITED BLACK FRONT!

THE DEVILS ATTACKED AND KILLED

On April 27, 1962, the Los Angeles' savage, brutal Police Force numbering nearly one hundred, c a m e into our Mosque No. 27, without warning, shooting and killing. Our Secretary, Ronald T. X. Stokes, was shot fatally and two other brothers are not expected to live.

One of the brothers who was shot in the back is now permanently paralyzed, having to spend the rest of his life in a wheel chair. The dying secretary, Ronald, was handcuffed and (he savage devils hastened his death by

beating him on the head with their clubs. Others, a total of five, while lying wounded and handcuffed were kicked in the face and mouth; they kicked-in the bottom bridge of one of the brothers mouth. The brothers who were shot and seriously wounded by police were not hospitalized or given medical aid until 48 hours after being shot.

"WE SHOT YOUR BROTHERS"

"While on the way to jail," said one of the brothers, "one devil officer said to his partner, 'I broke my stick on the (continued on page 3)

MR. ELIJAH MUHAMMAD

Dedicated to Freedom, Justice and Equality for the so-called Negro. The Earth Belongs to Allah.

MUHAMMAD SPEAKS

CIRCULATION OVER 310,000 WITH MORE THAN 1,250,000 READERS AND STILL GROWING

Vol. 1 No. 8   Chicago, Illinois — June, 1962   10c OUTSIDE CHICAGO 15c

UNITE FOR JUSTICE TO . . .

STOP RACE MURDERS!

HOW WHITE SUPREMACY COPS HANDCUFFED, BEAT A DEAD MAN

THE MAN YOU SEE LYING ON THE GROUND in the forefront of this picture, his hands handcuffed behind him—is dead. He is Ronald T. X. Stokes. He was shot through the heart by white supremacy policemen who continued to beat and kick him after he was dead—and then they handcuffed the dead man, along with two other brother Muslims who lie wounded and handcuffed. The Honorable Elijah Muhammad has called for a redoubling of efforts to secure justice for the black man in America.

Figure 2.10 June 1962. For years in *Muhammad Speaks*, the image of the dead and injured Muslims and the story of the violence that occurred in April of 1962 became a recurring touchstone.

slain and six others felled by police bullets before 75 officers quelled the riot on 5606 S. Broadway."[52] According to FBI reports, the officers were suspicious of two Muslim men who had (potentially stolen) clothes in the trunk of their car. While inspecting the car, which was parked a block from Muhammad's Temple 27, one of the policemen either physically intimidated the men or the men resisted. In any case, the Muslim men got away and one supposedly ran into Temple 27. In their patrol car, the police chased the man running toward the temple, which was the Nation's Los Angeles headquarters, and stopped. Hearing gunshots the Muslims came out and wound up either participating in the confrontation or being implicated in the violence.

The news reports that followed focused as much on the details of the officers' report, sketchy at best, as they did on impugning the character of the Nation. The articles contained descriptors such as anti-white, anti-Christian, and anti-integration. As anthropologist Claude Levi-Strauss notes in his theory of myths, they derive their meaning by juxtaposing opposing concepts, creating binary oppositions, and the articles about the shooting mythologized the Nation in just this way by contrasting the NAACP with the Nation.[53] "Police have estimated there are 3,500 Muslims in Southern California. The group has been denounced by officials of the National Association for the Advancement of Colored People and Negro Groups which advocate peaceful integration."[54] In response to the reporting, Malcolm X accused the police chief of using the press to spread propaganda and distort the facts.[55] Malcolm X and Elijah Muhammad then went to great lengths to assert that the Nation did not hate whites nor allow members to carry firearms. Their self-assessment fell on deaf ears.

In the 1990s Carolyn Rouse interviewed a number of African Americans who joined the Nation of Islam in 1962 after this incident. They rationalized that an organization that threatened the police must be doing something right. It turned out that the Muslim men harassed by the police owned a dry cleaning business, which explained the clothes in the car. But regardless of the facts of the case, blacks living in South Central Los Angeles equated the police shooting with similar injustices taking place around the country. The story's content mattered less than the form. The fact that the police feared the group, even described in the

Figure 2.11 September 1965. The Nation of Islam's perspective of the police.

negative press as well-dressed, was what impressed blacks who lived in fear of daily harassment.

What we learn from the media representation of the shooting is that by 1962 the conceptual categories surrounding race were becoming un-moored. Media, by or about African Americans, had multiplied, and with it so had the meaning of race. As whites learned more about the cultural, political, and religious life of African Americans, the inferior-black/superior-white binary morphed into new tropes of difference constituted relationally. If we filter the accounts of the incident in Los Angeles in a manner similar to Levi-Strauss's linguistic approach in *Structural Anthropology*, what we find is not a set of rigid binaries, but instead a constellation of shifting values.[56] The only "fact" stated un-equivocally in the mainstream press was that the police, a surrogate of the state, were beyond reproach. That was not the case, however, when it came to the NAACP, integration, or racial equality. Those words/ideas needed further explanation, and in 1962 few racial signifiers were stable.

In the *Los Angeles Times* article "police" as both an object and concept unambiguously signified goodness, truth, and social order. Taking for granted police accountability, the *LA Times* article spent no time addressing narrative ellipses or contrasting accounts and instead worked to reassert the need for violent police oversight of black radical organizations. What the *LA Times* failed to reflect was that televised images of civil rights struggles were boosting white readers' skepticism about the police, and for blacks disenchantment had reached its peak by the mid-1960s. The circulation of media images of Alabama Governor George Wallace trying to stop the desegregation of public schools and of cattle-prod-carrying Sheriff Jim Clark violently attacking protesters were chipping away at Americans' trust in the state and law enforcement.

Most members of the Nation of Islam supported segregation not because it represented an ideal. Ideally racism would not exist. Rather the concern was, if the authority of the police and the state remained unquestioned, then blacks remained subject to the whims of that authority (figure 2.11). The message of the Nation was not only that the struggle for integration was fraught with physical dangers, but also that it inadvertently reasserted the superiority of white society. Whites, importantly, were not seeking access to black establishments and black schools. Therefore, supporting integration meant continuing to seek the validation of whites, which was at the heart of the black community's vulnerability. Therefore, why not create an economic and religio-political system that is self-legitimating?

Describing the value of Elijah Muhammad's message, Imam Ali Rasheed (Captain Edward), one of the most important Muslim leaders in Los Angeles from the 1960s to 1990s, said, "It was a message so powerful and so basic in its concept that it dignified the man but most of all what it did was it pulled the fear out of him."[57] The problem the Nation had was that reversing the paradigm, or making blacks vulnerable to other blacks or more specifically the hierarchy within the Nation, was only a temporary solution to the problem of authority and legitimacy. What the Nation needed was to link its precepts to more accepted knowledge (such as scholarship on race, the civil rights movement), and more traditional forms of authority (as in orthodox Islam, Christianity). In a word, the Nation needed routinization.[58]

Figure 2.12 October 1964. This image offers a utopian vision of what the Nation of Islam could accomplish if African Americans could unite around Elijah Muhammad's religious, social, and economic program.

Figure 2.13 July 1965. This image of Islamic black futurism was reprinted in numerous editions of the Nation's newspaper.

Muhammad Speaks became a venue for trying to insure the permanence of the religion, but the routinizing of the Nation, or the bureaucratic rationalization of their faith, meant tempering the message so that it was understandable to others. The problem with attempts to do so in the 1960s (and even the 1970s) was that many members, including Malcolm X, were still fiercely angry. And much to the chagrin of Elijah Muhammad, Malcolm X used his position as the spokesman for the organization to vent that anger. It was his impolitic "chickens coming home to roost" comment following the assassination of President John F. Kennedy in 1963 that for Muhammad was the proverbial straw that broke the camel's back. In order to undo the damage, the Nation of Islam put out a statement saying, "We with the world are very shocked at the assassination of President Kennedy."[59] The leader of the Nation felt that Malcolm's oversized personality and use of the bully pulpit were undermining the public relations goals of the Nation. And Elijah Muhammad's tawdry behavior with women made it critical for the Nation to self-censor or risk losing members. After Malcolm X's assassination Elijah Muhammad said, "Who made Malcolm nationally and world known? Was it not I? Is it not also clear to the world, that for one whole year, Malcolm repeatedly scandalized me and the God, Master Fard Muhammad and the salvation of us all?. . . . He was a victim of his own vicious teaching of violence. I care nothing about the slander against me by one or by all. I said in the beginning that Allah is the best knower."[60]

The split between Malcolm X and Elijah Muhammad offers lessons in power, corruption, messaging, and "messengering," and there are wonderful historical accounts of those struggles.[61] But there are far too many myths pitting Malcolm X against Elijah Muhammad and turning the entire history of black Muslims into a parable about the evils of reverse racism.[62] Manning Marable was right to attempt to correct the record about Malcolm X. In his Pulitzer Prize winning book, Marable highlights the continuing education of the leaders and their struggle to make choices that had profound implications not only for the organization but for race relations in the United States.[63] But as compelling as Malcolm X and Elijah Muhammad are as historical figures, the meaning of the Nation cannot be defined solely by the leadership, just as the meaning of Sunni Islam cannot be defined by what religious leaders in the Middle East do or say. Rather, to understand African American Islam it is necessary to understand the tools used by Muslims to make religio-politico truth claims and to author a compelling redemptive narrative of political, spiritual, and corporeal salvation (figures 2.12 and 2.13).

Institutional Rebranding: The Road to Routinization

The first *Muhammad Speaks* published after the assassination of Malcolm X was attentive to the potential threat of organizational fracturing. In the image accompanying the article (figure 2.14), Elijah Muhammad is rendered a divine leader with an economic agenda to guide blacks out of the wilderness. In the text under the image, Muhammad is contrasted with Malcolm X: "Be it known that Malcolm had no salvation for you: he held no possible good for his followers in teaching them to arm themselves with the obsolete weapons of the white man. How can you attack a modern, well-armed people, as white America, with nothing to support yourselves in that attack? White America grows and stores your food and clothes and houses you in whatever way she desires." This simultaneous rendering of Malcolm X as a false prophet and Elijah

Figure 2.14 March 1965. This "Divinely Guided Leadership Is Best" cartoon explains Muhammad's message and was printed above an article published just after Malcolm X's assassination, which blasted Malcolm X as a false prophet.

Muhammad as a master builder attempted to appeal to the economic pragmatism that drew many converts to the Nation. "Our only future lies in being separated from a people who despises and hates us though we and our fathers have spent our lives here in sweat and blood helping them but not ourselves and kind. United we seek a place on this earth that we can call our own, and build a government of peace and equality among ourselves in the name of Allah, as other nations have done." This socialist utopia, where formally marginalized individuals unite around race and common interest, was in many ways similar to the postcolonial Pan-African ideals that imagined African states uniting around shared common economic interests and equality. Importantly, *Muhammad Speaks* set the stage for the intellectual and discursive global engagements that we see in twenty-first century Muslim media.

What African American Muslims in the 1960s and 1970s did through their media production was to unknowingly lay the groundwork for the eventual transition to Sunni Islam. With the exception of the religious arguments and political demands, the truth claims made in *Muhammad Speaks* were generally supported by first person accounts, exposés, and reissued news reports—standard journalism. In a 1966 four-part series entitled "Scientific Appraisal: Deadly Neglect of the Male Child May Mean Race Suicide," the conclusions about what black male children need educationally echo conclusions made by sociologists, educational theorists, and politicians in the twenty-first century. "'Schools are oriented and set up to permit girls to prosper while boys are left to flounder' is the explanation offered by most principals, teachers and parents for the fact that there are almost twice as many boys as girls in an area of 'slow learners.' . . . One sociologist said that the organization of schools posed particularly acute problems for Negro boys."[64] This article shared print space with an article about the development of a steel and iron industry in West Africa and an article announcing a call for research proposals by the federal government to study health issues including mental health. Throughout its fifteen-year run, *Muhammad Speaks* published many first-person accounts of members overcoming racism as a result of their conversion. And ads were sprinkled throughout reminding the reader of all the Muslim-owned businesses selling everything from logo-embossed paraphernalia to "natural brown rice" and "tender white rock fryers."[65] Then there were the articles that most people in the 1960s read as paranoid, but would now be read as mainstream. In one entitled "U.S. 'Aid' to Latin America Revealed as Bribery, Plunder and Genocide," the authors state, "U.S. industrialists, militarists and other exploiters take more out of Latin American countries than they put in. The people of the southern and central American nations are being driven into deeper and deeper poverty and debt even though they are providing more land and labor for the U.S. ruling elite."[66] Another article celebrated Egyptian President Abdul Gammal Nasser's refusal to be controlled by Western development aid.[67] By all measures, *Muhammad Speaks* disrupts the idea that the Nation was a cult whose only legitimacy was housed in the charismatic authority of one leader.

As radical as the organization appeared to outsiders, the Nation sought widespread acceptance first within the African American community and later internationally as it built economic ties with Peru and ideological ties with pan-Africanist and postcolonial leaders. In the end, the organization sought acceptance from the *ummah*, or world community, of Muslims.

While members began studying traditional Islam in the 1950s, the move toward Sunni Islam was finally realized when W. Deen Mohammad took over in 1975 and financially and ideologically disbanded and then repurposed the organization. In 1976 W. D. Mohammad changed the name of the Nation to the World Community of Islam in the West in an attempt to qualify it as a mainstream American religious organization; not so much led by a charismatic leader, as administered using traditional and legal forms of authority. In the end it was this impulse for routinization, driven in large part by a desire to connect with Sunni Muslims around the world and to take advantage of new opportunities for blacks in the United States, that turned an organization falsely condemned for its reverse racism in the 1950s and 1960s into a religious disposition that by the 1980s was as deracinated as it was deterritorialized.

Throughout the 1960s, the changes in approach are well represented in the Nation's newspaper, *Muhammad Speaks*, and in the stories covered by a Muslim television news program, *Muhammad Speaks* (1973–1976).[68] The leaders of the Nation made many mistakes, but one thing they did that helped to sustain the movement was to respond to real world issues such as schooling, taxes, police violence, and business promotion. They also opened themselves up to accepted tools of evidence, including Islamic exegesis, social science, and medical science.

The 2007 documentary *City of Muslims* nicely captures the spirit and arch of community change in Los Angeles from the 1960s to 2007, but this film is not meant to document an elaborate and complicated history.[69] Rather, it paints the picture of a unified community, glossing over the ruptures, dissention, and disaffection that make the community much harder to define or historicize. It is an unswerving, post-9/11, feel-good piece that takes on the inordinate task of trying to redeem the Nation, the race, and Islam.[70]

Early in the documentary, the filmmakers use the 1962 attack on Temple 27 to help explain why the Nation of Islam was an attractive alternative to Christianity. But the filmmakers refuse to explain the Nation's rationale for why blacks, as David Walker argued, have a right to defend themselves against state-sanctioned violence. The filmmakers also leave out the religious beliefs of the Nation, the unorthodox assertion that Elijah Muhammad was the last messenger of Allah, and the political demands for a separate nation. Instead, the film focuses on the substantial Muslim-owned businesses in Los Angeles, which in some sense formed an economy within an economy. Also highlighted are the educational programs that emphasized discipline and moral character, and were adopted and adapted by the Sunni Muslims after 1975. But missing are descriptions of the Afrocentrism taught as a corrective to white American and Eurocentric history or the struggles with the growing immigrant Muslim community that did not necessarily recognize them as Sunni Muslims.

A substantial amount of footage includes excerpts from the Nation of Islam's weekly three-hour show, *Muhammad Speaks* (1973–1976), broadcast on the local public television station. Left out are on-air discussions about the Nation's ideology—an ideology that Warith Deen Mohammed, Elijah Muhammad's son, rejected when he transitioned the community to Sunni Islam and formed the World Community of Islam in the West in 1976, renamed the American Society of Muslims in 1981. Instead what the audience sees is footage from the Black Business Bazaar, the Black Community Fair, and other events in which Muslims worked together with non-Muslims and public leaders such as Los Angeles Mayor Tom Bradley. And there is footage of Muhammad Ali, who had recently returned from defending his boxing title in Zaire (eventually renamed the Democratic Republic of the Congo). After describing efforts working with the "Messenger Elijah Muhammad" to build a much-needed hospital for "one million black people" in Chicago, Ali says:

> And all these black people in Hollywood, all these movie stars. It's time for them to unite, and quit smiling and showing their teeth, and get together and use all that fame and help these poor black people out here. Just 'cause they're in Hollywood with white women they shouldn't sell out their people just because they can be in good with white people. And I'm thankful for the Honorable Elijah Muhammad because if it wasn't for him I'd be up there with some white woman.[71]

With the exception of a brief history of events in 1962, issues of race and disenfranchisement are virtually absent from the film. Muhammad Ali, for example, is presented unequivocally as a national hero. His image on the cover of a box of Wheaties Cereal is how he is introduced in the documentary. Unexamined is Ali's refusal to be drafted into the

Vietnam War or his direct political challenges to the white establish-ment.[72] The history told in this documentary is of a community that became economically empowered and assimilated through an embrace of Islam, the work ethic, and capitalism. One of the last scenes is of a little Muslim girl reciting Al-Fatiha (the opening chapter in the Qur'an) in beautiful Arabic, providing proof of a seamless arch from Nation to orthodoxy, from a community defending itself against racism to a com-munity embracing American citizenship and entrepreneurship.

Of course the community in Los Angeles, like communities in other urban centers, was only occasionally at peace with itself. Many members in the Nation distrusted the leadership before Elijah Muhammad's pass-ing and were thankful for the transition to Sunni Islam. But with Sunni Islam came decentralization, and businesses that were relatively stable but in debt were sold off. So with the embrace of traditional Islam came a lack of coordination and financing to get projects off the ground. The struggle involved figuring out how to repurpose an organization built on principles of *Gemeinschaft*, or a society that enforces strong behavioral norms, into a religious ethic that encourages *Gesellschaft*, or individual self-interest. But perhaps the visual signifiers of unity in the 1960s and 1970s were mislead-ing. Imam Saadiq, a leader of a Los Angeles mosque who is interviewed in the documentary *City of Muslims*, once told Rouse that the collective wealth of African American Muslims was actually higher in the 1990s than when the Nation owned businesses. He was referring to the fact that there were many Muslims, from very wealthy people in sports and entertain-ment to middle-class professionals, whose collective wealth was probably much greater than in the past. This fact is impossible to prove given that we have no religious affiliation census data or accurate survey data. But the fact that the estimates for the number of African American Muslims in the early twenty-first century were somewhere on the order of two to four million and that many of them were most likely middle class suggests that it is more than likely that Imam Saadiq was right.

The African American Muslim community remained vibrant at the local level, and W. Deen Mohammed's *Muslim Journal* remained in print and online well past his death in 2008. Now on the masthead are two flags: the American flag and a flag with a moon and crescent. While the *Muslim Journal* reflects changes in how African American Muslims feel about the American government and their status as citizens, it maintains its critical voice. Describing his opposition to the impending war with Iraq in 2003, W. Deen Mohammed is quoted in the *Muslim Journal* saying, "Only the Iraqi people are punished by war, not Saddam Hussein."[73] A documentary that aired on the PBS *Religion and Ethics Newsweekly* show in 2003 tried to make sense of why a Washington Post–ABC poll showed that 78 percent of white Americans supported the Iraq war while only 35 percent of black Americans did so.[74] Support for the Iraq War among African American Muslims was most likely in the single digits. As religion scholar Aminah McCloud says in the film, "African Americans here see the world very differently from other Americans."[75] In this short six-minute news piece, produced by a non-Muslim, we once again see issues of citizenship ("I feel I'm an American Muslim and a Muslim American. That covers it all. Our ancestors paid the price. We paid more than the price to be what we are."), race ("There's no such thing as black Muslims. There's only Muslims. We're all one family from one God."), and the proper authority for making truth claims ("God says in the Qur'an . . .").

The embrace of Islamic orthodoxy, the *ummah*, and American values has generated interethnic, multiracial, and international engagements with African American Muslims. On paper, on websites, and at conferences and large religious events one can literally see the instantiation of W. D. Mohammed's efforts to routinize and deracialize the faith. As a result, the *Muslim Journal* (formally *Muhammad Speaks*) remains one of the few publications directed at African American Muslims. Muslim media is now produced, for the most part, by multicultural teams, which means that defining what constitutes black Muslim media requires some sleight of hand. The magazine *Azizah*, for example, was founded by a black Canadian living in Atlanta, Georgia. It was run and edited by a team as diverse as the women featured in its pages. But the *Muslim Journal* continues to feature stories that attend to the needs of urban Muslims who still live in segregated communities and who are situated socially and economically in ways that shape their experiences. For this community of Muslims, their weapon for self-defense continues to be knowledge.

Conclusion

Redeeming the race continues to be a political project in the African American Muslim community, and this imperative continues to be as liberating as it is constraining. An article published in the *Muslim Journal* on November 7, 1986, best articulates the stakes. Entitled "Muslims in Oakland Protest Showing of 'She's Gotta Have It,'" the article describes a peaceful demonstration in front of the Grand Lake Theatre in Oakland. Spike Lee's smash indie film had just been released and was one of the first African American films to break through to white audiences. In Lee's romantic comedy a black woman dates three very different and quirky black men. Rather than moralize, the film offers a character study of a small group of people living in Brooklyn in the 1980s. For many African Americans the story's specificity was unreadable because even mainstream cinema and television have almost always housed redemptive narratives. Julie Dash's *Daughters of the Dust*, Alex Haley's *Roots*, Bill Cosby's *The Cosby Show*, Robert Townsend's *Hollywood Shuffle*, and Lee Daniels's *The Butler* are just a handful of examples.

The article in the *Muslim Journal* equated the making of a film about black female sexuality to the making of a romantic comedy about the Holocaust or Japanese internment or AIDS. The author of the piece, A. W. Taha, argues that an African American film must be judged by one key question, "Does it address the African-American agenda, (the needs and dignified concerns of African-Americans)?"[76]

The idea that any African American media is a surrogate for the political, social, and dispositional goals of the race is a historical legacy. Since the first African American newspaper, media has been used to advocate for the race. To do otherwise is to validate stereotypes and racism. As one protester in the crowds is quoted as saying, "As a single black woman my purpose in coming here today is to make a statement, which is that there are some of us who are not asleep, and who take serious issue with the constant portrayal of black women as prostitutes, as whores, and as immoral people. What we need now is to see positive images of black people."

3

Divine Redemption

Hebrew Israelites and the Saving of the World

Ben Ammi Ben-Israel died in southern Israel on Saturday, December 27, 2014. He was seventy-five years old at the time, which is not really *that* old. At least not by "Western standards." And not for a messianic figure whose redemptive project had long been predicated on "physical immortality," a phrase that was both the title of his final book and a central goal of the transnational spiritual community he had helped to lead, inspire, and educate since the 1960s in Chicago.[1]

For just under fifty years, Ben Ammi (born Ben Carter) led one of the most successful emigrationist projects in the history of African American life, perhaps second only to the more famous West African settlements founded for newly freed slaves and their descendants during the eighteenth and nineteenth centuries through the efforts of a motley crew of white and black abolitionists, clergy, slaveholders, elected officials, and free blacks.[2] The nation of Liberia was created as a byproduct of ongoing fears—dating back to the American Revolution—that the newly decolonized United States of America could not accommodate a fully multiracial citizenry, especially since it was assumed that racial slavery embittered manumitted blacks and that deep-seated supremacist doctrines made it difficult for many whites to entertain the idea of sharing political authority with their erstwhile slaves.

The American citizens whom Ben Ammi helped to shepherd out of "the belly of the beast" in "modern day Babylon" (language mobilized by the émigrés themselves) and into a "New World" on the other side of the Atlantic Ocean in the 1960s began their journey snuggled self-consciously within the grooves of the migratory tracks laid down by the American Colonization Society and its varied collaborators in the construction of that aforementioned settlement turned nation-state, Liberia. The latter effort transpired in the early 1800s, a few decades after "black loyalists," former American slaves who fought for the British during the Revolutionary War, had been relocated from Nova Scotia to Sierra Leone by Great Britain. The brutalities and inhumanities of race-based chattel slavery (and assumptions about fundamental black and white incompatibility) convinced many people—on both sides of the abolitionist debate and both sides of the Atlantic—that a truly interracial polity was unimaginable.

By the 1920s, Marcus Garvey's Universal Negro Improvement Association had started to court Liberia's Americo-Liberian leadership to envisage that nation as a base from which to begin the process of what some called "African Fundamentalism" or even "African Redemption." Such notions could be said to traffic in the kind of hubris that allowed some free blacks in the United States to consider themselves perfectly situated and equipped (given their access to European-style education and religious forms) to humanely, even lovingly, civilize their continental African brothers and sisters. Since Africans could be imagined as relatively backward and unenlightened, as pagans with primitive and premodern beliefs, a missionizing ethos often animated responses to the continent from blacks (and whites) in the Americas. Garvey's pan-Africanism, described as an "Afro-Zionism" in many scholarly precincts, owed a great deal to the conceptual architecture of modern Jewish Zionism, which functioned as a model for effective diasporic solidarity. Although Garvey eventually abandoned his Liberia project and never made it to Africa himself, several Garveyites did relocate to that West African nation during the first half of the twentieth century. Ben Ammi's emigrationist push years later relied on Universal Negro Improvement Association forebears to help with his community's initial departure in 1967. It would be UNIA member James Flemister, already a Liberian citizen, who brokered land deals for Ben Ammi's group and allowed them to retreat to his farmland when they needed a break from their housing construction efforts in the Liberian jungle. The community's decision to leave Chicago for Liberia was based on a complicated calculus of race, religion, and popular media/culture that catalyzed and sustained their goal of reinventing themselves anew beyond America's shores.

Although black citizens' interest in "quitting America" for good would wax and wane over the decades, reflecting substantive and symbolic changes in the country's ostensible commitment to genuine racial equity and inclusion, there was general skepticism among many blacks in the United States about the goal of African repatriation.³ Even while Marcus Garvey was purchasing and christening ships for a journey "back to Africa" in the early 1920s, many African Americans were less sanguine about that idea. Harlem Renaissance poet Countee Cullen's first poetry collection, *Color*, included the famous poem "Heritage," which wondered aloud, "What is Africa to me?"—especially when the "me" invoked is "three centuries removed" from the continent's geographical and cultural landscapes.⁴

For the "saints" (as community members are called) who heeded Ben Ammi's call in the 1960s, and the many more Hebrew Israelites who contested his claim that it was finally time for Yah's chosen people to leave the United States, the entire endeavor was predicated on an investment in racialized and mass-mediated renderings of redemptive possibility.⁵ One can read the history of these racialized and mediatized investments as a profound recalibration of canonical and conventional African American responses to political and existential exclusion. For Hebrew Israelites, the reimagining of Africa and black identity was an attempt at collective resurrection from the throes (and legacy) of what sociologist Orlando Patterson framed as "social death."⁶ Over the past seventy years, much of the media produced by Ben Ammi, the African Hebrew Israelites of Jerusalem, and self-identified sympathizers has been a purposeful refutation of assumptions about blackness as preordained cultural impoverishment and inescapable abjection. African Hebrew Israelites explicitly reverse the story of human progress, proffering "Euro-gentiles" as an instantiation of the primitivism and backwardness that is to be transcended at all costs—and that is traditionally associated with black people.⁷

The organizing principle of their revitalization movement is hostility to what might be glossed as secularism in favor of a reinvigorated relationship with God, "the Most High," all while insisting that such a relationship is not reducible to those inadequate institutionalizations and compartmentalizations we typically label "religion."⁸ Some Hebrew Israelites are keen on explaining to the uninitiated that the term "religion" comes out of the Latin root *religare*," which they parse as "to bind, to tie, and to hold back."⁹ For them, etymology helps to explain the essential problem with religion. It holds people back from the Creator instead of drawing them closer to Him. This formal antireligiosity is coupled with a pointed critique of political liberalism's conspicuous hypocrisies as played out in the wide chasm between America's ideals and actual practices vis-à-vis democratic claims championing liberty and justice for all inhabitants.

The story of self-proclaimed African American "Hebrews," "Israelites," and "Jews" starts, as many scholars tell it, with historical figures that predate Ben Ammi by almost a hundred years, leaders with names like Cherry, Crowdy, and Matthews and with titles that range from Prophet and High Priest to Prince, Elder, or Rabbi. These varied and interconnected narratives pivot on a similar investment in challenging the presumptively privileged whiteness of mainstream forms of Christianity, a blinding whiteness that casts biblical narratives and personages in its monochromatic image. The symbolism of this racialized scenario is often acerbically articulated with skeptical invocations of a proverbial "blue-eyed Jesus" painted, framed, and hung on church walls above otherwise all-black congregations. Malcolm X popularized the idea that such imagery represented high irony at the cathected crossroad between race and religion. And although all of the varied spiritual leaders of past black Hebrew or black Jewish movements had distinctive ways of operationalizing their critiques, they shared some common politico-spiritual scaffolding constructed to dispute the lines drawn to separate ancient Israelites from contemporary black racial subjects.

For Hebrew Israelites, the Old Testament stories were not merely powerful ancient analogies that could be applied to New World struggles.[10] Instead, their nineteenth- and early twentieth-century tales of links to ancient Hebrew patriarchs, tales spun anew by the likes of Ben Ammi, eschewed the domain of metaphor for genealogy's more materialist moorings. It was not enough to consider the Old Testament characters models for contemporary black life; they were also literal progenitors and direct ancestors. The ancient scriptures were readily mined for proof that ancient Hebrews were decidedly "black," just like enslaved Africans. Even Christian preachers were making this claim. If the Egyptians were a dark-skinned people, "black" in contemporary racial terminology, they maintained, how could Moses pass for the pharaoh's grandson unless he looked just like those Egyptians? Ultimately, this thinking helped to ground their claim that the ancient Israelites are literally the forefathers and foremothers of those individuals sold into chattel slavery in Africa. It was a claim about racial pedigree that flew in the face of well-worn Christian justifications for cruelty against African subjects and assumptions about African inhumanity, all prerequisites for what was considered divinely ordained servitude. The "curse of Ham" was the most widely circulated and oldest argument about trans-Atlantic racial slavery's prophesied foretelling in the Bible, a slavery predicated on the actions of a misguided son and his drunken father. To some white Christians, dark skin became the sine qua non for "eternal slavery," a conspicuous marker of collective disfavor in the eyes of God, one powerful epidermal distinction between the elect and the damned.[11]

Many of the debates about human evolution and variation in the American colonies and in the early history of the republic were fueled by the scientific community's penchant for legitimizing folk assumptions about the absolute ontological reality of racial difference. Doubling-down on purported black inhumanity, such scientific legitimations even declared Noah's curse of his youngest son's offspring not nearly alienating and distancing enough from the status of "God's chosen people." Scientists such as Carleton Coon, Georges Cuvier, and Anders Retzius would argue that the origin story of blackness should be situated before—and entirely outside of—the birth of our species, which meant that the tale of black people's emergence was not knowable with recourse to post-biblical interpretations of Genesis.[12]

Polygenesis was one powerful argument for the claim that the term "man" (in an anthropological sense) portrayed the historical narrative of only non-black subjectivity, and the nineteenth-century public sphere was saturated with written and spoken claims to that effect. Pamphlets and fliers were organized around articulating the definitive difference that race made, a difference providing metaphysical cover for economic exploitation and political marginalization. The well-known "Life of Philadelphia" cartoon series, created by pro-slavery propagandist Edward William Clay in the 1820s, lampooned African American attempts to dress and speak like civilized and cultured white Americans, ultimately satirizing what many considered the absurd and insufferable pretense of black sociopolitical sovereignty.[13]

Stories told by black Hebrews/Jews/Israelites in nineteenth-century America were sharp rejoinders to declarations of black wretchedness and pre-humanity. If the Nation of Islam was famous for its purposeful and pointed reversal of white supremacist claims using an origin myth more akin to science fiction (with whites being understood as the petri-dish concoction of Yakub, a "mad scientist" and evil genius who genetically "graphed" whites to be evil and war-like "devils"), Hebrew Israelite communities tended to stick closer to sacred textualizations in their attempts to demonstrate the value of black people's lives. For them, the Old Testament provided a narrative logic for white depravities and propensities not too far afield from the kinds that the scientist Yakub was said to have manufactured in a laboratory.

The Torah-based tale of Hebrew brothers Esau and Jacob has long been central to various black Hebrew Israelite reclamations of race-based humanity and even racial privilege. In a recasting the oft-invoked Genesis story, Noah and his sons are already black before Shem and Japheth, Ham's older brothers, cover their father's intoxicated body without seeing his "nakedness," invalidating the argument that this little episode describes the advent of blackness. Noah's curse, then, has nothing to do with the emergence of racial differences, popular white Christians' interpretations of the affair notwithstanding. However, Hebrew readings of the Old Testament do, they argue, include a depiction of the creation of "white" skin, a phenotypical trait that various Hebrew Israelite communities have interpreted as a form of leprosy—tracing its emergence back to the birth of Esau and Jacob.

As Hebrew Israelites explain things, Isaac and Rebekah had twins, Esau and Jacob, who would be the progenitors of two nations, the Edomites and the Israelites, respectively. Before the little ones were even born, God let their mother know that the two fetuses were already fighting in her womb (which was why she was having a particularly difficult pregnancy), and he told her that their battles would continue throughout their lives and translate into animosity and war between the two nations they would produce, Jacob's Israelites and Esau's Edomites. "The one people," it was prophesied, "shall be stronger than the other people; and the elder shall serve the younger." The Israelites were destined to rule over their Edomite rivals, but their hostilities would begin with Jacob stealing his older brother's fatherly blessing, a tale retold with specific reference to physical differences between the siblings' bodies, which Hebrew-Israelites map onto visible distinctions between "blacks" and "whites" as racial groups. The Bible's rendering of Esau as "red" and "hairy" serves as a racialized physical marking of his distinctive and exceptional (and evidently singular, at that point in history) whiteness. Esau may have been his father's favorite son, but he is less favored in this Israelite retelling of the story.

Even after Esau has already sold his birthright to Jacob for a bowl of stew, Isaac is fooled into blessing Jacob (who is dressed up to look and feel like Esau) in an elaborate bit of trickery that their mother Rebekah helps to engineer. Arriving too late to foil the plot but in enough time to see what happened, Esau vows to kill his younger brother as a consequence. Ill-gotten or not, Jacob's offspring would benefit from divine blessings, and there was nothing Esau could do about it. If blackness is borne of a curse in one Christian reading of Genesis, the traditional curse of Ham claim, in this counter-reading of Esau and Jacob's escapades, white people specifically lose their blessing and birthright, their status and standing, in this pro-black rejoinder.

The entire trans-Atlantic slave trade is still preordained and sanctioned by God in the Hebrew Israelites' reading of the Old Testament, but now it is their chosen-ness that makes blacks the subject of such historical terror, not their utter insignificance. This fact comes off as strange and counterintuitive, Hebrew Israelites declare, only because people mistakenly deploy a kind of presumptive whiteness to ground their definitions of Judaic difference. Their community's scholars, books, and traveling museums are all organized around the goal of proving their claims about authentic Hebraic descent.

Israel had rejected Yah by serving other gods and blatantly disregarding his commandments, and their punishment would entail having their identity stripped from them and being cast out of the Holy Land and scattered across the world. Yet, it is a story prophesied to end with their reclamation by Yah's grace after centuries of trials and tribulations in a foreign land.

This is a fundamental recalibration. The ontological value of African chattel slavery at the hands of European slavers and ancient Israelite enslavement in Babylon and Egypt might be said to switch places, the latter becoming a metaphor for the former and not vice versa. The Old Testament explicitly describes what produces transatlantic African slavery and does not simply stand as an historical antecedent with certain suggestive similarities. The Christian trope of brotherhood is replaced by a literal declaration of national, familial, and ancestral kinship.

Anthropologist Marshall Sahlins argues that kinship has always been more than just a metaphor for (or extension of) biological procreation. Instead, he maintains that so-called blood ties are merely a metaphor for more expansive and universalist notions of kinship, which he parses as "shared being" or "mutuality of being."[14] In Sahlins's formulation, radical interconnectedness and social belonging produce a "transpersonal praxis" wherein "kinship is the *a priori* of birth rather than the sequitur."[15] Biology does not ground kinship, even if we think it does. Kinship gets concretized, after the fact, as shared biology. And what facts matter in procreation narratives are different in different parts of the world.

Thus, even though the Hebrew Israelite's claim of literal descent from the ancient patriarchs might appear to be an assertion of biological relatedness, it can also be read as an example of how fungible and accommodating such a shared sense of being is. That is, contemporary Israelites might be said to understand themselves not just as offspring of the ancient Israelites. Instead, their rereading of the Israelites' plight in the Old Testament is more like a short-circuiting of the distance between the two eras and communities in ways that make them much more correctly understood as "the same entity in discrete subjects," which Sahlins flags as indicative of what is found in communities with name-sharing traditions.[16] For Hebrew Israelites distrustful of traditional Christian interpretations of the Old Testament, history requires newfangled conceptual tools. The Western take on the historical global order more generally seems to them to be a plan to disempower. What is required, therefore, is a kind of semiotics of conspiracy to scaffold skeptical claims in racially meaningful ways. And this hermeneutics of hyper-suspicion circulates far and wide with the assistance of new and old media.

In the nineteenth century, pamphlets were used to carry black Hebrew rereadings of ancient passages to potential believers. Along with newspaper coverage in "the black press" and more mainstream media outlets, these mass-produced printed materials encapsulated a faith in the power of rhetoric known to attract disaffected black folk in urban America. One of their most popular rhetorical strategies was to challenge the taken-for-granted association of Christianity with whiteness by emphasizing dark-skinned messiahs and detailing all the ways in which white folks had historically squandered God's blessings. They did not call whites blue-eyed devils; their critique was far too grounded in Biblical exegesis, but to their respective audiences, the Muslim and Hebrew Israelite reinterpretations of whiteness functioned somewhat analogously.

For black religious groups that shared urban sidewalk space with the Hebrew Israelites, such as the Nation of Islam and the Moorish Science Temple, canonical counternarratives stitched the old to the new. Disparate musings and traditions were cobbled together with iconic and conventional sacred texts to produce distinctive versions of, for example, the "Holy Koran." Out of this bricolage emerged newfangled "chapter and verse," including Rosicrucian texts and *The Aquarian Gospel.*[17] Hebrew Israelites produced their own texts as well, mostly extensions of their specific interpretations of the Bible, especially the Torah. They read well-known biblical stories directly against the grain of mainline Christianity, repackaging familiar narratives, like that of Esau and Jacob, by giving them new object lessons and taking those tweaked teachings straight to the streets.

One of the most important initial venues for Ben Ammi and other Hebrew Israelites back in Chicago during the 1960s was the soapbox, a literal platform for public speaking set up right on a stretch of urban sidewalk space. And so, Ben Ammi began his most public interventions as many had before him, from earlier charismatic religious leaders to socialist political agitators. The soapbox allowed Ben Ammi to take his emigrationist message directly to the people, even if most were unsuspecting and disinterested pedestrians. The Hebrew Israelites were headquartered at what they called the Abeta Hebrew Culture Center on the second floor of an office building at Forty-Seventh and Cottage Grove. The culture center was where they taught history classes and Hebrew classes, threw parties, sold Sunday dinners, and organized bake sales to raise money for the community.[18] Prince Gavriel HaGodol, an elder in the community, recounts one of their weekly rituals this way:

Every Sunday morning a large group of us [Hebrew Israelites] would go down to Maxwell St. to an area known throughout Chicago as "Jewtown." Brothers Asher, Eldanon, Baruch, Elidode, Rockameem, Noahk, Mose, and I and Sisters Karmiah, Afrah Teretsah, Devorah and Ahdinah, all led by Ben Ammi, would assemble and set up a soapbox to stand on and speak to the passing shoppers. The majority of these passersby were Black, who each and every Sunday flocked to this area in search of a bargain at the discount Jewtown stores.[19]

This was their weekly routine, which also included such derogatory or resentful invocations of European Jewish establishments in the area ("Jewtown"). After setting up soapboxes a few hundred feet from the Maxwell Street police station, they preached their back-to-Africa message. To passersby, they loudly challenged "brainwashed Toms," declaring that "the so-called 'American Negro'" constituted the "lost tribes" of Israel and railing against the lies white America told—lies that made such claims so hard for people to swallow. Soapboxing allowed them to present their message as the living, breathing embodiment of an Afrocentric spirituality. Donning their own African-inspired Israelite clothing (Kente or Mud Cloth outfits with dangling fringes on cuffs and sleeves), preachers demonstrated their quick rhetorical skills during street-corner debates and passed out leaflets detailing their identitarian claims and emigrationist plans. It was finally time to leave America, they declared, and not just because of American racism and discrimination. It was also proclaimed in the Bible. And if they were in bondage far away from home, as the Bible predicted, then they would be at the end of their ordeal soon. True redemption for Yah's people required returning home and being restored to their native land.

Because such a return was destined, it was their responsibility to prepare themselves physically, mentally, and psychologically for the journey. There was much debate within Chicago's Hebrew Israelite community about the timing of that foretold homecoming, with biblical references to the "Ships of Tarshish" interpreted as a key to when modern-day Israelites in America were supposed to depart, but Ben Ammi was part of a relatively new guard who were unwilling to wait any longer before actively planning their escape. For him, leaving was the logical extension of Israelites' ontological claims about black people's authentic lineage, and his sidewalk soapbox was the necessary venue to urge people to accept that truth.

There was never talk of *choosing* Jesus as a personal savior; in that way the rhetoric bore almost no resemblance to Born Again Christianity. Indeed, conversion was rarely framed as a question of *choice* for the believer at all. It was about *accepting* the fact of one's ancestry and genetic birthright. It was all predetermined; history was recalibrated as the simple unfurling of prophecy. You were a Hebrew Israelite, by their calculation, whether or not you knew of or believed that fact. So the Israelites would address all of the Africana pedestrians they could find on those Chicago streets, proselytizing by convincing them of, rather than converting them to, the faith by reminding them of their connection to the ancient Hebrew tribes, especially Judah.

Whiteness was, for them, incompatible with authentic Hebrew Israelite identity, and "Jew," as an identificatory category, only highlighted the lies that were said to whiten Biblical patriarchs. Even though some of Ben Ammi's institutional forebears and contemporaries from other groups understood themselves as "black Jews," the term "Jew" was constantly contested. For different Hebrew Israelite groups, there was a conflicted commitment to traditional Jewish authenticity. Some acknowledged, even grudgingly, European Jews as "the keepers of the faith," but others dismissed them as "false Jews of Revelation," imposters. Though not a self-described "Israelite," Fleming Aytes, for example, wrote *The Teaching Black Jew* in the late 1920s, arguing that blacks were descendants of the ancient patriarchs while using the term "Black Jew" without qualification.[20] The "Jew" in question was always a black subject for Aytes as it was for many of the other late nineteenth- and early twentieth-century prophets and ministers who deployed the term. But this was a Jewishness to be distinguished from that of white "heathens," as Aytes put it, and imposters, or Edomites passing themselves off as Israelites in a masterful reversal of Jacob's original scam. Some used the term "black Jew" liberally while others, like Ben Ammi, preferred to relegate the term "Jew" to European subjects. Historian James Landing went further, carving out a distinction between "black Judaism" and "Black Judaism" to highlight differences in ideological commitments to normative Jewry. These differences aside, alternative positions on the status of "the Jew" pivoted on the sense that race was fundamental in the tale of ancient Hebrew Israelites.[21]

When Ben Ammi and about four hundred saints little by little left Chicago for Liberia starting in 1967, they spent much of that time telling their story to the mainstream black press. Black journalists were fascinated by the unconventional elements of their biblical claims, even though they knew many readers would ridicule the group because of them. Regardless of potential negative attention, mainstream media and black weeklies were useful in getting the word out about the return home of Yah's chosen people. The stories published in venues like *Ebony* magazine generally included an overview of Israelite beliefs, including their assertion that emigration had to happen right then because Yah would destroy America in 1970. At their 1967 arrival, the Liberian press descended as well. Some of them mistakenly thought that their new guests were Muslims given both how they dressed and the fact that journalists abroad mostly knew about postcolonial, anti-imperialist black radicalism in the United States of that time through figures like Malcolm X and Elijah Muhammad.[22]

Much of this early press coverage was specifically framed as a discussion of race and citizenship. Liberian President William Tubman was an outspoken supporter of African American migration to his country, as long as those new arrivals were willing to become Liberian citizens and fully integrate into that society, which the émigrés expressed interest in doing. His nation's constitution included special provisions allowing immigrants to purchase land upon accepting citizenship. They even received an allowance from the state without an otherwise mandatory two-year waiting period. "The government will take care of them for three months," President Tubman told reporter Era Bell Thompson. "When they become citizens, each family will be given 25 acres of land and a lot in town. If they can till the soil, they can always plant enough to eat. As a matter of fact, you Negroes belong here. You had no business being there [in America] to begin with."[23] Thompson's *Ebony* feature on the community is chock full of photos of saints at work in Liberia, clearing bush, building wire hangars for export throughout the country, and planting crops. The magazine article also stages a debate between African leaders like Tubman, who welcomed masses of African American migrants, and leaders like Tanzanian President Hasting Banda, who believed that black Americans were too culturally different from Africans for such migration to work. "I don't think they'll fit in," Banda quips in the piece. "We haven't got a cinema, you know."

African leaders such as Senegalese President Leopold Senghor, Dahomeyan President Emile Zinsou, Ugandan President Milton Obote, and Ghanaian General Joseph Ankrah each made a more pointed case about why the Hebrew Israelites should consider staying put in the United States, which had mostly to do with America owing them full and unconditional citizenship. According to General Ankrah, "Ghanaians would like to see black Americans, like all citizens of the United States, enjoy all rights and equal opportunities to which citizenship entitles them."[24] Other leaders made related arguments about America needing to reckon with its racial hypocrisies at home in ways that could ultimately make the nation truly inhabitable to black residents.

Despite Tubman's support, the Hebrew Israelites had a rough time in Liberia. Some of that was a function of their anti-assimilationists decisions. For example, they chose to rely on their UNIA benefactor to purchase land on their behalf instead of becoming Liberian citizens. Adding even more levels of complication, they stayed together on a three-hundred-acre plot of bushes, shrubs, and trees, "the jungle" they called it, rather than moving into the capital, Monrovia, some one hundred miles away, and integrating into the larger community. The Liberian jungle also proved to be more difficult for the émigrés to negotiate than many of them had imagined. Disease and even death would strike their little camp, and within eighteen months over 75 percent of the people who had left America for Liberia with Ben Ammi returned to the United States. Those community members who had not returned by 1968 began preparing for one last move to Israel. Rather than narrate this early part of their journey as failure, they recast Israel as "Northeast Africa," not "the Middle East," and described it as the final leg of a multipronged journey to their true home. Liberia is characterized as the location where Yah separated "wheat from chaff," true believers from those who lacked the genuine commitment to follow him through the most arduous circumstances. So, the community went from West Africa to Northeast Africa and deny to this day that they would have stayed in Liberia (and never considered journeying any farther east) if their efforts had met with more success in 1967 and 1968.

With their relocation to Israel in 1969, the media descended again, pondering this strange group of black Americans landing unannounced at Ben Gurion International Airport and intending to stay in that new nation under "right of return" auspices. Some scholars have read the identification with ancient Israel and the move to Israel as a flight from blackness.[25] They characterize it as a form of internalized anti-black racism, and as evidence that black Jews or Israelites did not want to be considered black at all.[26] Actually, the opposite was true. Ben Ammi's community of Hebrew Israelites embraced an extreme commitment to race that allowed them to reread Israel as part of the African continent (and themselves as Africans) rather than disavowing any connection to Africa as other contemporary Israelites (those unaffiliated with Ben Ammi's group) currently do. However, even these anti–African Israelite communities articulate their claims to Israelite identity with a concomitantly unmitigated anti-whiteness—and even black supremacism—that is all the more fascinating for its lack of investment (historically, genealogically, symbolically, or otherwise) in any African grounding for such racial ontologies.[27]

Elderly saints from the 1960s provided John Jackson with accounts of these early years, and they noted that from the very beginning their community had an intriguing relationship with media. For example, the press outlet that paid the most attention to the exploits of the African Hebrew Israelites in Liberia, and later in Israel, was the Nation of Islam's weekly newspaper, *Muhammad Speaks*. It ran a number of sympathetic stories on the experiences of the Hebrew Israelites overseas, including critical coverage of their treatment by the Israeli state. For the Hebrew Israelite community, framing their message for the media became part and parcel of an iterative process of self-reflection and self-formation that was always in critical dialogue with other black religious formations. Studying a community like the Hebrew Israelites, therefore, demanded recognition of their self-conscious deployments of race- and Bible-based rhetoric through the media and their ongoing attempts to redefine their beliefs and cultural practices over the years, attempts moderated by audience responses. The goal of redeeming black people globally eventually developed into a more ecumenical version of Ammi's Israelite cosmology, in large part as a function of living on the margins of Israeli society and remaining invested in the plight of those black Americans they had left behind.

Upon arrival in Israel, the community began leveraging the most monetizeable human skills and expertise they possessed, which included construction and music making. In the Negev Desert, they built homes for nomadic African Bedouin who needed stationary addresses so that they could be taxed by the Israeli state. Community members' competency in construction had developed during their failed attempt to build a city from scratch in the Liberian forest. And some early émigrés had a very elaborate history of engagement with the music business. Several Hebrew Israelite émigrés had been established recording artists and session musicians for famous R&B acts of the time. Once they arrived in Liberia, and continuing throughout their time in Israel, the community would send these musicians on the road to raise funds for the collective by playing soul music throughout Africa and Europe. Indeed, the community became famous in many places around the world for its Hebrew-singing gospel choir. Some members of the community even created a new form of musical notation, a coding system that they argued was less contaminated by the problematic ethos, spirit, and negativity of mainstream musicality. Nothing was innocent, not even the ways in which artists rendered notes on a staff.

To be clear, the black Hebrew Israelites from the United States did not leave the country they called home since birth simply because of discrimination. Their justification for leaving pivoted on a discussion of cultural pathology, specifically *black* cultural pathology. One version of what Ben Ammi and the other Israelite pro-emigrationists were arguing on those Chicago sidewalks in 1966 was a belief that blacks had to leave the United States because their cultural practices and assumptions in that country were dysfunctional, even evil. They did not believe that black cultural pathology was necessarily the outcome of structural or interpersonal racism, though the notion was sometimes thematized that way on those soapboxes in Chicago. For them, it was the cost of living in such a vile and damned country.

Everything about life in America was a spiritual contaminant. What blacks ate, especially traditional soul food, was literally deadly. Most of the music they listened to was lewd and ungodly. The religion they had disproportionately adopted was a conspiratorial rewriting of history with the expressed purpose of obscuring the truth about God's chosen people. The clothes they wore showcased their lack of respect for the holiness of their most precious resource, the human body. Every aspect of their cultural universal was skewed, alienating them farther and farther from Yah. In almost every respect, the Hebrew Israelites' thesis about black pathology mirrored the Nation of Islam's thesis about black brainwashing. One of the few exceptions was how differently each group articulated their relationship to the nation-state. Members of the Nation believed that they had a future in a sovereign state in North America and that the United States could be redeemed, even as they appreciated the courage it took to leave

For many Hebrew Israelites, the cure for these aforementioned ills rested exactly in the opposite direction from embracing mainstream cultural practices. That logic and sensibility was precisely the problem. They needed to get out of Babylon and let go of the negative cultural attributes they had inherited as a function of having been tainted by white American cultural values. Black culture was not so problematic and pathological because it was so different from white America's cultural beliefs and practices. This was not simply a "culture of poverty" perspective. The problem they saw with black culture was that blacks had adopted, too easily, white cultural predilections. Leaving America was redemptive because it allowed black Israelites to avoid the racist animus of individual Americans and the lingering biases of their most powerful sociopolitical institutions, but it also (and most importantly) provided blacks with the opportunity to rebuild every dimension of their cultural and spiritual universe.

When they landed in Israel in 1969, only a couple of years after the 1967 war, they pronounced themselves home. This was their forefathers' land, they said. So it rightly belonged to them, blacks from Chicago and other American cities.[28] They would not convert to Judaism, symbolically or otherwise, because that would be conceding to the assumption that they were not who they said they were, descendants of the ancient Hebrew Israelites. So, they were at an impasse given Orthodox Jewish authority on what constitutes state-sanctioned proof of Jewishness. They could not be Israeli citizens as a function of their identificatory assertions. They certainly did not have the requisite documentation to satisfy the adjudicative tests for determining the veracity of such claims. They would publicly renounce their U.S. citizenship many times over the subsequent decades, even supposedly burning U.S. passports for dramatic effect. At the same time, however, they proved to be quite savvy diasporic Americans, leveraging their continued status as United States citizens to invite a bevy of American and West African politicians to their *kfar* (village) in southern Israel over the decades, to raise money for continued community-member migration from America to Israel by working their transnational links to places like Atlanta, New York, and Chicago (including infamous airline ticket fraud scams and money-laundering schemes that financed their ongoing trips), and to get U.S. congressional funds for the construction of a million-dollar school building in Dimona, Israel, exclusively for their young people.[29] There was symbolic and substantive value to being American, their renunciations of that citizenship notwithstanding, and it was a value that they were able to mobilize strategically to survive as temporary residents in a state that would not allow them to work legally since they were not permanent residents or citizens.

In addition to the newspapers, pamphlets, music, photographs, and videos used to tell the story of their faith, community members have written and published books addressing their experiences in America, Liberia, and Israel. Ben Ammi's many publications explain the theories they espouse about the world and black people's place in it. Published and marketed by the community's communication arm, their Ministry of Information, these books intersperse biblical verses with detailed exegeses of how those passages support the community's contentions and justify their coining of new terms and concepts: Evolutionary Corrective Force (those whose spirits "have been formed by and given the protection of the Divine principles of Love, Truth, Justice, Mercy, Equity and Peace"), Plants of Renown (specially farmed vegetables that can unlock the secret to cellular immortality for human beings), Euro-Gentiles (an explicit description of Europeans' lack of Israelite ancestry), and much more. The community labels this "the power to define," and they use such power in all of the media they deploy to educate the masses.

Even during the 1960s, the community relied on communication technology to make their connections across continents possible, from landline phones to the post office. By the early twenty-first century, the community's original one hundred or so migrants to Israel grew to over 3,500 in that country alone, while cheap cell phones, "magic jack" apps, and varied social media platforms helped them to keep their transnational spiritual community connected. Of course, Ben Ammi's books continue to be available online after his death. His lectures long circulated the globe on DVDs, even as YouTube and other media-sharing sites showcase many of those videos for an exponentially wider audience today. Videos of annual ceremonies in Dimona were posted online to be downloaded by enthusiastic community members all over the planet. Their freestanding websites include audio recordings of speeches, free giveaways, prayers, blessings, and links for donations and gifts. Their Facebook page profiles videos of their New Jerusalem Gospel Choir and historical footage of Ben Ammi speaking as a much younger firebrand. Some of these media representations were organized in a decentralized manner, produced by volunteers committed to the Kingdom of Yah. Some of it was centrally organized by the Ministry of Divine Information in Dimona, Israel.

Explicitly situating their religious messaging within a "ministry" underscores the fact that a group rejecting its national homeland can mobilize tropes of the nation-state to frame collective rebuilding efforts: Ministry of Divine Transportation, Ministry of Divine Health, Ministry of Divine Agriculture, and so on. (The community methodically places "Divine" in front of many important nouns—Divine Marriage, Divine Pleasure, Divine Education, and the like—to signal the fact that they are reinterpreting these terms in ways that are meant to bring glory to God and reflect his deific principles.) The Ministry of Divine Information's role is to help disseminate the community's story, and the kingdom's own Communicators Press has been publishing their written offerings since Ben Ammi's first book in 1982.[30] Many of their videos are produced by the Ministry of Divine Information's Audio Visual Truth Center, which is both a production facility based on the *kfar* in Dimona and an archival space where Hebrew Israelites monitor and store television programs from the United States and Israel. They also have a traveling exhibit/museum of "Hebrewisms in Africa" and of the community's journey from the United States to Israel, which they are trying to adapt for online curation and/or a full-length documentary film.

On January 4, 2015, Ben Ammi's memorial service was streamed online for over four hours as community members sang songs and gave testimony to the greatness of his vision. A lot of community members in the United States tried to make it to Israel for the ceremony, but many more could not. A few Israeli officials came out as well, and the community declared its love for their messiah on a global stage. We might imagine such online streaming as a modern/digital form of soapboxing, but the traditional soapbox remains valuable to other Hebrew Israelites today in places like New York, Philadelphia, Minneapolis, and elsewhere. They continue to distribute audio cassettes and DVDs of sermons curbside, though much of that material is also online. Even depictions of their contemporary sidewalk-based soapboxing are YouTubed. Indeed, many Hebrew Israelite groups still use sidewalk space to make their impassioned case against Christianity (as a purposeful attempt to hide the truth about ancient Israel), against American hypocrisy (as a fundamental poison pill at the center of its body politic), against "Jews" (as Edomites pretending to be Israelites), and against conventional African American cultural practices (as examples of Yah's chosen people continuing to disobey his edicts). In fundamental ways, it remains possible to boil down their project to the task of "redeeming the race" and declaring black people's undeniable humanity. And that declaration was always aimed at two audiences simultaneously, the folks who stopped to listen, the ones who wanted to know, and the many more who walked right by those soapboxes and often found themselves harangued more forcefully as a function of their indifference to the message. "Why you ignoring the Truth, sister?" In such urban exchanges, "the truth" is often described as black women demeaning themselves with, say, fake hair, skimpy clothes, and white partners on their arms. Like that link to the live streaming of Ben Ammi's memorial service, a link that was posted on Facebook and tweeted to thousands on Twitter, community members have always been conscious of their different audiences. They have been well aware that some blacks might see them as crazy, that many whites would agree with such an assessment, and that other black Jews or Israelites dismiss Ben Ammi as an apostate and false prophet. And all religious/spiritual communities, not just Hebrew Israelites, must think more carefully about potential eavesdroppers or hecklers listening to their messages in the public sphere—eavesdroppers and hecklers increasingly forced to reckon with their vehement, unapologetic and contested definitions of black emancipation.

PART II

Religious Media and Black Self-Formation

4

Reimagined Possibilities

Prosperity and the Journey to Redemption

Journeying Home: Local and Global Flows

Thirty-two years looked different on Shonda. We greeted one another in the local mall, a building we had both seen develop from the thick of woods in the early 1980s. It crept upon the landscape like the spattering of other consumer stores lining the path of the new Broad Street extension. Before the expansion of the town's city center, we all shopped on Main Street, the type of Main Street that centered small communities across the South. "Brody's on Main" was where my mother took my sister and me (Marla Frederick) to make our annual pilgrimage to purchase one sturdy pair of burgundy, strapped Aigner sandals for the summer; clothing, she ordered almost exclusively from the Sears catalogue. Shopping then was pragmatic, not extracurricular. With the advent of the mall, however, life changed for such municipalities. Social life now centered on consumer shopping. Teens hung out in the mall on the weekends, senior citizens walked the periphery for exercise on weekday mornings, and bored residents spent their day socializing in and around the food court. Running into Shonda on this particular day, over ten years after our high school graduation, was in many ways, no surprise.

We greeted each other warmly and caught up on life quickly. My thirty-plus years were (as the biblical text might suggest) barren; hers, full. Just out of her twenties, she laid claim to three children and two grandchildren. I on the other hand made room only for an expanding cadre of nieces and nephews. But these points were not the primary focus of our conversation. We talked unexpectedly and almost exclusively about the dynamic way that Shonda's life had changed given her rekindled faith. Through a series of life's ups and downs, she found herself attending one of the fastest growing and most popular neo-Pentecostal churches in the area. As she explained, this church experience renewed her hope, deepened her faith, and brought clarity to her life's ambitions.

Shonda's story was not the first time we had heard such piercing testimony.[1] Not surprisingly, her story reflects other stories heard in other locales, both national and international, over the past decade of studying religious movements. Small for its size, Sumter, South Carolina, like other cities across the South and around the world, has been influenced by the neo-Pentecostal explosion that has reshaped the American religious landscape during the latter part of the twentieth century and first portion of the twenty-first. In this short span of time neo-Pentecostal megachurches have experienced phenomenal growth, while mainline denominations and many black mainstream churches have been in decline due both to this charismatic renewal and to increasing American ambivalence toward organized religion. Shonda's faith journey had meandered between stints at traditionalist and neo-Pentecostal churches before she settled on Morning Star, with its neo-Pentecostal ethos, charismatic leadership, and admonitions to prosperous living.

Reflecting the zeitgeist of the religious mediated moment, everyday church women were undergoing a revival of sorts built around an attention to the individual, not the structures. They were being encouraged to see themselves as "the head and not the tail," "above, and not beneath," "a lender, not a borrower," in the words of popular Word of Faith songs and scriptures—new people not tied to tradition nor limited by circumstances.

This chapter examines the lives of women like Shonda and the work of religious broadcasting in the redemption of "the race," particularly of black women of the race. It looks specifically at how religious discourses made popular by the media speak to the ongoing concerns of black women in the U.S. South. The intense focus on race within mainline churches throughout the Civil Rights era and beyond, which did not include a complementary emphasis on its gendered inflections, allowed space for the advancement of more "felt needs" ministries that spoke directly to individuals' concerns. Such ministries, largely present in word of faith, neo-Pentecostal, and evangelical communities, have focused more intensely on addressing the discrete concerns of adherents to the greater exclusion of discussions around structural challenges to unjust systems of exclusion and oppression. In other words mainline churches wedded themselves primarily to a racialized discourse of progressive social uplift that paid limited attention to the growing concerns of individual women enveloped in conflicting and confining social contexts. Meanwhile, ministries that were attuned to media, self-help and entrepreneurialism and tapped into the zeitgeist of the moment—namely, those seen on television and those associated with the neo-Pentecostal movement—found a way to construct answers to women's challenges that seemed, based on the prevailing logic, to proffer remedy. They responded, as one religious broadcaster explained, to followers' predominant concerns about family, finances and health. Standing in the mall, a tremendous symbol of America's shift toward consumerism, and encountering Shonda were both indicative of the times and instructional for our work. In exploring Shonda's life and the faith lives of women like her we can discern how women understand the notions of "redemption" meted out through televised prosperity gospels.[2]

Race, Gender, and Redemptive Media

Research on the rise of Pentecostalism both in the United States and abroad offers numerous explanations for its growth, from relief from the anxieties caused by economic vulnerabilities and indifference toward mainline religion, to attention to personal redemption and increased media capacities.[3] Indeed, among religious groups neo-Pentecostalism has been particularly successful. For their part neo-Pentecostals affirm the spiritual affects of classical Pentecostal doctrine—exuberant worship, glossolalia, and other magico-religious practices—while jettisoning its avowed denominationalism, its aesthetic commitments to strict dress, makeup and jewelry codes, and its historical rejection of the accoutrements of worldly success, given the scriptures' warnings against greed.

Indeed, over the past few decades neo-Pentecostals' more cosmopolitan adaptation of media and their attention to narratives of personal redemption have dramatically influenced their rise. Televangelists like Oral Roberts, Kenneth Copeland, and Kenneth Hagin once dominated the airwaves with their messages of seed-faith giving tied to supernatural financial increase and miraculous healing; however, over the past thirty years, "black televangelism," as ethicist Jonathan Walton explains, has become central to the making of religious life in the United States. Personalities like Creflo Dollar, T. D. Jakes, and at one time, Eddie Long, have dominated the airwaves.[4] Their variations on the prosperity gospel notwithstanding, they exhort people to strive for business and financial success in this world. Nevertheless, they are only a part of the story of the dramatic increase in neo-Pentecostal expression on television and across electronic media. Over the same period of time, female televangelists like Joyce Meyer, Paula White, and Juanita Bynum have also gained significant sway. While the ministries of Long, Bynum, and White have waxed and waned over the years, given sexual, marital, and economic scandals, three of these televangelists still maintain controlling dominance of the electronic airwaves: T. D. Jakes, Joyce Meyer, and Creflo Dollar. Their prominence on television, along with social media outlets like Facebook and Twitter, speaks to their ongoing legacy. Yet, it is the story of the women—Bynum, Meyer, and White—that illuminate our concerns here. These female evangelists have contributed tremendously to the development of a neo-Pentecostal ethic that eschews social limitations and encourages, particularly for women, personal advancement.

In many ways each exudes characteristics of the "religious dandy" that emerged out of the heyday of late twentieth-century religious broadcasting.[5] Such personalities, who promote the idea that their wealth is first and foremost from God, often perform their own wealth through their dress style and acquisition of fine houses, cars, and/or private jets. Yet, most importantly for this discussion, they offer piercing narratives of personal struggle and redemption.

Raped repeatedly by her father as a child, Joyce Meyer now controls a multimillion dollar religious empire. T. D. Jakes and Serita Jakes, barely able to scrape together money for a decent car or to keep the heat on in his fledgling first church, now own a multimillion dollar media empire, producing books, movies, and conferences. Sleeping with various men to help meet her financial obligations in her youth, Juanita Bynum managed to cast aside her past and become a platinum-selling gospel artist, drawing massive crowds to her preaching revivals. Thrust into poverty after the death of her father and raped by caretakers whom her mother trusted, Paula White "should have gone crazy," as she explains, but has instead become a household name in religious circles, commanding high speaking fees and serving as a spiritual advisor of sorts to billionaire real-estate mogul Donald Trump, while crisscrossing the country and exhorting audiences to trust God and "spin out" of their troubles. It is these "victim to victor" narratives of tragedy and triumph and rags to riches that bolster their stance in the marketplace of religious broadcasting. As they insist, their success attests to the limitless possibility of those in the viewing audience, for whom redemption and uplift could occur with the proper amount of faith and for some, hard work. Such narratives emerged in tandem with the rise in the America's self-help industry.

Yet, long before prosperity gospels dominated mediated religious discourse, notions of black uplift in progressive U.S. churches were found in organized struggles for civil rights as well as the drive for black self-reliance. Within these discourses, race served as the central rallying cry for redemptive efforts by black organizations. The perniciousness of racism allowed civil rights organizers to focus almost exclusively on the redemption of the race with sparing consideration given to the questions animated by gender. Furthermore, patriarchal leadership of the movement reinforced black masculinist ideals, thereby also reinforcing the notion of female submission and with it the secondary nature of women's concerns. The fixation on racialized oppression so characteristic of progressive black mainline churches that laid claim to the history of civil rights advocacy indeed galvanized communities for progressive change in the mid-twentieth century. Protest marches seen on television largely pointed to the ways in which men and women fought together against racial discrimination in the South.

Nevertheless, as Gloria Hull, Patricia Bell-Scott, and Barbara Smith indicate in their 1982 volume, *All the Women Are White, All the Blacks Are Men, but Some of Us Are Brave: Black Women's Studies*, the popular problem with the framing of civil rights efforts is that "all the women are white," and "all the blacks are men."[6] In other words, to talk about racism has been to address the concerns of black men and to address gendered oppression has been to talk about white women in ways that amplify the challenges of establishing and sustaining an intersectional discourse. Indeed, in efforts to recognize the work of women in the long history of the Civil Rights movement, scholars have pointed to the ways in which "Men Led, but Women Organized."[7] Such scholarship takes a closer look at the role, particularly of churchwomen, in the advancement of the race. At the same time that churches effectively advocated for racialized uplift, the church itself remained largely closed to progressive causes on behalf of women. Scholars like Cheryl Townsend Gilkes have pointed out the peculiar ways in which women had to struggle for leadership roles in churches, challenging the very assumptions of their gendered social positioning all the while maintaining what she deems the "dual sex politics" of the church, which allowed certain freedoms while constraining others.[8]

Despite challenges, black women from the earliest founding of the black church effectively engaged in ongoing efforts toward the redemption of black men, women, and children. According to historian Evelyn Brooks Higginbotham, such efforts to bring about social change in the late 1800s and early 1900s were often constructed through a discourse of respectability.[9] This discourse valorized women's positions as wives, mothers, and social servants and exacted a persistent requirement that they live morally upright and clean lives. Social attitudes thus frowned upon sexual engagements outside of marriage and released a cloud of shame over those who fell beneath moral standards. Speaking against the backdrop of a charged history of racial and sexual constructivist projects, which worked to subjugate black people, race leaders adamantly promoted the ideals of sexual purity and restraint. "Respectability," Higginbotham asserts, "demanded that every individual in the black community assume responsibility for behavioral self-regulation and self-improvement along moral, educational, and economic lines. The goal was to distance themselves as far as possible from images perpetuated by racist stereotypes."[10] Their convictions were bolstered by both moral and political imperatives.

Women who were dedicated to the cause of the Civil Rights movement were also largely concerned with respectability, as evidenced by the selection of Rosa Parks as the face of the NAACP's legal challenge to Jim Crow. Several women prior to Parks had refused to give up their seats on buses, but none was as connected to the movement as Parks and none embodied the principles of respectability quite like Parks, a married and childless seamstress. "Unlike Claudette Colvin or Mary Louise Smith, Parks was the *perfect* woman to rally around. . . . She could 'stand on her feet, she was honest, she was clean, she had integrity.'"[11] Mediated images of Parks and other civil rights protestors are striking because of the very contrast between their respectable behavior and the violent, brute behavior of white Southerners. These images of women in modestly adorned dresses affirmed their humanity and dignity through their attire and often quiet, nonviolent behavior, which in turn validated the approach of protestors, making for compelling nightly news reporting. Respectable blacks, and respectable black women, to boot, entered public spaces as "deserving" of equal rights. And, although such rights are guaranteed by the Constitution, the attention to respectability politics at once aided in the securing of these rights, while inadvertently reinforcing the idea that the prerequisite for African American full citizenship is respectability.

Collective action in these instances served as a policing mechanism in black communities and black churches especially. While the emphasis on respectable behavior was expected by the church, and especially women, given scriptural emphasis on peace, grace, submission, and the like, for African Americans the stakes of not performing such behavior were amplified. In the context of a hostile white environment, lack of deferential behavior toward whites could mean loss of employment or death. The Civil Rights movement built its public mediated image on these fault lines, broadcasting the sharp contrast between black respectable citizens and white animalistic citizen councils, police departments, and other extensions of the state. Collective commitment to amplifying this drama was critical. And, yet with the passage of civil rights legislation in the 1960s and the growing emphasis on individualism in the 1970s and 1980s, the shape of response to social inequality changed.

America's turn to consumerism and individualism, marketed by rapidly growing media, shifted forever discourses around respectability and black redemption. By the 1980s the emergence of a consumer society, committed to self-help logics, changed the way in which people came to understand themselves as social agents. According to media scholars Sasha Torres and Christine Acham, the media's portrayal of blacks changed dramatically during this period as well. While some might contend that media by and large took the side of protestors, showing their abuses to a shocked American public, "evidence reveals that with the shift from civil rights to the black power agenda and the rising frustration of the black urban populations, television was no longer seen as an ally to the black community."[12] For Torres, the alteration in media's portrayals of African Americans from the 1960s through the 1990s was based on an attempt to advance more neoconservative politics and attacks against civil rights achievements without directly signaling race:

During the civil rights years, the alliance between news workers and the movement produced a particular set of coded identifications linking disparate televisual information texts: television asked its viewers, black and white, to identify with nonviolent black protest and against the violent representatives of the southern state. By the early 1990s, though, television was asking its viewers to perform identifications that were precisely the opposite of those we find in the earlier period, to identify against blacks, who are now generally associated with criminality, and with the state power of the police.[13]

Troubling images of the lazy "welfare queen" and the violent, drug-running gangster further contrasted with increasingly popular representations of Asian Americans as the "model minority."

Into this moment, television programs like *The Cosby Show* and *A Different World* emerged and became wildly successful, underscoring notions of black respectability and American meritocratic individualism. Success was possible for all with hard work and elbow grease. Cosby's celebrated television series mirrored the ideal of smart, black, socially well-adjusted people living the American dream.[14] As one of America's most watched sitcoms at the time, it affirmed the prototypical American narrative of sacrifice and hard work as keys to success, with the state no longer primarily held culpable for social inequality. Added to this moment, popular television shows like *Oprah* helped everyday people figure out how they could personally change in order to reap the benefits of the "good life"—better finances, better homes, better bodies, better love lives.

Christians were not immune to the fixation on individual transformation; after all, the rise in evangelicalism ensured an attention to individual salvation as the source of meaningful, enduring change. Moreover, while white evangelicalism began increasingly to reach out to African American communities and multicultural churches began to crop up around the nation, sociologists Christian Smith and Michael Emerson point out that these same white evangelicals found it difficult to understand or challenge the effects of structural racism. "Despite having the subcultural tools to call for radical changes in race relations, [evangelicals] most consistently call for changes in persons that leave the dominant social structures, institutions, and culture intact."[15] And, while the religious right gained momentum during this time, advocating socially conservative religious agendas relating to marriage and family, which were shared by many African Americans, most black Christians stayed away from such advocacy, enshrined as it was in conservative policies that further undermined the advances of the Civil Rights movement. Nevertheless, increasing attention to individual uplift and self-help mantras took hold and movement away from collective action for racial justice was swift. People could individually affect their own lives by living right, eating better, purchasing the right products, and exemplifying great faith.

Scholars like Mara Einstein and Heather Hendershot argue that the concurrent rise in consumerism further influenced how Christians, particularly in the white evangelical business subculture, understood their faith, producing and purchasing items like t-shirts, bumper stickers, and coffee mugs to "brand" and effectively promulgate their religious commitments.[16] Consumerism emphasized the need for not only tailor-made consumer products, but tailor-made ministries given to answering the specific individual concerns of parishioners about their family, their finances, and their spiritual growth. Popular mediated African American religion tended to look inward, rather than outward in addressing issues of social inequality, economic injustice, mass incarceration, or education inequity. For African American ministries, the shift was indeed swift as aging civil rights icons were less attuned to media and new religious personalities emerged who enthusiastically embraced media and its demands.

These new media stars focused on prosperity messages that affirmed human possibility through a type of radical individual faith. One could put faith in action to redeem any and all situations. Interestingly, prosperity gospels did not mete out success based upon gender. Men and women were equally qualified and equipped for abundance, if they just believed. Whereas civil rights advocacy focused mostly on the advancement of the race, prosperity gospels placed possibility and upward mobility at the forefront of individual change, regardless of gender. Anyone could be a millionaire if he or she just believed and practiced faithful giving.

While the progenitors of early prosperity messages were largely white charismatic male figures, a new cadre of black and female preachers began to emerge on the scene in the 1990s and focused on an abundance of possibility in their preaching. Interestingly, these men, particularly Jakes, and women talked about gender and sex and abuse. In some ways it is possible to argue that the program of the Civil Rights movement lost sway not only because of the achievements of civil rights legislation and the emergence of a hyper-consumer society, but also because it continued to place the issues and concerns facing women on the back burner. As McGuire's "new history of the civil rights movement" reminds us, the concerns of women were always, at the very least, central to women. The shortsightedness or unwillingness of Martin Luther King, Jr., and others to integrate gender issues into the larger public discourse around racial justice could explain in part the disenchantment of younger generations of women with the traditionalism of mainline churches—and, thus women's attraction to prosperity gospels and the new cadre of preachers leading the charge.

Believing for Transformation

"Who tried to encourage you to have anything? I never had one [pastor] encourage me." Ms. Canty's words still resonate. In her late seventies, she had spent her entire life in black Baptist churches working for the cause of racial justice and serving her faith community only to be preached to by a pastor who "didn't think women should do this and do that; didn't think women should have their own businesses." For her, T. D. Jakes tells the world "what the women can do!" By the mid-1990s, Jakes's "Woman Thou Art Loosed" movement, as a public mediated event, had reset the tone and tenor for how black churchwomen were to think about their own spiritual and social progress. Tens of thousands of copies of Jakes's video-taped message, as well as a book of the same title, were sold across the country and around the world as he challenged women to take off the masks of perfection, come to terms with their sordid lives and their histories of abuse, brokenness, and socially reinforced inferiority complexes. Church work, children, and husbands had all too often conspired against women, requiring their total sacrifice while leaving them too broken to deal with their own pain as they healed everyone else and too busy to focus on their own dreams. Jakes's message went viral. And, yet, his movement also exemplified the spirit of the moment with its attention to hyper-mediated, self-help, consumer-oriented messages of redemption. Promoting individual faith and initiative, with limited attention to public policy, Jakes's ministry offered an increasingly popular paradigm for how African Americans, and African American women in particular, could achieve the "blessed" life. The purchase of the next book, the next video series, the next ipod message would help to catapult their lives to total transformation. The emergence of neo-Pentecostal style ministries to meet the felt needs of individuals became the trend driving national and international messages of redemption.

Jake's success with *Woman Thou Art Loosed* was followed closely by his introduction of Prophetess Juanita Bynum at his Singles Conference in Dallas Texas in 1996. There, Bynum revealed her history of sexual indulgence and search for redemption, promising women similar transformation if they would but come out of the "sheets" (a metaphor for premarital sexual relationships), live in faith, and give generously to the ministry. Bynum's testimony was awash in the types of daily struggles that single Christians navigate, and it resonated with them. Standing for most of her ninety–minute sermon, thousands of women hung onto Bynum's every word as she reveled in her story of failed attempts at love, disheartening falls into sexual sin, and costly sacrifices for the sake of her soul. Women saw themselves in Bynum—in her plight and her attempts at wholeness—and Shonda was one of them.

Shonda grew up the daughter of a pastor and mother, who also served as a minister. "I grew up in a church. My father was a minister, and my grandparents, all of them kept me in a church," she explained. This church was about thirty minutes away from the heart of Sumter in a more rural part of the county. After the birth of her children, however, Shonda felt that she "wasn't getting fed" in her family church. Its respectability politics ran afoul of her sense of self, and she left it for a more contemporary, media savvy neo-Pentecostal church. Finding Morning Star gave her freedom and new direction. "I was like fifteen when I had my first [baby], seventeen when I had my next one, nineteen when I had the last one. And, you know, when I went [to Morning Star], people didn't judge me." The idea that "people didn't judge" at her new church is indicative of the neo-Pentecostal move away from respectability politics signaled in Jakes's and Bynum's sermons. "I was struggling a lot," she continued, "'cause sometimes, there were times I felt that I failed, you know, and I was just trying to do my best and look like I was just going through so much and, when I started going there, I started getting fed and getting the word and that life wasn't over and that everything I was doing . . . was on the right track, you know. Sometimes when you go up to the old churches, sometimes they kinda steer you like, kinda, like you failed."

And, the message was not simply that she had "failed," but rather that she, as a woman, had failed. Respectability politics at local churches can exact tremendous moral demands from black female bodies, while virtually ignoring the sexual proclivities and often the invisibility of male partners complicit in the conception of children. Shonda's shame was a particularly gendered one. Such politics and the embarrassment that attends it also too often render older women silent, including those who may have had similar experiences. Respectability politics can mute women's (counter)voices, those voices that disrupt the party line; thus, young people live in solitude with perceived failure. Neo-Pentecostals, at least those in public leadership, conversely, testify about their own shortcomings—endlessly. And they do so with adages like, "Without a 'test,' there is no testimony.'" The promise of supernatural blessing dictates that believers must be tested and must attest to God's intervention. Thus, dark, dreary situations are a prerequisite for witness, for breakthrough. Indeed, televangelists have built thriving electronic and print media ministries from testimonies of God's supernatural intervention into the most desperate areas—finances, health, family, and sexuality. Triumphant stories of redemption affirm the possibility of overcoming struggle. Whether intentionally or not, such testimonies work well in hyper-mediated contexts.

Juanita Bynum's extraordinary success as a black female televangelist in the late 1990s was telling itself. Her "No More Sheets" message broadcast her experiences with multiple men and God's power to redeem her from sexual promiscuity. The worst of her story took the audience through the pain of her economic dependency upon men. Sex became a commodity of exchange, allowing her access to clothes, furniture, and housing.

As Shonda explains, such a message resonated with her given her life experiences.

I have a lot of tapes. . . . I used to watch Juanita Bynum. . . . She played a big part in my life. She really did. When she came out with the No More Sheets . . . that's before I moved in this house . . . I watched and just the things I was going through at the time and she was talking about being single and the stuff that you go through . . . with life in general. . . . Like with me I had kids, I always thought I needed a man to really help me to be a family and to help me with the kids and all that . . . and I was going through all kind of mess with that man trying to hold on and when I watched, I was like, oh my God! I said, I can do this 'cause you know, just listening to her and learning about being single and the things you have to go through to get, you know, to where she was.

For followers of Bynum, her willingness to reveal her own personal story of failed relationships provides a means for them to identify and choose alternate paths for themselves, while for those maintaining celibacy, it affirms their choice and the struggle therein. Shonda's story is no different. She found in Bynum mimetic possibility. As Simon Coleman notes in his study of Pentecostals, "Great preachers mediate in an amplified fashion between the everyday and the impossible. . . ."[17] Bynum's capacity to tell her common story of personal struggle and magnify it to an audience of tens of thousands, convincing them that they too could have an "impossible" life transformation, proved remarkable. They saw her not as a renowned preacher, but as one of them, and thus believed that they, too, were capable of redemption.[18]

Famous African American televangelists and many local pastors who broadcast their shows on television, replicating nationally syndicated televangelists, follow this pattern. Despite their prior struggles, they display for their viewing audiences their own tremendous success stories, which are often marked by strong faith, powerful ministries, model marriages, and abundant resources. As religious television scholar Razelle Frankl notes, televangelists "appear, at least in the image conveyed by press and television reports, as affluent corporate chiefs—wearing custom-made suits, traveling in personal jet planes, and living in comfortable and well-furnished homes."[19] They have arrived at their measure of success after great trial, performing wealth in the face of Pentecostalism's traditional rejection of outward signs of "worldliness."

The potential evinced by such displays of worldly success speaks to men and women alike. Black religious dandies in particular have wedded notions of religious faith to ideas of racial uplift, performing for their audiences a type of religiously sanctioned narrative of social uplift that offers new conceptions of selfhood. Some such dramatic performances by televangelists provide a means of aesthetically affirming black uplift and social mobility while simultaneously critiquing perceived notions of black religious complacency with regard to the economic status quo. Women navigating their own lives, often through divorce and/or single parenting, find the messages empowering.

Shonda's story, like that of countless men and women interviewed in Christian communities in the United States and Jamaica, turns on the profound influence that such television ministers as well as her own local pastor have had on her life. Like contemporary media ministries, which espouse prosperity and encourage an attention to individual development, Shonda's pastor offered a steady diet of prosperity and "common sense" approaches to life, like the importance of debt-free living. His ministry, aired on the local television station, drove visitors to the church from Sumter and surrounding areas.

To walk into Morning Star is to feel the excitement. "The more you're under attack, the more the word of God will work for you!" the pastor attested as musicians played in the background. "Somebody told me the other day, 'Pastor I'm going through hell.' You know what I told him? 'Don't stop!'" Applauding wildly, the members leapt to their feet. It was the type of transformative message that Shonda had talked about. Keep pressing was the idea. Trust. Believe. God will deliver. Or, again, the "greater the test" the "greater the testimony." The idea sinks into people's consciousness at every level. One church member, when giving out her email, indicated that her contact information is "gmillioinaire@ . . ." Professing one's possibility, despite current circumstances, is key to attaining it.

Jones, the pastor of Morning Star, had done that in his own way. Deciding to step out in faith, he left the Church of God in Christ (COGIC), the largest Pentecostal denomination founded and led by black Pentecostals, to establish his own entity. With locations now in Sumter and Spartanburg, his is in some ways a mini-denomination. Having moved out from under the COGIC denominational structure because of financial obligations to and oversight from the larger body, he now serves as the head pastor, chief executive officer, and chief financial officer. Nothing occurs at the church unless he approves. This type of autonomy, and loose accountability to larger denominations, is often central to the neo-Pentecostal movement. This "independence" undergirds the entrepreneurial spirit of launching out on what God has called "YOU" personally to do, regardless of history, tradition, deacon boards, and the like. Faith alone, as "you" have experienced it and the ability to "walk in" what "you" hear have been the calling card of leading ministries.

As Shonda explains, the transformation in her own vision of herself as a productive, self-sufficient citizen was inspired by this ministry of prosperity. After working for someone and receiving public assistance to help with the rearing of her children, she decided to do things differently.

> I was like, I cannot work for anybody, I want to just be self-employed. And, hair was what I wanted to do. . . . I didn't want to be broke, and my pastor was a pastor who always talked about prosperity . . . and being rich, and not just in money. And that's why I was like, okay, I want to find something I want to do . . . and I always saw my vision, my salon . . . but I just never knew how to get there.

Envisioning herself as wealthy, Shonda took a leap of faith and decided to pursue cosmetology and open up her own shop. The pathways to her self-employment are laced with moments she describes as supernatural; she also expresses an ongoing commitment to imagine her life as prosperous, reinforced by her pastor and favored televangelists.

> So suddenly . . . you know, when he speaks something, it's already there, he just tapped into it, to kind of pull it out of you. And when I went to church one day and this was just about a year or so ago, and I just left the hair show and I bought this picture for my salon and I said God, I'm claiming my salon next year cause I just paid off all my debt, all my bills and I said I'm debt free, my car was paid for and all that and I just want to take this year and save my money for myself. . . . I came back from the hair show that Monday, that next following Sunday, when I came back, I had an accident and that Sunday when I went to church, he just called me out and got to prophesying to me about my salon and it was gonna

happen this year and I was like . . . next year, but, obviously he means this year. God said this year!

Shonda's presumed failures as a teenager, having children and not completing her education, were stumbling blocks in her home church, but they were the seedbeds of prophecy at her new church. Sociologist Milmon Harrison documents similar sentiments among former members of mainline churches who attend word of faith churches in California. As he explains, "The positive thinking, the sense of personal power and of agency to bring about and realize the biggest, most unlimited goals 'within the realm of what God wants'" are what draw adherents to these new churches and away from traditional ones. "Virtually all of the interviewees," he contends, "said either directly or indirectly, that they wanted something more than what they were getting in their previous churches. . . . They did not say something 'different,' they all said something 'more.'"[20]

Others in Shonda's church had traveled a similar path and the ongoing prompting of the pastor to envision themselves as prosperous encouraged Shonda to "tap into" a vision that she said she always had for her life. One might call that vision the American dream. Taught to Americans at a young age, the ideal of a stable family life, solid career and relative wealth are ideals that are encouraged throughout grade school and amplified through the media. Shonda's experience was no exception. She had simply taken a brief detour that she found corrected at her new church home and reinforced by televangelists like Bynum.

Now, living in an immaculately kept brick home at the end of a cul-de-sac, Shonda reminisced about its purchase. "This house . . . I bought it by myself, there was no husband, no nothing, just me and my kids and all of that was just faith. I just stepped out on faith. Yep." The satisfaction of securing her home, on her own, without the help of a man, was testament to the workings of faith. She had stepped out on it, and God, she concluded, responded.

Similar to Shonda, Belinda moved from her traditional Baptist church to Morning Star. She explained that the service at Morning Star made her "dig deeper spiritually" and "find out more about myself." "The traditional church," she lamented, "you know they mainly center around the way you dress . . . whether you wear makeup. . . . For a long time I thought that if I wore a dress a certain way . . . God is not going to love me. God is not going to forgive me." Belinda, like Shonda, felt judged by her family church. Older people led the service, rarely allowing young people's full participation. They sang the same hymns and went through the same liturgies. And, most destructive for Belinda, they seemed to judge recklessly. "They would just take one particular scripture . . . and use that little scripture to really batter you and I used to feel that I was never worthy. For a very long time I felt that I wasn't worthy of God's love."

At her new church, however, Belinda experienced more freedom and felt as though God spoke directly to her about her personal circumstances. Between Morning Star and televangelists T. D. Jakes and Meyers, she felt her life getting more on track. "In the morning, one in the morning I'd be up to watch [Jakes]. If I didn't get him that night, if I overslept, [then] Joyce Myers the next morning. You know I just had to hear him." She listened even more attentively to them as she separated from her husband and started raising her children as a single parent. "I had really severe bouts of depression and I really leaned heavily on [televangelism] because I knew I needed something that could really carry me through because I just was never the type of person who just goes to friends and says this is what's going on with me." Evangelists spoke directly to her. They skipped over expectation of where she should be and spoke directly to where she was.

Living now in a single-wide trailer in the country, where she pays $435 per month in rent, Belinda counts her blessings. The trailer is furnished and her children have a comfortable bedroom in which to sleep. The air conditioning is paid in the summer, and the heat in the winter. When she has missed a rental payment, her landlord responds in grace, trusting that she will get the rent to him as soon as she is able. Neighbors are likewise generous. "I've had people that have stopped to offer to help me removing the leaves, bagg[ing] leaves off the front yard. The man that owns the home that I'm renting . . . I fall short sometimes a month, not having the rent and he just encourages me, don't worry about it." Stepping above hard circumstances might not be the ultimate demonstration of prosperity, but having minor blessings throughout the process counts. Bynum, Meyers, and Jakes demonstrate in their testimonies that prosperity is a process and that one's self-perception and the perception of one's circumstances are fundamental to change.

Like Shonda and Belinda, Veronica was "drawn to" televangelists by the struggles that they profess to have overcome. Sometimes, their trials are understood as the very "price" they had to pay for the presumed anointing on their lives. As Veronica explained, "One thing I liked and I admired about . . . Juanita Bynum . . . was like, when I heard, when I learned of some the things that she went through . . . I was like, no . . . not this beautiful lady, she went through all this stuff." The telling of "No More Sheets" elicited empathy. "You look at somebody and you just assume they don't go through things like that but when I read some of the things, I was actually, like, she's been there and done all those things and so she ministers out of her hurt and what she's been through and what God has taken her through and . . . that's one of the reasons I was drawn to her, her ministry." In the end, Veronica concluded that "you just never stop to think the price they paid for the [anointing] upon their life." It is clear that the testimony of struggle is seen as the prerequisite for tremendous blessing. Neo-Pentecostal televangelists have narrated this trajectory, explaining the redemptive possibilities meted out through trials and tribulation and grounded in deep personal faith.

Testimonies of God's supernatural blessing in times of crisis abound. The blessings often come in physical form, one by one, believer by believer. As Veronica explained while seated in her new home, $95,000 was the limit for what she could afford on a home. She purchased the home for "$95,400 with three percent locked in interest." But, that wasn't the end of her story. She walked away with two thousand dollars because "all I had to do was pay $500 for my closing." Still that wasn't enough of a blessing. The house was purchased *and* furnished within budget. Her energy raised even more, "I got on Highway 378. Spirit of God told me to go to the furniture store. . . . all seven pieces you see here [cost] $2,000." At the store, she explained, "We put $200 on everything to put it on hold. While it was on hold, they discontinued the line and so everything was half off." The store called and as she tells it, told her, "Girl, come pick up your checks!" "When I stand and tell you God is taking care of me and my family and giving me favor with man, it's true. All this stuff happened after I got under the ministry, the teachings of Morning Star." The exuberance Shonda, Belinda, and Veronica feel comes not only from the messages they hear from televangelists, but also from what they hear from their pastor. The zeitgeist of the moment reflected the anticipatory faith of those ministers who had experienced trial and came out better on the other end. The supernatural, individualized approach to faith that characterizes much of the prosperity gospel is evident in each testimony. God comes through for particular people based on their faith and their faithfulness. The spirit of this personalized faith frames the lion's share of religious broadcasting.

Limitations of Mediated "Redemption"

Working against social expectations of her place in society, her limited financial success and limited capacity for self-realization, Shonda left her mainstream church and entered into the space provided by a new, neo-Pentecostal church she felt "ministered" to her. This ministry, focused on prosperity and given to the dynamics of personal testimony, she attests, spoke to her situation in a way that her home church could not. Respectability politics, which contribute to notions of the "deserving" or "undeserving" poor and hinder self-disclosure, operated for Shonda against her sense of self-worth. Instead, identifying with the struggles of televangelists as well as those in need within her church worked for her.

This "felt needs" approach to life, which does not directly attend to dynamic social change through active organizing or advocacy on the part of society's most vulnerable, seemed to help Shonda to achieve her individual goal of self-sufficiency. The hyper-attention to individuated faith, however, taken to natural conclusions, can also lead to overindulgence and encourage a lack of accountability, as critics of the prosperity gospel often point out. The free-market entrepreneurial spirit of the current neo-Pentecostal moment comes with its own challenges as television ministries have been called to account for the large profits rolling into their doors. Senator Chuck Grassly's (R-Iowa) investigation into the finances of noted televangelists Paula White, Joyce Meyer, Creflo Dollar, Eddie Long, Kenneth Copeland, and Benny Hinn did not yield any significant judgments against their ministries, but it did revive the question as to whether such ministries should continue to operate as tax-exempt.[21] Given that Joyce Meyer's ministry reportedly brings in over $95 million annually, that Eddie Long's ministry empire collapsed under allegations of sexual misconduct and financial malfeasance, and that even locally, Morning Star struggled to meet the financial demands of lenders after poor economic decisions, the need for greater accountability in the financial world of neo-Pentecostals persists. Nonetheless, the words of transformation that they offer their followers continue to reach new cadres of believers, speaking to both men and women with messages of redemptive possibility, regardless of the sin or problem or circumstance. Everyone has transformative possibility, and anyone can attain tremendous prosperity regardless of social location. For followers to constantly hear affirmations that they can have more, that they deserve more, that they will receive more, however, can lead to a myopic vision that overlooks and underestimates the need for structural change.

In 2015, popular best-selling televangelist Creflo Dollar launched a Go Fund Me page imploring followers to send him $300 per person to help him purchase a $65 million dollar jet. Followers of his ministry interviewed on television adamantly supported their pastor's request under the auspices of ministry. He believes in excellence. He deserves "excellence" in travel. The image he created for himself and the sense of worthiness he has poured into his congregants caused them to adamantly reject claims that his request was excessive. One woman interviewed on a local Atlanta news channel was asked as she walked to church, having just stepped off a public transportation bus, whether she would support her pastor's initiative. Without hesitating, she confirmed that she would because she believed in him and his ministry work. After public outrage and constant criticism, the ministry finally dismantled the page. Nevertheless, Dollar himself entered his pulpit shortly after the scandal and proclaimed that his critics were dream killers and enemies of God's work. "I dare you to tell me I can't dream. I dare you to tell me I can't believe God. . . . Because with God all things are possible, to him that believes."[22] "I can dream as long as I want to. . . . If I want to believe God for a $65 million dollar plane, you cannot stop me from dreaming!" Tying his vision to the historic work of spreading the gospel, Dollar opined that "if they discover life on Mars" he will have to believe God for a billion dollar spaceship to go and spread the gospel there. He then went on to dare his followers to "dream about what the devil says you can't have"; whether it was the "best house" or the "best car," his logic insisted that God wanted them to have the best. The enemy wanted them to settle, but God's vision for their lives was the top of the line. By

REIMAGINED POSSIBILITIES | 139

and large popular black televangelists have mastered this art of persuasion, encouraging believers in their mediated audiences that prosperity is their road to personal redemption.

Such preaching, while evidently reframing socially constructed visions of individual possibility, also runs the risk of enormous self-indulgence. The balance between the two is the ongoing challenge of religion in this media age. In his discussion of the rise of the prosperity gospel, Harrison contends that "perhaps most important in understanding the Faith Message as an ideology of transition is the fact that its power and resonance are not dependent upon its followers' actual attainment of material prosperity. Rather it is the pursuit of it, the process by which one yearns for and then works toward achieving, through faith, self-improvement and self-actualization with tangible results to follow."[23] Black redemption on these grounds is always, thus, in process.

5

Race, Islam, and Longings for Inclusion

Muslim Media and Twenty-First-Century Redemption

The voice of Muslim women.
Masthead of *Azizah Magazine*

To please Allah (subhanahu wata'ala) by providing a platform for orthodox thought leaders to affect positive change.
Our mission is to make MuslimMatters a safe, online community which shares and discusses relevant issues along
with practical solutions, shaped by the experiences and
viewpoints of its writers.
MuslimMatters website

Many African Americans who transitioned from the Nation of Islam
to Sunni Islam also shifted their focus from racial uplift projects in the
1960s and 1970s to questioning whether race should have a place in contemporary redemptive projects at all. This attempt at postracialism is
boldly represented in *Azizah Magazine*, founded in 2000. Its articles on
food, fashion, Islamic exegesis, and stories of personal success target
middle-class Muslims of all races and ethnicities. The goal of the magazine is to help women shape their American lifestyles such that they are
in keeping with the faith. The magazine provides examples of how to be
both devout and successful, and the visual eye candy in this sleek magazine makes the choices seem entirely pleasurable. The magazine reads
like Oprah Winfrey's *O*, in which consumerism and personal enlightenment are cast as co-constitutive.[1]

Like much of the new media, *Azizah* crosses so many racial and ethnic borders that to classify it even as "African American Muslim media"
is a bit of a stretch. At the beginning of the twenty-first century a growing body of Muslim media similar to *Azizah* attempted to reach multi-

racial, multiethnic audiences. MuslimMatters, an online news platform for young Muslim journalists, for example, was founded in 2007 and quickly developed a reputation as one of the most highly respected forums. Then there were critically acclaimed documentaries such as *Fashioning Faith* (2009), *Journey into America* (2011), and *The New Muslim Cool* (2009), as well as films by Michael Wolfe, president and executive producer of Unity Productions Foundation, including *Allah Made Me Funny* (2008). These films feature diversity not only on the screen, but also behind the screen. In the case of each of these films, the production staff was as multiethnic as they were ecumenical.[2] Finally, newer venues such as YouTube and blogs have not only been giving Muslims a platform for authorizing knowledge about Islam, but also, in the case of blogs, turning media explicitly dialogic.

Within American Muslim media the sense of racial common cause was replaced in the late twentieth century with a deterritorialized ideal of *ummah*.[3] This media attempted to speak for all Muslims, as *Azizah's* masthead, "The voice of Muslim women," indicates. But given the audience's lack of shared history or cultural values, is this media legible to most readers and viewers? And if its legibility is partial, does it have the power to redeem? In the past, African American Muslim media pivoted around issues of race, knowledge production and authority, and citizenship. Do these topics continue to be focal points of debate and contestation? And if not, what has taken their place? Does the new postracial ideal reflect what Muslims experience in their daily lives?

As religion scholar Jamillah Karim describes in her book on relations between African American and South Asian Muslims in the early twenty-first century, racism within the community mirrors racism that exists generally in the United States: "At the same time that Asian and Latino immigrants cannot become white, they refuse to identify as black. In response to a racial hierarchy that demonizes blackness, nonwhite immigrants construct ethnic boundaries that separate them from African Americans."[4] On the website MuslimMatters author Safia Farole describes the same phenomena in an article on "Race Matters: Colorblind Racism in the *Ummah*."[5] Farole concludes by asserting the authority of Islam to diffuse colorblind racism: "One thing that easily slips from our minds is that the Prophet (Peace Be Upon Him) was a revolutionary man, and that through the revelation of the Qur'an, he was an agent of societal change, targeting acts of discrimination, as illustrated by the hadith involving Bilal and Abu Dhar. We Muslims have a great religion of racial and class inclusivity to be proud of; lets [sic] uphold those standards in our daily interactions."[6]

What we see in twenty-first-century African American Muslim media is that the issue of race, at least at a personal level, has largely been settled. The message sent to the African American Muslim community is that only those who are ignorant of history and geopolitics are vulnerable to white supremacy. Essentially, abjection is for the weak. The refusal to revive the types of racial redemption projects of the mid-twentieth century is rooted in an appreciation of Islam as a global faith that crosses all ethnic and racial boundaries. At least that is the story the American Muslim community likes to tell itself.

Behind the scenes, however, many issues concerning race, Islam, and the state remain unsettled, producing a need for redemptive projects of various kinds. For example, post-9/11 efforts to redeem the religion read a lot like efforts by the Nation of Islam to redeem the race. Also, cleavages around proper forms of piety are observable in social media, as are efforts to manage them discursively.[7] Finally, ambivalence with respect to citizenship continues to complicate the political commitments of African Americans and inspires some of the faithful to travel or migrate to theocratic states. Moreover, this travel seems to be an enactment of the Nation of Islam's utopian ideal of cultural membership in a state built on nonarbitrary rules of inclusion.

This chapter provides examples of how African American Muslim media strives for postracialism while acknowledging racism; celebrates America while rejecting American exceptionalism; and does all of this while debating authority in Islam and proper practice of the faith.[8] In other words, this chapter explores what we somewhat jokingly call a post-postcolonial racialized postracialism in the mediated digital and material global spaces marked by Islamic idealism. The African American Muslim media we highlight was in no way unique in its refusal to attend to borders, either territorial or conceptual, and was, we argue, the logical outgrowth of the Nation's exegetical approach to questioning dominant discourses, including those pertaining to identity and citizenship.

Anthropologist Arjun Appadurai coined the term "mediascapes" in his 1990 article "Disjuncture and Difference in the Global Cultural

Economy."[9] In the article Appadurai interrogates the effect global flows have on social dispositions in five dimensions: mediascapes, technoscapes, ethnoscapes, ideoscapes, and finanscapes. He uses the suffix "-scape" to "indicate first of all that these are not objectively given relations which look the same from every angle of vision, but rather that they are deeply perspectival constructs, inflected very much by the historical, linguistic and political situatedness of different sorts of actors."[10] Appadurai's analysis disrupts the over-inflation in scholarly debates of the threat of Americanization and commoditization in the context of increasing globalization.[11] Throughout the world people have more immediate concerns than the United States or neoliberalism, and therefore even the most pervasive corporate and imperialist propaganda is often read and interpreted in unintended ways. Given this indeterminacy, it is not enough to analyze the texts alone. The influence of mediascapes can be understood only ethnographically, by asking the reader how he or she interprets these "proto-narratives of possible lives, fantasies which could become prolegomena to the desire for acquisition and movement."[12]

In order to draw connections between the media and emerging dispositions toward race, faith, and citizenship, we both studied the work of and interviewed African American Muslim bloggers and journalists. For researchers, working with digital media is tricky methodologically because of the vastness of media sources, the ease with which people lie, the fact that people select what they reveal about themselves online, and the sampling error caused by inequities in Internet access. Given the vastness of the material as well as the issues related to how people represent themselves online, we had to figure out how to be selective without cherry-picking examples that supported our hypothesis about the redemptive potential of media.

What we found was that for African American Muslim writers their social identities and histories often made it difficult for readers to hear their redemptive message. As one of the most expressive bloggers among our sample, Umm Adam, put it, "I feel that my comments on that blog are not taken in [sic] consideration by others, because . . . they feel that as an African American woman . . . I must have been raised in the ghetto with no education, father and mother on crack. . . . Covering up in hijab and moving to Saudi Arabia must obviously be an extreme form of expression."[13] ("That blog" was *American Bedu*, published by a white American ex-pat living in the Kingdom of Saudi Arabia.) Likewise, scholar and blogger Margari Aziza describes the legibility issues that arise not only between African American Muslims and others, but also within the blogger/scholar world as well. Discussing issues such as these, this chapter also explores the interconnections between the writings of an African American Muslim journalist and her decision to migrate to Dubai.

Religious Border Policing

The Internet, as anthropologists have come to note, is not a utopian space of racial neutrality. In describing what race means in Second Life, an online virtual world, anthropologist Tom Boellostroff writes, "Though there was a sense in which one chose to appear African, Asian, or any other race, whiteness acted as a kind of default."[14] The game offers players opportunities to adopt personas not available to them in real life through the creation of an avatar, or virtual identity. Designed by users, avatars can talk to other avatars through ims (instant messages), get married, have sex, purchase land, and buy products like cars. And in these two-dimensional worlds, pixels imitate life. Players interviewed by Boellostroff were aware that racism and forms of exclusions present in real life carried over into the virtual world: "Some residents who tried wearing nonwhite skins reported racist responses, including friends who stopped answering ims and statements that nonwhite persons were invading Second Life. It was not surprising that some residents who were nonwhite in the actual world engaged in forms of racial passing, so that at least one of their avatar embodiments was white."[15] Boellostroff's research on online communities revealed that rather than being an exceptional space of tolerance, it is one in which racism, sexism, and homophobia prevail.

For African American Muslim bloggers, discovering that racial identity still matters on the web often comes as quite a shock. Most want to be taken seriously as scholars or lay scholars of the faith but instead find themselves, like Umm Adam, being characterized as "ghetto." How then is identity reenlisted in efforts to claim one's authority to speak about Islam? How are race and nation signified such that they are simultaneously cast as irrelevant and yet absolutely essential to knowledge production? And what do these media producers hope to gain through these global conversations? A look at a Muslim blogger's somewhat funny, somewhat cruel, rant against her audience helps us to glean some insights about how Muslims police themselves and one another by signifying their identities and thus their authority to make particular truth claims.

In 2009, a popular Muslim blogger known as Sunni Sister wrote a sardonic send off to her readers. The blog began, "Dear Muslim Blogger," and then proceeded with a list of dos and don'ts that revealed deep contempt for the Muslim blogging community. The premise of the letter was that in order to be a popular Muslim blogger, one must present a particular set of views. "Hijab. Super bonus points if you are a man telling women how to dress. . . . Music. Pro or con, but if you're con, remember to throw a lot of Qur'an and Sunnah at people. . . . Our corrupt, terrible society. Note: This can be about either the Western country you live in or any Muslim country. Double points if it is about both."

Other topics mocked by Sunni Sister included disavowal of *and* identification with Western society: "This works better if you are one of those types who insists on wearing an over the head abaya or a thobe, gives your children impossible to pronounce names, and in other ways, constantly gives the impression that you would much rather be lounging in a goat hair tent in Arabia than living in your illegally subdivided flat in Philadelphia / Brixton / Sydney / Toronto." Sunni Sister also advised Muslim bloggers to note their support for the veil (niqab): "'I don't wear niqab, but I support people who do.' Because my opinion matters that much."

Other popular blogging topics identified by Sunni Sister included Muslim women marrying non-Muslim men and parenthood. About parenting she wrote, "'Natural parenting.' Attention niche bloggers . . . schooling, vaccinating, bottle feeding (at any time, including supplements), epidurals, using OB/GYNs, etc.—all of these are the hallmarks of the mainstream culture of the shaytanic kufar (satanic non-believer)—oh feel the many topics coming together. This works super best if you can manage to twist some ayat (Qur'anic verse), hadith (deed or saying of the Prophet Muhammad), or scholarly rumination into making it seem as though women who send their kids to pre-school after having vaccinations are sending their children on the playtime path to eternal hellfire."

Then Sunni Sister hones in on identity politics:

MY IDENTITY! There are so many things you can do with this one which is by far the most popular blogging topic of our Gen-X Muzzle blahgers. . . . Your nationality, race, ethnicity, gender, sexual orientation, sect identification—all of them are ripe for the pickin's. Remember, you are always to speak "as a (white / black / South Asian / British / con/re-vert/ Californian / Sunni / Sufi / gay / etc) Muslim." Make sure to remind people, over and over again, that you have an identity. . . . BONUS points to white people blogging about being white and how they are now "Oth-ered" even though, of course, white Muslims are still white and unlike, oh say, Black or South Asian Muslims, have the option of taking off their scarf and blending in completely. Double bonus points to whites who have been "othered" and now claim the authority to tell blacks / Lati-nos / Arabs / South Asians all about themselves and what they're doing wrong. Super triple bonus points to gay White Muslims. I take off my hat to you. However, trend setting bloggers should note that "my identity" is overdone.

Sunni Sister saved her final harangue for bloggers who interpret Islam as a form of protest, acknowledge the rationale of terrorists, or complain about other bloggers—which ironically is the act she was engaged in. At the very end, she wrote, "Now you have benefited from my deep wisdom. Go little grasshoppers, and populate blogistan with self-important rant-ings about your precious egos—er, I mean, identities. And bring me a frappuccino." Soon after posting her invective she deleted it and all of her old posts. She left in its place a YouTube video of the opening of *Apo-colypse Now* with the lyrics for a song that opens, "This is the end, Beauti-ful Friend, This is the end, My only friend, the end." Those who are part of the Muslim blogging community were more sympathetic than not.[16] Clearly, she had captured the character of the online Muslim community.

As Sunni Sister noted, the Muslim women's blogosphere has niche blogs addressing topics such as dress, hair, makeup, cooking, homosex-uality, home schooling, progressive politics, and polygyny. Others are more general, focusing on the observations made by a Muslima living abroad and or by someone with an explicit religious/political/social per-spective. But all topics relate, in one way or another, to identity, dress,

Qur'an and hadith, proper religious exegesis, gender roles, marriage, religious politics, and parenthood. This repetition provided easy fodder for Sunni Sister's comedy, but humor aside, besides religion, identity, and family life, what is there to discuss? And if identity is central to online conversations, how does one avoid racializing or ethnicizing oneself or others in exchanges over religious exegesis and orthopraxy?

In 2009, Muslimah Media Watch listed over five hundred English-language websites dedicated to Muslim women's issues.[17] The number of English-language websites founded by Muslim men was almost as impressive. As one can sense from the dramatic and poetic denouement of Sunni Sister, many of these websites were started by young people in their twenties.[18] While the young seem unintimidated by the technology, the content of some of the older bloggers, who were in their thirties and forties and had more life experiences to share, seemed to attract more readers. If one can judge the popularity of a website by the number of comments made to posts, the most popular websites generated as many as one hundred comments for a provocative essay. The relatively high response rate indicated that relationships were forged between Muslim bloggers and their readers. Many of their readers were fellow bloggers, friends, or virtual strangers engaged in ongoing conversations. The intimacy often came at a price. Some thin-skinned bloggers struggled with negative feedback and lashed out at their critics. Some blogs died slow deaths after months or years of inactivity. Others began to screen users, and this increased privacy took the media out of the public realm.

What Sunni Sister objected to about Muslim blogs is actually their reason for being. The blogs that we studied in 2009–2010 explored how to perform daily acts of piety and therefore operated similarly to the mosque movements described by Saba Mahmood in *The Politics of Piety* (2005). Many of the women and men who created these websites wanted to share their personal journeys with their faith (*imaan*), and part of that journey involved struggles with identity, interpretation of Sunnah, raising children, and marriage. The blogs became the place to receive feedback and hopefully affirmations that the choices they made were the right ones. But at times the performance of vulnerability and feigned humility masked a righteousness that drove Sunni Sister away.

By definition Muslim bloggers are confident that they have something to say that might be of interest to other Muslims. All want to be acknowledged by other Muslims for how well they practice their religion (*deen*) or at least for their good intentions (*niyah*). Some bloggers, however, described their blogging as a near obsession, a need to make sense of their lives by writing their thoughts and sending them out like messages in bottles. At times, the responses by readers were far from affirming, and some bloggers tried to block critical feedback by blocking access to users whom they considered abusive. Some were so disturbed by negative feedback that they stopped blogging altogether after making sure that they told their readers how hurtful the comments were. On the other hand, the most popular bloggers tended to have very thick skins and seemed to enjoy setting off heated debates.

The most compelling blogs had the potential to inform a reader's exegetical practices and thus mediate a Muslim's perspective on the world. These sites often welcomed people into a hard-won life, in which sacrifice, humor, and religious discipline laid the foundation for a life rich in experiences and familial happiness. Successful Muslim bloggers could make a Qur'anic verse or hadith come to life by juxtaposing it with beautiful images of life in the Atlas Mountains or images of family life in Saudi Arabia. Similar to advertisements, some Muslim blogs were able to generate desire by bringing together the abstract, in this case Islam, with the tangible, such as a successful marriage, career, or migration to a Muslim country, or *hijrah*. Muslim bloggers modestly claimed that they were speaking only about themselves, but readers rarely responded as if the blogger's actions spoke only in the singular. Readers would regularly censure bloggers for making mistakes in their personal life.

In August 2013, MuslimMatters posted a video lecture by one of its founders, Omar Usman, entitled "The Shaykh 'n Bake Shame Grenade: A Muslim Internet Phenomenon." The article described a "shame grenade" as "a rhetorical object hurled into a conversation to compel someone into a certain action via complete embarrassment. When detonated it causes everyone within its 'shame radius' [sic] want to give up on life."[19] The lecture identified seven categories of shaming that vividly captured the risks of censure. Usman's example of "toxic negativity" included a response to a cute picture of a Muslim writer's very young daughters at the zoo posted on the Internet. A reader replied, "So many younger Muslim kids around the world wear hijab—a sign of obedience to Allah and which distinguishes from the believing Muslims who

Allah loves from the sinning, evildoing unbelieving women whom God Allah hates." As demoralizing as it was for the writers, from an anthropological point of view these responses were a tactic used to negotiate the borders of the faith. And the power to control religious borders through shaming, or calling someone out as not being Muslim enough, replicated itself both in digital media and on the ground in communities. For African Americans this mattered because they were often seen as inauthentic Muslims; unorthodox Nation of Islam Muslims versus orthodox Sunni or Shia Muslims. Rather than uniting disparate communities, social media seemed to exacerbate these divides.

More subtle forms of policing can arise from the confusion between audience interest (popularity) and religious authority. Thus, blogs that focused only on the positive were often seen as inauthentic or condescending, as if the writer did not recognize his or her own fallibility. Particularly for the women's sites, revealing one's vulnerability and imperfections was essential for the writer, who adopted an ethic of self-confession that recalls Susan Harding's experiences with born-again Christians in *The Book of Jerry Falwell*.[20] Representing weakness established a sense of equality between the writer and the reader and facilitated a kind of "If I can do this, you can do this too." ("If I can wear *hijab*, you can too." "If I can wear *niqab*, you can too." "If I can migrate to KSA or the UAE, then you can too.")

Among the vast numbers of Muslim bloggers was a smaller subset of African American bloggers. What distinguished them was their tendency to bring an African American political and social sensibility to their blogs. Margari Aziza described her blog as "an exploration of the intersection of race, religion, and gender from the perspective of a black American Muslim woman." Halim Naeem, PhD, on the other hand, dedicated his site to Muslim masculinity and Islamic manhood, refusing to highlight his racial identity, although his readers nevertheless saw it as central to his concerns. The more conservative male bloggers, those who identified as Salafi, defined the borders of their community narrowly. On these sites, "progressive Islam" was often denounced as inauthentic. On one blog Islamic scholar Hamza Yusuf (often called upon to represent the voice of moderate Islam in mainstream media) was dismissed as a "fag" for his "progressive" interpretation of Islam. Another difference between men and women was that male Muslim bloggers tended to be less personal and generally spoke in the third person or claimed an authority that came not from experience, but from serious engagement with authoritative knowledge.

Why do bloggers seek affirmation about their exegesis and ortho-praxy, and more importantly why do these negotiations over religion continue given how toxic they can be? At a functional level, sharing a common set of goals and values makes it easier for groups to cooperate, and conversations in the media facilitate the development of a shared set of beliefs and values. But one could make the reverse argument that new social media is actually sowing discord and dysfunction. Generating strong feelings in viewers and readers is necessary not only for changing minds, but for competing for viewership. Subtlety and nuance are often the beginning of the end for most blogs, and this pruning impacts the availability of quieter voices.

Importantly, how the faith is represented in blogs, books, documentaries, news, and cartoons has the potential to change perceptions of the inclusiveness or exclusiveness of the *ummah*. Passive crowdsourcing can give a relative sense of what is and is not acceptable within the *ummah*, which is why the existence of gay Muslim websites and pro-Israel Muslim websites can change both how Islam is understood by outsiders and how insiders feel about their own faith. For our purposes, more important than the amount of advice trending in one direction on the Internet is the question of what triggers a viewer to rethink his or her beliefs and to act upon his or her newfound sense of religious purpose. The question of which media sites, artists, and writers have the power to inspire directed us to the question of authority, or who is given permission by the viewer to speak for the faith and why? If Muslims submit to ethical precepts that then become embodied, who is allowed to name those precepts? Authority to speak for the faith is bestowed on some but not others, and what we saw in Muslim media is that race still matters.

Regardless of their schooling or religious sincerity, in the United States African American Muslims were not often seen as exemplary members of the *ummah*. In mediascapes this meant that they had less power to persuade or inspire. But this did not stop them from trying. In the next sections we focus on the work of two African American female bloggers and one white male blogger who grappled with identity and authority as they attempted to insert their voices into conversations about faith.

Umm Adam: The Marked Blogger

Umm Adam was the blogger for *Soliloquies of a Stranger: The Life of an African American—Muslim—Muhajirah (expat)—From the Hood—In an Inter-Racial Marriage. It Doesn't Get Stranger than That!* In a very moving entry about her black neighborhood in Chicago entitled "It's So Hard to Say Goodbye to Yesterday," she wrote:

> Almost every boy from the backyard was eventually killed. This was a good community. Many two parent homes and if it was a single mother she was hardworking and trying to raise her kids right. The last time I saw my friend was around 1994 at the funeral of her next door neighbor, Jason. Jason was a very good kid (he was about 24 when killed). Nobody knows who killed him or why till this day. I remember at his funeral his mom asked all of the "backyard" kids (who were now young adults) to stand up. It was a very moving moment. About a week or so later their neighbor, Carol invited us all to her house for Kwanzaa. Shortly after her son, Lateef was killed. Two other boy's [sic] from the backyard, that I know of, were also killed.[21]

Some readers responded to this entry and blog by assuming that Umm Adam was from the ghetto. This inspired her to pen "My America: A Tale of Two Worlds" to correct the record. Despite positioning herself as "from the hood," Umm Adam is actually from a solidly middle-class family in Chicago. She reported that she received her education at some of the best public schools in the United States and graduated with honors from college. Her family includes prominent lawyers and academics, and as she noted in an entry entitled "My America Part 3," she even lived "NEXT DOOR" to President Barack Obama.[22] Her parents were members of the Nation of Islam (what Umm Adam called "the Nation of Idiots/Ignorance so-called Islam") before they transitioned to Sunni Islam. Her parents identified as Muslim but never really practiced. Against her parents' fervent advice, Umm Adam spent some time in the Nation of Islam in the early 1990s. She eventually transitioned to Sunni Islam after

rejecting what she considered the strange idol worship of Louis Farrakhan and the continued insistence that W. D. Fard was the embodiment
of Allah. In both instances, she was welcomed into the faith, the NOI
and mainstream or Sunni Islam, by prominent leaders in Chicago. In
the first, she was allowed in the ministers' private dining room and Farrakhan's wife sewed her NOI garments. In the second, she was welcomed
into a local *masjid* by Jabir Herbert Muhammad, the grandson of Elijah
Muhammad.

Despite her relatively privileged upbringing, race issues in Chicago
were such that geography did not shield her friends and neighbors from
the undertow of racialization. Umm Adam's blog readers, who were not
primarily African American nor particularly attuned to racial issues in
the United States, seemed to miss the subtlety of this distinction. After
revealing these details about growing up in Chicago in her blog, Umm
Adam felt that her authority to speak as a Muslim or for the faith diminished. Umm Adam voiced frustration at not being taken seriously when
she commented on other blogs. She cited as an example her attempt
to engage in a discussion on *American Bedu*, a blog written by a white
American living in Saudi Arabia. A number of Umm Adam's most devoted followers, many of whom let slip that they too were African American, came to her defense: "Asalaam Alaykum, Great post-masha Allah! I
couldn't have said it better. Thank you for putting these 'troublemakers'
in check. (African American + Muslim = crack baby, loser, terrorist, bad
childhood, abused, brainwashed, criminal . . .)"[23]

In digital media, race is potentially a more powerful signifier than
class. Umm Adam's audience could not hear her speak nor examine how
she carried herself in public. She could not distinguish herself from other
African Americans who were less educated or less well off. In the world
of four dimensions and human interaction, African Americans can dis-
arm racism by being "articulate," by demonstrating tastes that align with
higher economic classes, and by performing the unexpected.[24] Umm
Adam may have worn *niqab* (which she did), she may have known the
Qur'an backward and forward in Arabic (which she seemed to), and
she may have lived by the Sunnah based on the teachings and deeds of
the Prophet Muhammad (as she claimed), but none of that mattered
in the two-dimensional world of blogs. While Umm Adam wanted to
participate in debates about how to live according to the faith with all

women in the *ummah*, she was perceived as a voice primarily for African American Muslims.

Margari Aziza and Umar Lee: Authority Rendered in Stark Relief

In order to get an ethnographic sense of the racial tensions visible in social media, Carolyn Rouse sat down with Margari Aziza at a Starbucks in a Barnes and Noble near the University of Pennsylvania campus. Aziza was a blogger and a brilliant student, and we wanted to know more about her motivations for blogging. We were particularly interested in how bloggers respond to one another. Rouse started by asking her about Umar Lee, a white taxi driver from St. Louis who developed a large following of African American Muslim readers.

CAROLYN: You read Umar Lee?

MARGARI: (laughs) yeah

CAROLYN: He's so controversial and fun how can you not?

MARGARI: I remember when I first came across his blog I had a friend
who was a recent convert. It was recommended because she was very
strident in everything and they told her in a class, "Well why don't
you read Umar Lee. He has something to say about the Salafi burn
out."

And when I read it, a lot of his stuff that was sometimes funny
really angered me. I thought he was full of stereotypes especially
about culture. He took a lot of liberties about other people's culture,
especially black culture and Arab culture. His misconceptions about
masculinity it was kind of cartoonish. And then he's like, "The Paki-
stanis, they are emasculated."

I think he's a likable person, you know, you can engage with
him in discussion. I actually met him. For all his faults he's a likable
person. But the other thing that's problematic about his blog is like,
if I were a black taxi cab driver writing this blog nobody would read
it. But he has a legitimate voice because he's a white convert. And he's
actually smart for his lack of training. At the same time his critical thinking is very limited. I mean he just paints everything with
broad brushes. So that's why initially I spent a lot of time on his blog.
Wasted a lot of time with debates with people, but became very frus-

trated with the level of discourse. It makes him an authoritative voice
about our culture. He doesn't seem very reflective about that. . . .

I remember when I went back to California in the summer
and took a *fiqh* (often translated as full comprehension of Islam)
class with Hamza Yusef (president and co-founder of Zaytuna
College). With the Salafi movement it was like, "All these years
of distortion we need to get back to Qur'an and Sunnah." No
acknowledgement of 1,400 years of tradition and intellectual
rigor. Taking a class at Zaytuna it really opened up a lot. It did
acknowledge that there is this rich tradition that you need to
engage with. I mean we can operate without reacting to colonialism and everything is not about Westernization. It's like, "No we
have our own traditions, we have our own thing." That kind of
awakened the historian in me.

In the discussion of Umar Lee Aziza identified Lee's authority to
speak for the faith as emanating both from his body (his race and religious signification) and from his textual practices (how he interprets the
faith). But given that there were a number of other African American
male bloggers, why did Lee capture the imagination of so many?

Umar Lee, a white taxi driver in St. Louis, gained respect for his prize-
winning online article entitled "Rise and Fall of the Salafi Movement."
The Salafi movement, which took off in the 1990s in a number of cities,
encouraged Muslims to adopt a rigid interpretation of Islam and was
itself bolstered through media. Salafism (often used interchangeably
with Wahhabism) is named for the Salaf, or the first three generations
of Muslims starting with the *sahaba*, or companions of the Prophet Muhammad. Salafis believe that the practice of Islam was perfected during the time of the Prophet but has since become corrupted. Salafis use
Islamic history, primarily Qur'an and hadith, to revitalize the proper
practice of Islam, marking and shunning innovative ideas or practices
(*bid'a*). In his history Lee writes:

In the early to mid 90s, we witnessed a period in which lots of people
were becoming Muslim after the new interest in Malcolm X brought
mostly by Spike Lee's X hats and the movie. . . . There was so much hope
that "knowledge of self" would bring blacks out of the rut they'd fallen

into. . . . The strong yearning to be a part of something positive . . . I cannot understand it as well as a black person, but I do know what this yearning is like. This point is important because many of these new Muslims from the influx would find that their next "great hope" was in the salafi dawah.[25]

In addition to enabling the movement to emerge simultaneously in several major cities, the Internet produced new forms of textual engagement. Lee characterizes it as the "cut and paste era" when "a brother could . . . look like a scholar if he knew the right sources to cut and paste from." Self-styled leaders in the Salafi movement began creating and distributing their own magazines, tapes, books, and even clothing such as *kufis* and *thobes*. This religious paraphernalia sold especially well at their two conferences, Islamic Assembly of North America and Qur'an and Sunnah Society of North America.

Lee's history continues:

By the late 90's, the Salafis had clearly established themselves as the most dominate [sic] Islamic presence on the internet. There was a vast worldwide network of articles and audio lectures that interlinked to one another and were sent on numerous email lists. Even people who were not necessarily part of the salafi group often referenced this vast network [sic] salafi websites. It was kinda funny to walk into an "ikhwani" run masjid and see fatwas or articles from salafi websites posted on the board. . . . The internet presence along with the grassroots efforts the conferences produced was [sic] second to none at the time. . . . The groups of salafis in the cities outside the east coast would come together to listen to tapes, have their own make-shift classes or listen to "ilm-online" which was a tele-link to classes in East Orange.

The dedication to the movement produced its own economy facilitated in large part by the Internet. Unfortunately, by 1999 the movement began to break apart over seemingly meaningless differences, such as whether or not one must call oneself a Salafi or demonstrate loyalty to the Saudi throne. People who took the wrong position were slandered, and eventually people were asked to sign the equivalent of a loyalty oath clarifying their position with respect to the faith and Saudi Arabia.

The penalty for not complying? . . . The dreaded boycott. This meant that no one would give you the salaam, nor speak to you, your wife or even your children. That being the case, this created a lot of problems inside homes as the wife would not appreciate being boycotted by her friends because her husband is not "taking the correct position" or vice versa. The obsession with "clarifying one's salafiyyah" reached a fever pitch.[26]

The ways in which members policed and censored one another was one of the reasons many people left the movement by the early 2000s, sometimes by migrating abroad. In the years following the online publication of this history, Umar Lee called out several of the worst offenders online. Eventually Umar Lee was thought by some to be an FBI informant and by others to be a truth-teller. Muslims who knew his work generally either loved him or hated him; both made him a popular blogger.

Aziza's movement away from conservatism was less about personality struggles and more about her growing exposure to the rich diversity of opinions and experiences throughout Islamic history. At a personal level, this knowledge diminished the historical importance of colonialism and Western imperialism. Relative to the 1,400 years of struggle with religious exegesis and political authority, the particular social and economic dilemmas of today seemed less surprising and unique. From that perspective, the immediacies of contemporary concerns faded. In many ways Aziza's path of self-discovery followed that of Muslims like W. Deen Mohammed and Malcolm X, who recognized that while spiritual dispositions are informed by politics, African American Muslims must find a space for imagining moral possibilities within the faith that are not simply a reaction to contemporary concerns. Aziza makes no claims that America is a postracial society; instead she argues that as a Muslim she refuses to allow race to define her or how she chooses to embrace her faith.

At the same time that she had conditioned herself not to react to the racial hang-ups of others—that is, to essentially free her faith from the conceptual prison born of America's racial history—she described her blog as an exploration at the intersection of race, religion, and gender. This was not a contradiction; rather, it was an appreciation for the fact that her perspective, or her *scape* as Appadurai would say, on her faith and the world could never be separated from the most critical parts of her identity.[27] This honesty was refreshing, but it also was a requirement if she was going to be taken seriously. Black women in particular are rarely given the freedom to speak as an objective voice of authority. This is as true in the world of American academia as it is in the world of Islamic social media. Therefore, Aziza constantly reminded her readers that her authority stemmed from her experiences, which could not be denied.

The relationships between religious authority and the raced, gendered, and differently abled body stand in stark relief in a space that ironically was supposed to render these distinctions meaningless. The social media experiences of Umm Adam and Margari Aziza were not unique, and what we learned from them was that authority in Islam is not singularly tied to proper Islamic *ijtihad* (interpretation), but is linked to other signifiers including race. Proficiency in Islamic jurisprudence, history, or the religion is often not enough to give blacks the authority to speak for the faith. This is ironic since many African Americans are drawn to the faith because of how race is discussed within it. Notably, one of the Prophet Muhammad's last speeches describes how Allah created race simply as a way to mark tribal differences but not inferiority. "All mankind is from Adam and Eve, an Arab has no superiority over a non-Arab nor [does] a non-Arab ha[ve] any superiority over an Arab; also a white has no superiority over black nor [does] a black ha[ve] any superiority over [a] white except by piety and good action. Learn that every Muslim is a brother to every Muslim and that the Muslims constitute one brotherhood."[28] This historical speech was useful for African American Muslims bent on opening up a space for themselves within the *ummah*. Indeed, since September 11, 2001, efforts to redeem the religion have become as critical as efforts to redeem the race. After 9/11 African Americans took on the role of the decidedly American Muslim who could translate the faith for the skeptic. Suddenly their citizenship meant something, and Muslims like W. Deen Mohammed were poised to take advantage of their new role as translators of the faith. Mohammed had already encouraged his followers to embrace their American citizenship, which meant that they had a ready vocabulary for explaining how it was possible to be both Muslim and patriotic.

The hip hop song by Native Deen "My Faith, My Voice" (2010) embodies Mohammed's mainstream ethic celebrating God and country.

The group essentially repurposes language used to redeem the race to redeem the faith. The word "faith" is easily substituted with the word "race," and "Muslims" with "black men."

> This is senseless, and it's gruesome,
> Please don't let this, be a Muslim.
> Awww maaan . . .
> We're all vilified, They're saying we're savages,
> Uncivilized. Islam means peace? Na that's a front!
> It's all a deceit, till they get what they want.[29]

The lyrics tap into the frustration that through media Muslims, like African Americans, are held responsible as a group for the actions of individuals. One can see this when "moderate" Muslims are condemned for not speaking out against Muslim terrorists, while white men are never asked to speak out against mass shootings by white men in the United States

Mediated Global Religious Orthopraxy and Personal Redemption

One can only understand the uniqueness of black Christian prosperity ministry when considering the absence of black Muslim prosperity ministries. While most black Christians continue to embrace American exceptionalism and to trust in the American dream, Muslims and black Hebrew Israelites continue to articulate a relationship to the United States complicated by scale. Black American Muslims, for example, most certainly identify as American, but not to the exclusion of a sense of global citizenship that harkens back to the anticolonial and anti-imperialist struggles of the twentieth century. This dual citizenship encumbers them with ethical obligations that supersede place. In practice this means that many consider it their moral duty to call out American aggression, racism, xenophobia, and imperialism wherever they see it. Digital media has made it easier to cultivate an audience when speaking against injustice, and globalization has made it easier for U.S. citizens to migrate.

To be clear, contemporary Muslim critics of American exceptionalism do not reject their U.S. citizenship; there are no modern-day calls to create a parallel nation run by blacks. Unlike some Hebrew Israelites who have indeed renounced their U.S. citizenship, most Muslims affirm their rightful place as descendants of black slaves, exploited laborers, intellectuals, entrepreneurs, inventors, and artists who built the country too. America is what it is because of African Americans, not despite them. Speaking eloquently to this sense of belonging in the documentary *The Black Power Mixtape 1967–1975*, poet Abiodun Oyewole states, "We make love to America. There wouldn't be an America if it were not for black people. And so, you have some dedicated black Americans who will die a million deaths to save America. And this is home for us. We don't know, really, about Africa. We talk about it in a romantic sense, but America is it."[30] For most African Americans, Africa, like Xanadu, is a hauntingly beautiful mirage. But for Muslims, their faith has allowed them to traffic between Africa rendered in religious media as a place of racial possibility and Africa as a real destination.

Notably, the late twentieth and early twenty-first century has been marked by an exodus of African American Muslims who chose, for some length of time, to leave the United States in order to live in a state where race and racialization operate differently and, some might argue, more benignly. Their hope is that in these postcolonial theocratic spaces they can free themselves from the burdens of political race-consciousness in order to make room for a spiritual identity that is, for lack of a better descriptor, postracial or more accurately an *ummah* consciousness idealized in African American Muslim publications like *Azizah*. Emotionally many Muslims are tired of the battles and want to simply focus on their faith. For those frustrated souls *hijrah*, or migration to an Islamic state, offers a way to escape American racism because ideally Islam organizes the rights and duties of citizens such that wealth and power are distributed justly among people regardless of race or gender.[31]

As noted previously, the core aspect of African American Islam is its continued unsettling of (racial) identity, (historical and religious) truth claims, and (rights and duties of) citizenship. These constituent elements were clearly in play in 2007 when Carolyn Rouse traveled to Dubai to meet with an African American expat journalist, Maryam. Maryam had read Rouse's book on converts to Islam and contacted her. The writing of this present volume was already in progress, so Maryam was asked if she would be willing to be an interlocutor for it. We wanted to know more about expats and their disenchantment with the United States and more importantly how the project of racial redemption in the mid-twentieth century had developed into a discourse of justice privileging religion over all other identities. Toward that end, Rouse and her two-year-old daughter spent two weeks at a pristine, newly built Holiday Inn in Sharjah overlooking the Khalid Lagoon, after which they spent one week in Yemen meeting more African American expats.

That same year, 2007, the *New York Times* published an article entitled "Seeking the Real in a Desert City Known for Artifice."[32] The title of the travel article cleverly evoked Slavoj Žižek's famous piece in *Re: Constructions*, "Welcome to the Desert of the Real."[33] In the essay published only four days after the World Trade Center attacks, Žižek writes, "If there is any symbolism in the collapse of the WTC towers, it is not so much the old-fashioned notion of the 'center of financial capitalism,' but, rather, the notion that the two WTC towers stood for the center of the VIRTUAL capitalism, of financial speculations disconnected from the sphere of material production. The shattering impact of the bombings can only be accounted for only against the background of the borderline which today separates the digitalized First World from the Third World 'desert of the Real.'"[34]

Dubai breaks apart Žižek's binary. Dubai is a Third World desert of virtual capitalism. The media's fascination with this city, designed to belittle American pragmatism and European elitism through extravagant mimicry of both, is understandable. Like a good therapist, the leaders of the United Arab Emirates understand us better than we understand ourselves. But in this desert of optimism gone awry are stories of horrific worker exploitation, a hierarchical system in which the 20 percent who have citizenship are supported by an immigrant population that is not entitled to the same rights to business ownership, land ownership, or schooling. And those are just the legal immigrants. Immigrants entering the country already know that the chances that they will ever attain citizenship are slim to none.[35]

Citizens in the UAE must be generationally tied to the land. By refusing new members the state evokes what is essentially an imagined primordial tribe, but then instantiates the tribe by rewarding citizens who practice endogamy with free land, healthcare, education, and access to capital. The 20 percent who have rights as citizens assert their citizenship by wearing "traditional" dress in public, which categorically distinguishes them from a confusing hierarchy that juggles class, race, religion, and nationality. Because citizenship laws discourage naturalization, what one sees in Dubai conforms to Ulf Hannerz's thesis regarding global ecumene, a term coined by historian William McNeill to describe the development of hybridized peripheral cultures with the technology and organizational capacity to be taken seriously by those in power. Hannerz describes how this global ecumene works in cosmopolitan spaces like Dubai, which have significant intercultural social and economic exchange. Dubai is an interesting case study in that the marginalized are the majority, and the state must therefore make concessions by granting noncitizens significant rights.[36] Diverse identities and subcommunities could threaten current hegemonic structures, and the state is well aware of the potential of a growing disenfranchised population to destabilize the UAE. In order to protect the interest of citizens the state regularly re-patriates unwanted visitors. Before Rouse arrived, an African American Muslim ex-pat received a knock on his door and was told that he was no longer welcome in any Gulf Cooperation Council country.

Given the capitalist decadence, draconian citizenship rules, and country and class segregation, why do some African American Muslim converts or reverts make Dubai their home? Importantly, are these journeys the residue of utopian ideals rendered in *Muhammad Speaks*? And how does the quasi-socialist economic program of twentieth-century African American Islam fit within this neoliberal, theocratic state? To begin to unpack what citizenship and neoliberalism mean to converts living in Dubai, it is important to understand how being part of the *ummah* provides a discursive opening for negotiating rights through Islamic exegesis and for insuring equal protection, something African Americans continue to fight for in the United States in the twenty-first century.

In *Politics of Piety*, Saba Mahmood disrupts the "imaginary of freedom." [37] She argues that religious interpretation is at the heart of Islamic tradition and that what is produced through this everyday exegesis are forms of agency tied to negative and positive liberties. For Mahmood, the stable object is the Aristotelian subject who is open to enlightenment and self-improvement through the cultivation of the self. This self-conscious actor, Mahmood implies, uses Islam as a tool of self-creation.[38]

The experiences of African American Muslim women stand in contrast to the experiences of Egyptian women. For African Americans, engagement with Islam has never been only about cultivating dispositions and proper orthopraxy. Engagement with religious exegesis has to be coupled with the political project of reclaiming their humanity, something we see taking place simultaneously in media and on the ground. This reclamation is driven as much by a desire for spiritual peace as by a need to bring form and reason to a political struggle for citizenship. Redemption, in other words, is never simply the end result of orthopraxy and the feelings of religious purity that accompany right practice. Redemption also requires laws, structures, geography, and an economy. Meeting up with Maryam in Dubai, Rouse was able to consider how media, faith, the city, and law came together to produce forms of citizenship desired by African American Muslims.

Maryam and Wajda's Longing for Citizenship in a Theocratic State: Making Dubai Home

Maryam, who grew up working class in Newark, New Jersey, was a gifted student. Becoming a wife and mother in her late teens, however, she found herself struggling to nurture her two young sons and her intellect while holding down a job. Eventually she received a BA at Rutgers University at the age of thirty and an MA in Sociology and Historical Studies at the New School for Social Research at the age of thirty-three. (Because she is a journalist, we retain her name in this account.) In the UAE, Maryam lived in an apartment with a small living room that tripled as an office, dining room, and bedroom for her six-year-old daughter, Zahra. Off the living room was a postage-sized kitchen, bathroom, and small bedroom that she and her husband shared with their four-year old daughter, Tajma. But this modest space, which the family could afford on the husband's salary alone was, Maryam reiterated numerous times, enough for her. Maryam was very proud of the fact that the rent was so low that, as is prescribed in Islam, her salary as a teacher was for her to spend as she pleased. Never mind the lack of space, the constant battle with cockroaches, or the fact that the government could at any moment knock on her door and tell her to leave. Moving to a Muslim country was her *hijrah*. Now in her mid-forties, Maryam would not exchange Newark,

New Jersey, for her current life with her daughters and husband from Tamil Nadu, India. As far as Maryam was concerned she was living her faith.

Maryam's apartment was on the third floor of a fourteen-story building. From the narrow balcony outside her living room, she had a view of the neighborhood mosque where five times a day the *adhan* was recited over a loudspeaker calling Muslims to prayer. In the United States Maryam found numerous excuses for missing prayer, but in the UAE there was always a place to pray. Even the shopping malls have designated prayer spaces, and if driving, one could simply pull over and with the ubiquitous desert sand make *tayammum* (dry ablution preceding prayer). Maryam lived in a country where she did not have to explain or apologize for her religion and where her race was not conceptually linked to a troubled social history. Maryam was indistinguishable from all the other brown-skinned, *hijab*-wearing women from India, Africa, and other parts of the Arab world. Race mattered, but in a way that was different and disconnected from American sociobiology's linking of racial disparities to genes, which comes across as self-serving nonsense outside the United States. The UAE did not simply represent her *hijrah* toward a more committed religious orthopraxy. It also represented her escape.

Maryam was large, in her words "thick," and light-skinned, and spoke quickly with an accent that made very real the fact that after having lived in Turkey and the UAE, and being a speaker of Turkish, Arabic, Spanish, and French, she embodied what Appardurai describes as the "ineluctable globalization of experience."[39] After returning to the states from Turkey, she met her current husband, Ali, online. Ali, a civil engineer, could not believe how badly he was treated in the United States. Whether this treatment was on account of his faith, his dark skin, his nationality, or all three, the reasons did not really matter to Ali. As soon as he got a job offer in Dubai, he and Maryam packed up their eighteen-month-old daughter without a second thought and left to live close to his parents and siblings.

When Maryam wanted her children to stop whining or when she thought that it made no sense to debate or deliberate, she would say, "That's it. Finish." When thinking about Maryam's decision to leave the United States, we imagine she said, "That's it. Finish," referring both to the debate about whether to leave as well as to future efforts to carve out a niche for herself in the United States. The struggle in the United States was simply too great: "That's it. Finish."

Maryam introduced Rouse to Wajda (a pseudonym), who had recently moved to Dubai and was teaching at the same international school with Maryam. Wajda, Maryam, and Rouse became joined at the hip during her short stay, and after Wajda charged a fellow teacher with slander, Rouse accompanied Wajda on an unexpected trip to the police station.

Wajda was both beautiful and a complete mystery to people in Dubai and Sharjah, or more generally to people who were unfamiliar with America's race history. But for those who knew, Wajda's accent, diet, and cultural knowledge were unmistakable. She undoubtedly grew up in a poor African American community. One night Maryam and Wajda joked at a Baskin Robbins, "You can take the girl out of the ghetto, but not the ghetto out of the girl." Wajda, who was only twenty-two, was a younger version of Maryam. Their commonalities were probably the reason why in the ten short months Wajda had been living in the UAE, they had become fast friends.

Wajda flew to Dubai to meet an African American man who lived in Saudi Arabia. Wajda had every intention of becoming his second wife and living in what Wajda considered to be the ideal Muslim country. Her fortune, however, took a different turn at the airport. Upon meeting his future wife, the groom-to-be decided that they were not compatible and so he gave her enough money for three months of expenses and left. Wajda, who was profoundly resourceful, spent her first night in a rental car and then quickly found both employment and accommodations.

Within minutes of meeting Wajda, she began teaching Rouse about how Muslims get blessings in order to be accepted into *jannah* (heaven). A gifted teacher, Wajda used metaphors to explain the faith. For example, she used the bright light under the shade of a table lamp to denote God's mercy. "People who have strayed from the path are in the dark, beyond the reach of God's mercy." Wajda's extraordinary concern for the afterlife was not something Rouse witnessed in the African American Muslim community until after 2000. For Wajda, this was less an indication of an erasure of the this-worldly liberation discourses that energized the Nation of Islam than of a new syncretism bringing international discourses into conversation with what Islamic scholar Sherman Jackson calls Blackamerican Islam.[40] For Wajda, knowledge of Allah's rewards kept her on the straight path, but her reason for being in the United Arab Emirates had everything to do with her distinctly American liberationist consciousness.

After picking up a McDonald's dinner and sitting in dense traffic for over an hour, Wajda, Maryam, and Rouse finally located the mall they had been searching for. A friend of Maryam, Asma, had invited her to her son's wedding, and she needed to find something to wear. Both Asma and her son were African American ex-pats, and he was marrying his second wife, a Sudanese woman. After dropping Maryam off at the mall, Wajda and Rouse wound their way through the darkened streets of Sharjah to the police station. Wajda had an appointment at ten o'clock at night with a police lieutenant.

Just days earlier, Wajda had filed a complaint against a colleague at the school where she had just resigned her position as a kindergarten teacher. The colleague had accused Wajda of beating up another colleague and pulling out a knife. One might assume that the accuser, originally from Pakistan, employed the stereotypes of African Americans to effectively ostracize and stigmatize Wajda, who happens to be from "the projects" in Pittsburgh. But a history of race and abjection does not exist in the United Arab Emirates, or at least it exists differently and on a much different scale than in the United States. When it comes to race, everyone is essentially a different shade of brown. Wajda's legal rights existed despite the fact that she was part of the 80 percent of the population who were residents and not citizens of the UAE.

The entire evening Wajda nervously anticipated the hearing with the lieutenant. She repeatedly told Rouse that she needed her there for reassurance and to act as an ally. Also with them was Rouse's two-year-old daughter, who remained quiet and curious the entire time. After parking in the lot of the new municipal building, Wajda silently performed a *dua*, or invocation. Once inside, Wajda, who always wore a *niqab*, and Rouse were escorted to the police sergeant's office. They sat alone for about twenty minutes while Wajda filled out paperwork. When the sergeant arrived, he asked Wajda to describe what she wanted from the meeting. Wajda controlled her emotions and spoke very clearly about the slander and potential damage to her reputation. In the UAE slander is punishable. The laws are derived from injunctions against gossip in the Qur'an and hadith.

Wajda's former colleague, Azita, finally arrived with her mother, father, and brother. Azita, who normally wore only a scarf, arrived fully veiled. Her parents and brother wore "Western" clothing. The contrast was striking. Wajda was then given a chance to speak. Despite the presence of two males in the other party, the two African American women, Rouse included, were treated with tremendous deference, and Wajda's story was never doubted. At that point, the benefit of being an African American Muslim in a theocratic state began to be clear. With a nod of her head affirming her guilt, Azita signed an affidavit that she would never commit slander of this sort against Wajda again. The sergeant expressed bafflement as to why two "reasonable" young women would take their grievances to the police. He asked that in the future they work things out on their own. In Pittsburgh, where Wajda is from, no police officer would ever call her reasonable.

From the point of view of Wajda, who grew up in an era of mass incarceration under the direct surveillance of the Pittsburgh police and the justice system, the UAE offered legal protections unavailable to her in the United States. As a child, Wajda was repeatedly taken away from her abusive mother and placed in various foster homes. When she reached adolescence, she had had enough and ran away. She worked various jobs during the day and crashed at friends' houses at night. She would return to foster care only when she needed medical or dental care.

Despite her patchy education, Wajda was smart enough to attain proficiency in reading and writing, which enabled her to get and retain her job in the UAE. Wajda had raised herself and therefore had a resourcefulness that surpassed even Maryam's. Describing her work history, Wajda told Rouse that she started a jitney business (akin to Uber) in Pittsburgh before cell phones were ubiquitous.

As a teen-ager, while wearing what Wajda described as suggestive clothing, she found herself attracted to a Muslim brother selling wares on the streets. Rather than engage Wajda in conversation, which might have appeared to be a come-on, the brother directed her to a *mosque*. His restraint impressed her, and so she visited the *mosque* and eventually took some classes on Islam. In short order, Wajda publicly declared her faith by taking the *shahada,* or profession of faith, and she embedded herself in a conservative African American Muslim community.

Ultimately, it was her mother's accusation that Wajda stole $25 that cemented her decision to leave the United States and possibly never return. The police had a warrant out for Wajda's arrest before she left, and the absurdity and injustice of the warrant spoke to her almost complete lack of support. Wajda had lived her entire life under the gaze of the police, and like most vulnerable black adolescents from her neighborhood, she risked being cherry-picked off the streets and warehoused in prison if she stepped an inch out of line. Wajda saw her future, discovered a Muslim matchmaking scene online, and decided that she had to leave. She left behind a younger brother whom she adored.

Wajda reasoned that a theocratic state offered her more rights than her secular one. She knew the Qur'an, understood the edicts, and liked the idea that her rights would be guaranteed if she lived according to her faith. The UAE, like the Middle East in general, is not a paradise. For many ex-pats other issues emerge. For example, some described to Rouse that while race issues recede, gender issues come to the fore. And race still matters, although in a way that is usually tied to citizenship and wealth. For example, a tall dark-skinned American whom Rouse met in Yemen kept hearing the word *akhdam,* or servant, said in his direction as he walked the streets of Sanaa. This derogatory word is thrown at poor blacks, often homeless migrants from Somalia, Ethiopia, and Eritrea.

In many ways, the humanity afforded Wajda was tied to her U.S. passport. This was made patently clear in the airport where American and European citizens were separated and quickly processed for entry, while long lines of brown people waited for hours to be processed. What Wajda felt in the UAE was a sense of belonging that felt liberating. Because of her citizenship Wajda distinguished herself from the economic refugees who had come to build skyscrapers and remit money home to South Asia. As a result she got to experience the privileges of whiteness.

Maryam was also very aware of her privilege and highlighted it in an article published in *Time Out Dubai*.[41] The article, entitled "Flying Rickshaw," describes her experiences riding in a rickety plane cobbled together from the carcasses of dismembered jets. In the article, she wonders why it is that after 9/11, some populations are sacrificed in order to feed the insatiable demands of globalization. Her article speaks to states' ambivalence about the global flows that they themselves encourage for their own wealth creation. It also speaks to the randomness of privilege. The article ends as the rickety plane begins to shake and sputter.

> *Should I cry, scream, throw my hands up and run into the cockpit?*
> *Ah, the cockpit.*
> How ironic, post 9/11 and it's held open with a dirty shoe string. The heat in here is so intense that I am sure that he would smother to death if he closed it.
> *AC?!*
> It got cooler and wetter. Water dribbled down my arm, soaking it.
> *Allah, cool the co-pilot.* His shirt is open down to his shiny pink belly.
> *Refreshments?*
> Our flight attendant carried a tray of small, white, plastic cups. A half a cup of cola. Alhamduillah.
> "You see, I told you it would be OK." My neighbor says.
> "Thanks, but why have you been on this plane fourteen times?"
> "I have to change my visa every two weeks."
> "Every two weeks?"
> "I have a Nigerian Passport."
> Oh, what a shame I think.
> "Where are you from?"
> "America."
> "Really?"
> "Really."

Maryam was drawn to Islam in the United States because of its articulation of the links between colonialism abroad and racism in the United States. Her article demonstrates her continued appreciation for the geopolitics that lead to precariousness for some and wealth for others.

Reading Azizah *in Dubai*

In an attempt to study the legibility of this post-postcolonial racialized postracialism within the African American Muslim community, Rouse took copies of *Azizah* magazine with her to Dubai. A week into the visit with Wajda and Maryam, Rouse gave them copies of editions spanning three years, covering topics as diverse as *deen* (faith), *ayah* (Qur'anic verses), fiction, food, and decor. A popular magazine among Muslim women in the states, *Azizah* sells itself as "The voice of Muslim women." Given this claim, Rouse wanted Wajda and Maryam to comment on the magazine, to give us a sense of whether this magazine spoke for them.

The uncomplicated layout of the magazine welcomes readers, and the seeming simplicity of the articles—"Girl Scouts—So Much More than Cookies"—belies the difficulty the editors have creating a magazine that speaks to a very diverse community of Muslim women. The founder of the magazine, Tayyibah Taylor, is an African Canadian transplant to Atlanta, Georgia, via Saudi Arabia. African Americans are well represented in the magazine, but like much of contemporary Muslim media, it attempts to appeal to an international cosmopolitan audience.

When Rouse brought *Azizah* to Dubai, she anticipated that her interlocutors not only would be sympathetic to the magazine, but would engage with each article and advertisement. Naively, she thought she was bringing them a piece of the African American Muslim community, which they may not have been seeking to return to, but were nevertheless longing for. Within seconds of handing Maryam a copy of *Azizah*, Rouse's *ummah*-utopian hopefulness was laid bare. "They try to appeal to all self-identified Muslims," was Maryam's split second response to the magazine. Maryam was looking at the back of Volume 4, Issue 1, where there is a picture of an African American woman wearing a beautiful red hijab. The long red and white scarf flows in the wind, and the model's face, with eyes closed, registers deep spiritual contentment. The photo is the centerpiece of an advertisement for the magazine: "Informed, Inspired, Illustrious: The Azizah Woman. Catch the Spirit."

Maryam took exception to the woman's dress. From other conversations with Maryam and Wajda, Rouse knew that they both believed that a solid black or dark blue *jilbab* with matching head covering is the only proper form of dress. All other colors reveal shadows that hint at body form. From Maryam's perspective, the model's attractiveness and clothing were clearly being used to sell the magazine. What the image reflected was the magazine's compromise position on Islam. From the editor's perspective, simply employing some coded signifiers to express sincere but "progressive" identification with the faith was considered enough. When Rouse handed the younger Wajda, the magazine she was excited. She had never seen *Azizah* before. Quickly, however, Maryam's criticisms became Wajda's, too.

In order to put Wajda and Maryam's response to *Azizah* in perspective, it is essential to return to the Salafi movement. There were many African American Muslims like Maryam who desired the goals of the Salafis and took from the movement the passion for pure practice, but whose outlet became not personal attacks on members of the community, but migration. Wajda and Maryam do not directly link their practice of faith to the 1990s Salafi movement, but one way of being Muslim that was encouraged during that time in the African American community was a return to a perceived pure form.

For Wajda and Maryam the problem with *Azizah* was not the individual stories. They were quite sympathetic to the articles that narrated personal triumphs. What offended them is the magazine's sensibility, which tries to make Islam seem compatible with a "Western" lifestyle increasingly defined by consumerism. From the vantage of the UAE, *Azizah*'s redemptive framing of the religion simply did not make sense. From that perspective, there was no reason to redeem the religion or the race. Essentially, Wajda and Maryam had moved on. Constantly having to work to validate one's authority to speak for the faith or validate the legitimacy of the faith had worn thin over time.

In some ways, however, Wajda and Maryam's sense of liberation was illusory. The UAE in no way represents a social paradise of religious and economic inclusiveness. Moreover, the state welcomes Americans as consumers and professionals in service to its economic interests. In "Empty Citizenship: Protesting Politics in the Era of Globalization" Ritty Lukose argues that global citizenship is rooted in consumption.[42] Similarly Ulf Hannerz notes in *Transnational Connections* that the benefits of citizenship in neoliberal states like the UAE are difficult to differentiate from the benefits of credit-card ownership.[43] Freedom, particularly in the case of the UAE, has become freedom to shop. In the words of

Wajda, "When I order bacon, I don't have to ask for turkey bacon. It is always turkey bacon." That is, she need not worry that the food she buys and consumes is *halal*, or pure, since living in a theocratic state means that the products she purchases are likely to be produced and sold in ways that align with Islamic values and edicts. The problem with the overlay of consumption, citizenship, and religion is that unlike a public park or a public building, the space of the mall (a necessary oasis in hot and humid Dubai) is privately held and therefore is not, as James Holston articulates, a place for transgressing the state. Corporations are not compelled like states to legally articulate consumer or worker rights.

However, despite the UAE's best attempts to treat immigrants as disposable facilitators of capital accumulation, Islam opens a space for state redemption. Maryam and Wajda can choose to be citizens of Visa or Mastercard, or they can participate in critiques made possible through religious exegesis and media attempts to name and shame. As Muslims they have a sense of a shared destiny with the Muslims who control the UAE.[44] Maryam and Wajda have cultural membership, but a cultural membership that differs from "cultural citizenship" as articulated by Renalto Rosaldo. Rosaldo describes cultural citizenship from the vantage point of second- and third-generation immigrants in the United States expressing their diversity while simultaneously participating in democracy.[45] In the case of the UAE, the situation is inverted. Maryam and Wajda have few legal rights, but they can utilize universal notions of human rights as articulated in the Qur'an and hadith.[46] In two weeks of intense fieldwork, Rouse witnessed numerous encounters in which Maryam and Wajda asserted their rights through Qur'anic exegesis. This instrumental use of Islam was represented most significantly at the police department. African American Muslims in the UAE have what is best described as "soul citizenship." In "Soul Citizenship: The Black Hebrews and the State of Israel," Fran Markowitz, Sara Helman, and Dafna Shir-Vertesh describe this form of citizenship as one in which one accepts his or her legal exclusion, but then challenges state symbols used to define membership.[47]

The types of citizenship afforded Maryam and Wajda in an Islamic theocracy are desirable for two reasons. First, African American citizenship in the United States is complicated by secular discourses about racial inferiority. Scientific and social scientific theories of cultural and biological differences saturate American understandings of race and provide rationales for structural inequalities.[48] In contradistinction, Islam very explicitly articulates the humanity of all races. Second, in theocratic states religious appeals to justice provide a buffer against the most exploitative and destabilizing effects of neoliberalism. Maryam, for example, had health care in the UAE well before the Affordable Care Act was fully implemented in the United States.

The generation of African Americans born during or just after the civil rights struggles in the United States witnessed disappointment after disappointment. Backlashes against the new legislation came in the form of mass incarceration and economic and social retrenchment. Rather than replicate the discursive battles waged by the Nation of Islam, many Muslims simply moved on, casting for new futures free of U.S. racial politics. Maryam found a place for herself where she was someone other than an African American from the inner-city and where racial and religious redemptive media read like an unnecessary apology to an all too powerful state.

Conclusion

What are the threads connecting Walker's *Appeal* to contemporary blogs in which Islam is debated in global forums? In the case of both, authority is not the enemy; rather, state institutions that exclude blacks from participation as equals are to be feared. For African American Muslims specifically, authority is housed in the faith, recorded in texts that then become the basis for how citizens negotiate rights and duties. For African Americans in general, like Walker, that authority rests in the founding documents of the United States and in the three Abrahamic faiths. Importantly, it is through authority that black subjectivity is made and rights and non-arbitrary paths to citizenship are given.

Contrary to Al Qaeda's horrific misreading of Malcolm X, the Nation of Islam divided blacks into "field negroes" and "house negroes" for purposes of healing and to inspire change. The distinction was meant to link behaviors that helped to sustain slavery with behaviors that helped to sustain Jim Crow. Centuries of attempts at assimilation had generated only more violence. In an effort to pull blacks from the mud, the Nation articulated the role black agency and subjectivity played in perpetuating black disfranchisement. The subtlety of this attempt at reshaping black dispositions in order to topple abjection was completely lost on Al Qaeda.

More than any other media platform, the Internet is currently used to debate and reset the borders of the *ummah*. Media producers who successfully signify their religious authority are given permission to speak about what the faithful can and cannot do, how they should and should not feel. What we find in contemporary Muslim media is that marking one's authority in order to make claims about the faith involves more identity politics than scholarly exegesis. Race, in other words, still matters, but African American Muslims have found ways to be taken seriously such that they can participate, like other Muslims, in redeeming the faith. This is not a great leap forward from redeeming the race, but for many African American Muslims it is a labor of love rather than one imposed on them.

From the desert of virtual capitalism, Maryam took the time to reflect on this history in a remembrance of Malcolm X. In her article, Maryam presents a postracial ideal of an *ummah* built on brotherhood and submission to the faith and includes critiques of capitalism, media, politics, and violence. This blurring of the secular and the religious, the political and the economic, comes straight out of African American religion. To conclude this chapter, we have decided to give Maryam the last word because her article articulates so clearly how iconic media moments have become touchstones for personal self-formation and political critique. At the center of Maryam's analysis is her faith, which provides the compass for making sense of seeming randomness. Rather than endorse Maryam's critique, the point of presenting her article in its entirety is to demonstrate how black religious media continues to inform African American identity and political subjectivity. Her analysis also works strongly against Al Qaeda's use of Malcolm X as a foil for Barack Obama in the YouTube video described in the introduction.

There is a Malcolm X whom many would like to forget. Whatever passions this man inspires, for better and for worse, we might remember his journey to become Malik El Hajj Shabazz. This month he would have turned 85 years old. Near the end of his life, the Hajji let go of the past and strove for a better future, or at least one better than the world has endured. It was during the Hajj, seeing Muslims of different races and from all over the world joining together, that he understood the profound need for a universal faith and universal mission. Of course, his mission was cut short when a year later he was shot and killed as he gave a speech on African-American unity in New York.

What would the figure whom history and Hollywood will remember as Malcolm X have thought of the world today if he had lived to see it? Malcolm X was one of the few African Americans of his time who travelled through the Muslim world seeking to build a coalition between African-American Muslims in America and Muslims everywhere else. You could say he was ahead of his time. His larger mission was to create a fair and open political arena. Without human rights, he believed, civil rights could not be achieved.

Yes, the world has done much to strengthen civil rights since his passing. In regard to how people understand race, there has been a 180-degree turn in many places. Malcolm X had to travel a similar personal journey. For most of his life, race and class were two mountains that he had to climb. Once he had reached the mountaintop, he saw with clarity how Islam had no racial codes and that those who had accepted Islam were brothers. No matter their colour, Muslims ate from the same plate and slept side by side. His ultimate vision of human rights, one that did not just target one sphere of life or one demographic while leaving the other to fend for itself, was cemented by what he saw and experienced in Mecca.

It is interesting how the world changed so quickly after Malcolm X was murdered, as America endured its most restive decade. Three years after Malcolm X was shot and killed, so was Martin Luther King, Jr. Just months after that, Robert F Kennedy suffered the same fate. One man was a Muslim, one a Protestant and the other a Roman Catholic. All three might have made their country and their world far better, or at least more aware of its own ills, if they had lived.

If he were alive today, Malcolm X might not have been as astonished by how things have changed as he would be about how things can be so easily twisted around when people are less aware. Forty years ago police killed anti-war protesters at Kent State University in the US. Is the world better because in the run-up to the Iraq war, the millions who protested were largely ignored? In my daughter's fourth grade social studies book, there's a lesson on the benefits of globalisation. What it does not include are its risks. It doesn't mention worker exploitation, the elimination of fair wages or unemployment. There is 24-hour news and yet there appears to be much less awareness, and perhaps, even less empathy.

On the blog, The Last of the Iraqis, there is a video of one of the car bombs as it blows up. People are running for their lives; a man is on fire, and he strips off his clothes before he begins to run again. What would Malcolm X have thought of a world where we are more numbed to this kind of violence and despair? I remember watching images on my black-and-white TV of tired soldiers going home, of a man shot point blank in the head, and of ravished Vietnamese. I wasn't able to have an opinion for or against what was happening because I did not understand the images; I was only a child. Many people react without a response or without an opinion as they witness the world's troubles happening live on TV, but these people are fully grown. What would Malcolm X have thought of a world where matters of class, race and faith that he wanted to confront are often ignored in favour of news items on what Lady Gaga is wearing?

Think what you like about Malcolm X, but he wanted his opinion to matter about the things that matter most. We could use some of that passion today. [49]

6

Citizens as Stewards

"On the Air, Online, and in the Community"

When John Jackson, Jr., first met Laura and Michael, the husband and wife team responsible for producing *The Green Hour*, a weekly radio show broadcast out of Philadelphia, they were still living in California. The couple had just moved back to America from Israel, where they had previously been making a life for themselves by braiding European tourists' hair. On their days off, when they wanted a little break, they would reconnect with other African Hebrew Israelite "saints" in southern Israel on trips to the Dead Sea for leisurely swims. Or they might head up to the Jordan River to assist in some small way with "sacred visitations," tours of the Holy Land that Hebrew Israelites organize for foreign guests. Life was good in "Northeast Africa," but once Ethiopian hair-braiders started competing with the couple for customers and cutting into their profits, Laura and Michael realized that they would need to find new ways of earning money.

The duo eventually relocated to America's West Coast and opened a vegan-based soul food restaurant in Los Angeles, which seemed like a sensible way to operationalize the skills that membership in the African Hebrew Israelites of Jerusalem's Kingdom had cultivated. Like other saints, they were committed to healthy living and spent years developing an expertise in nutrition and vegan cooking. During his first visit with them, Jackson ate a meal at the couple's brand new restaurant and learned more about what had compelled them to leave America for the Negev Desert in the first place, only to return many years later with a fine-grained appreciation for healthy decision-making. Health starts, for saints, with veganism, but it hardly ends there.

Even though many community members who left Chicago in the 1960s and 1970s still ate the foods of their childhood, the leadership weaned saints off of meat by the 1980s and 1990s in favor of what Adam and Eve consumed in the Garden of Eden. Nuts, fruits, and vegetables replaced barbecue ribs and fried chicken as new health-based rituals reconstituted the practice of their faith. Members were mandated to exercise three times a week "to the point of sweating." They periodically treated themselves to community-administered colonics, created no-sugar weeks and no-salt days, and performed weekly fasts on Shabbat. And this was all on top of a growing list of other health-conscious norms adopted by saints.

The couple had been following these health mandates stringently in Israel and during stints working with other saints in places like Ghana. They were truly two of the Kingdom's best food innovators, credited by some saints with developing a popular vegan-based drink that was a hit among community members in Israel and the United States. So, in many ways, it was not a surprise that this husband and wife team eventually took their culinary talents back to the United States in their attempt to start anew. This return to the States also helped to grease the wheel for their own deployments of electronic media in service of the promotion of more racially inclusive understandings of national citizenship and global redemption, understandings tethered to the African Hebrew Israelites of Jerusalem's ongoing commitments to the interrelatedness between human and planetary health.

Before opening their LA restaurant, they used farmers' markets to sell their freshly made organic soul food all around that city, cultivating a loyal customer base for some of their favorite vegan dishes. When Laura published a cookbook with recipes for the dishes they prepared in their West Coast restaurant, she described the food as "inspired by her family's traditional Sunday dinners" and predicated on her training with Soul Veg chefs at AHIJ-affiliated vegan restaurants all around the world.

The flagship of the AHIJ's Soul Veg restaurants, Original Soul Vegetarian, opened in Chicago in 1982 and quickly became an iconic fixture on Chicago's South Side. While not technically a restaurant chain, Soul Veg establishments standardized their menus. In places such as Atlanta and Washington D.C., saints would converge for training in the latest preparation techniques sanctioned by the community. Not all the restaurants succeeded, however. There were other community-affiliated restaurants that struggled. Soul Veg West, the restaurant that Laura and

Michael launched in Los Angeles, fell victim to an extremely competitive restaurant market.

After shuttering the doors of their LA cafe in 2007, the couple moved to Philadelphia and began focusing their attention on a company they had started earlier in 2002, which specialized in selling healthy and environmentally sustainable cleaning products. Ultimately, the two chose to take their message of health and environmental stewardship to the public by way of a weekly radio program.

The Green Hour, a radio show that began in 2008, broadcast from the only African American–owned independent black talk radio station in Philadelphia. WURD, pronounced "word," self-identifies as a station unequivocally committed to covering the issues that most impact the lives of black Philadelphians and championing the political causes of racial justice and inclusion in contemporary American society. Regularly featured were sermons from Reverend Jeremiah Wright, made famous during Barack Obama's first campaign for president, and news commentary from Reverend Al Sharpton. For these Philadelphia-based broadcasters, their station represented one of the last holdovers from a bygone era, a time before media consolidation swallowed smaller media outlets. Bridging faith and politics, WURD maintained its commitment to broadcasting "truth to power" even if their relatively faint voice on the AM dial was often drowned out by larger media conglomerates. WURD's owners, Laura's relatives, would say that such a mission was all the more relevant in an age when the corporatization of media seemed to readily reinforce the claim that mass mediation was little more than a purposeful distraction from serious political engagement and organization. In fact, if one listens to many of WURD's hosts and callers, it is clear that for many of them considering questions of social justice and inclusion starts with the premise that neoliberal logics of a transnational media industry are complicit with the continuing marginalization of black lives all around the globe. Indeed, WURD exists as an explicit counterpoint to many normative claims proffered by the mainstream media industry, a counterpoint aimed at helping to facilitate critical and constructive responses—even potentially revolutionary responses—to such race-based marginalization.

"The revolution," as they say, "will not be televised," especially if left to broadcasters who have a vested interest in maintaining the status quo.

In 1974, poet Gil Scott-Heron put that 1960s Black Power slogan together with a fusion of jazz, blues, and funk, turning it into one of the most iconic spoken-word recordings of its time. A frenetic critique of corporatization, political opportunism, and popular culture's ability to seemingly anesthetize its viewers, "The Revolution Will Not Be Televised" traffics in a discussion of what some academics took to calling "the hegemony of vision."[1] In the Scott-Heron anthem, "televised" stands in for a neoliberal logic that would aspire to domesticate and dissipate revolutionary possibility, relegating "the political" to what fits inside network TV's standardized corporate-sponsored programming.

Proffering a romantic notion of revolution perched beyond any and all mass mediated cooptation, the song includes dismissive references to broadcast coverage of looters stealing TV sets and nightly news recaps of urban unrest. There is also a specific allusion to recurring media imagery of police officers killing young black men. "There will be no pictures," Scott-Heron declares, "of pigs shooting down brothers on the instant replay. There will be no pictures of pigs shooting down brothers on the instant replay."[2] The line is repeated for emphasis. Particularly striking is its unapologetic use of a derogatory term for law enforcement. More provocative still is its suggestion that killing "brothers" can be likened to recreational hunting, complete with instant replays for bloodthirsty fans.

Scott-Heron's tune is a powerful soundtrack for the kinds of political possibility that WURD imagines to be its most fundamental mission. From its perspective, the revolution requires mass mediation. Indeed, the issues that animate his tune are precisely those that made WURD such an important and atypical media institution. Listeners tuned in to WURD because they knew they would hear DJs, show hosts, and callers rail against police brutality, vehemently defend public education, espouse race-based conspiracy theories, and demand that the voices of poor black people be heard and taken seriously by politicians in Philadelphia and on Capitol Hill.

In this respect, WURD continued in a longstanding tradition of mobilizing broadcast media as a tool for promoting black dignity in the ongoing struggle for political recognition and full inclusion. Electronic media—radio, television, and the Internet—have picked up where the more traditional black press left off. Newspapers that highlighted abolitionist debates and antilynching efforts in the nineteenth century were followed by newsreels and photographs that iconically captured the Civil Rights movement in the twentieth century. Now in the twenty-first century cell phones and surveillance cameras capture the police brutality that Scott-Heron despaired would remain untelevised, and the Internet has provided a platform for mass dissemination of "pigs shooting down brothers on the instant replay." Throughout, self-consciously "black" institutions like WURD actively linked racial politics to the potential power of mass media to disseminate, distill, resignify, and on occasion adjudicate the complicated politics of interracial tension and contestation heightened by videos documenting the police killings of unarmed black men.

The Hebrew Israelites would be incomprehensible, in terms of their philosophies, cosmologies, and everyday practices, were it not for the race-saturated distrust punctuating their religious ethos. Echoing some of the same concerns addressed by the Nation of Islam in the 1960s, state government, public education, medical science, and law enforcement, even in the twenty-first century, were to be distrusted. While many in the black community recognized that state institutions still had to be monitored and reformed, these same people dismissed AHIJ discourse as irrationally paranoid, as examples of misplaced cynicism out of proportion to the concerns that produced them. One would be hard-pressed to find a Hebrew Israelite who did not know about, say, the Tuskegee syphilis experiment (1932–1972). This forty-year study, funded by the United States government, allowed black men with syphilis to go untreated simply to determine the natural course of the disease. What was already known about the disease before the experiment started was that it tortures its victims, leaving patients with a ravaged neurological system after years of pain. The experiment continued even after penicillin was known to cure syphilis in 1943 and in the end contributed virtually no new information about the disease.

For the Hebrew Israelites, medical experimentation on blacks represented the norm. Blacks, they argue, were categorically excluded from the "do no harm" ethos in medicine. And there is proof to support their claims. In *Medical Apartheid: The Dark History of Medical Experimentation on Black Americans from Colonial Times to the Present*, Harriet

Washington documents three centuries of medical abuse and experimentation on blacks, from slavery to the early 2000s.[3] Taking a slightly different but related tack, *Unequal Treatment: Confronting Racial and Ethnic Disparities in Health Care* (2003) demonstrates how racism impacts access to treatment and the quality of that treatment, indirectly resulting in increased morbidity and mortality among blacks.[4] These texts systematically and authoritatively document the devaluation of black bodies. But even these offerings fail to capture the smaller and more difficult to document ways in which a physician's presumptions and disposition contribute to a willingness to let black bodies die. And for the Hebrew Israelites, the act of letting black people die was often qualitatively indistinguishable from actively attempting to kill them. Indeed, to more than a few WURD listeners, even the infamous Tuskegee experiments did not fully capture the level of race-based disregard and hostility toward blacks that continued to animate contemporary Western medicine.

When Hebrew Israelites approached their relationship to new media platforms, it was generally to prove that mainstream facts about social life and history were wrong, understated, or purposefully deceptive. Black Jews, whether from Ethiopia or Atlanta, always felt the burden of having to prove their seemingly farfetched claim about black Jewish authenticity. The claim itself, that African Americans were descendants of the original Jews, seemed so counterintuitive to North Americans, given the astigmatic collapse of northern European-ness with bona fide Jewishness, that one of the consistent mechanisms for explaining its incomprehensibility was to point to conspiracy theories about the purposeful hiding of historical facts.

For the Hebrew Israelites based in southern Israel, remember, this meant understanding "the Middle East" as "a geographical fiction"—a falsehood intended to symbolically excise Israel from the rest of "northeast Africa," which is where the Israelites claim it rightfully belongs. The community boasted a "traveling museum" highlighting "Hebrewisms" all across the continent of Africa, and these historical (re)placements were meant to demonstrate a ubiquity of such cultural practices. It was to the existential detriment of black Americans, they maintained, that their historical ties to Jewish practices were not better known. If facts of black African history can be purposefully and actively concealed, they argued, how much of a stretch would it be to think about black people as the potential victims of more material, and not just symbolic, forms of injustice?

Their mission to correct misinformation was the central dynamic organizing Hebrew Israelite media. This meant that as ethnographers we had to take seriously their audio and visual investments, from Facebook to Youtube to websites, from originally produced programming to the archiving and broadcasting of media produced by others. In an effort to get the word out, the community spent a lot of time monitoring and mobilizing new media technologies such that the products were understood to embody AHIJ principles and goals. Our need to treat the media as agentive, as authorizing alternative truth claims, pushes at the limits of traditional ethnographic methodology.

Much has been said about online or virtual worlds like *Second Life*, which anthropologists can study using fairly traditional ethnographic methods.[5] Platforms like Facebook, Twitter, and Instagram were fundamentally constituted at the nexus where online and offline converge—and by the sparks that fly when they do. Many anthropologists, therefore, have been unsatisfied with the idea of simply studying such worlds online—without substantive engagement with the offline processes, people, and practices that make the online world possible.[6] Media ethnographies, therefore, require anthropologists to think through cultural worlds that crosscut the online/offline divide.

One interesting manifestation of this phenomenon came together at WURD, given its ties to the African Hebrew Israelites of Jerusalem. In the early 2000s, independent radio stations of any kind had a difficult time surviving at a moment of increasingly varied and sophisticated media competition. Even conglomerates that owned a series of stations across the country struggled as online offerings such as podcasts became increasingly popular. In such a context, independent stations had to be even more savvy in their attempts to attract and maintain audiences. For the owners of WURD, increasing competition required them to think about their niche or what separated their station from their competitors'. The station's response to that challenge was distilled in their slogan: "On the air, online and in the community." The line captured both their investment in "old" and "new" technologies as well as emplaced them as local actors in Philadelphia.

With some notable exceptions, radio has become an understudied media form these days, easy to ignore given the excitement over digital technology and Web 2.0 possibilities.[7] But this would be a mistake. While radio broadcasting remains an early twentieth-century technology, how people connect to mass-produced audio relies now in part on digital technologies. Local stations, like WURD, provide apps allowing listeners to tune in from their smartphones or live-stream content on their computers. And for people who can both see and hear, hearing has a more profound impact on our emotions and sense of temporality than sight.[8] Moreover, there is much to be said about the particularities of radio broadcasting that has allowed it to still function in the twenty-first century as a galvanizing force in local communities, particularly low-income communities of color.

The public activism around Trayvon Martin's death at the hands of George Zimmerman in 2012 was in part spurred on by black radio stations. They helped to make the shooting of an unarmed black teen a national news story and then helped to advertise town hall meetings and other local public events aimed at active and ongoing protestation. WURD's market being primarily local as opposed to national meant more fine-grained attention to neighborhood and city-specific responses and organizational efforts. Ultimately the station became one of the nodes in a national network of like-minded radio stations. Translating news into activism, these stations engaged local actors, facilitated dialogue, and advertised political events, often by broadcasting at local community venues in real time. In discussions about the vulnerabilities of the black body vis-à-vis the indifferences of the state apparatus, there are many people who would emphasize the role of black radio in political mobilization.

In keeping with this use of radio to mobilize, Laura and Michael used *The Green Hour* to highlight linkages between activism and a specific instantiation of the Hebrew Israelite ethos. Specifically, the one-hour Sunday morning show promoted one of the pillars of that community's cosmological claims: that we should all take very seriously our species-specific role as stewards of the planet (as exemplified by Adam and Eve in the Garden of Eden). The program aimed at raising the consciousness of black Philadelphians around environmentalism and its links to personal health and well-being. In fact, part of the show's project was to expand definitions of "the environment" by linking traditional environmentalist themes with specific concerns about quotidian aspects of urban living, aspects of urban living that spoke to core—even existential—concerns about belonging and community.

This more holistic definition was predicated on the African Hebrew Israelite community's overarching commitment to connecting the dots between the Bible and secular concerns related to issues of health and well-being and social justice globally. The show described its mission as interrogating "topics ranging from GMOS and food deserts to global warming and disaster recovery." It raised awareness about our collective condition and offered listeners lifestyle solutions for regaining control over their health. It encouraged people to incorporate "'sustainability" into their lives on a daily basis, and identified different domains of sustainability: "health, environment, social justice, culture and economics."

The Green Hour took on many different subjects from week to week, all with a decidedly holistic spin. For instance, they produced an hour-long interview with hip hop scholar and English professor James Peterson to promote his spoken-word album. The point of that segment was to educate listeners about the value of intellectual rigor to discussions about how black people should be thinking through questions of social health. The broadcasters meant to redefine green-ness by bringing it into critical dialogue with blackness as a way of recalibrating discussions of African American history and politics. In many ways, unless one was listening closely and knew the presuppositions that organized AHIJ's philosophy and approach to politics, the racio-political logic of their weekly program could easily be missed. They meant to normalize the relationship between black subjectivity, on the one hand, and questions of authentic citizenship and global stewardship, on the other—ironically enough, by making the case for black listeners being valid participants in seemingly "white" domains like environmental activism and health-related self-help discourse.

One of the most interesting things to note about the Hebrew Israelite saints dwelling in Dimona, Israel, is that they adamantly denied any "political" implications of their revitalization project, environmental activism, and cultural critiques. Indeed, if you asked saints in Dimona about politics, they would tell you that their project had nothing whatsoever to do with politics. To call their work political was even considered a kind of insult and trivialization. Saints were not disavowing politics as much as elevating the stakes of what they were doing above and beyond the mereness of a certain compartmentalized notion of "the political." Politics is about jostling for power, and the Hebrew Israelites considered themselves above that fray—with all of the power they might ever need firmly in Yah's able hands.

The Green Hour shared a similar perspective. What listeners may have mistakenly interpreted as politics, Laura and Michael would have more precisely described as consciousness and awareness. For them their discussions about urban policing, food insecurity, deep poverty, and more were about maintaining the earth's health. They described this perspective as "clean living from the inside out," which included "what you eat, what you wear, what products you use on your body, even how you clean your home. What you drive. Basically, all of the decisions you make every day." They encouraged their audience to "[get] informed about the connection between good health and what is happening in the world around you." They also used the show as a venue to promote health-conscious products designed by members of the Kingdom in Dimona.

Each episode was specifically about a theme linking human health to planetary health, physical well-being to environmentalism. During the second half of 2014, when much of black talk radio around the country focused with laser-like precision on the murders of Michael Brown, Eric Garner, and an increasing list of unarmed black men killed by police, *The Green Hour* showcased its anti-politics approach to social problems. As other news outlets were hosting national conversations on race, full-length episodes of their Sunday morning show were devoted to expounding on the benefits of Ayurveda yoga, debating varying definitions of sustainability, articulating the value of outdoor recreation, and asserting the importance of minority architects thinking about questions of urban design through the lens of health, environmental sustainability, and conviviality. In the latter episode, from October 26, 2014, the hosts spent that hour discussing the health benefits of children and adults running, playing, and otherwise exercising in parks and local green spaces. The theme focused on the underrepresentation of African Americans in such activities. There was also explicit mention of the perception that many outdoor recreational spaces in contemporary Amer-

186 CITIZENS AS STEWARDS

ica were not as welcoming to black folks as they should be. In general, however, the racial dimensions of the problem were understated and presented with little elaboration.[9]

The Green Hour's central intervention was to argue that there was nothing about environmentalism that should make it seem like a white issue. When discussing the value of a massage, various water filtration processes, or cold-pressed oils, Laura and Michael were making a case for the fact that all of these practices have implications for how black people in Philadelphia should think about their everyday decisions. Their aim, as they said, was to "get people literate about health and the environment" in ways that are specifically relevant to urban Philadelphians. The show consistently maintained that "emphysema, asthma, cancer are all connected to air quality, water quality, medical practice, pest management, you name it and are as important as civil rights, human rights, gender equity."[10] *The Green Hour*'s logic was linked to the assumption that sustainability was at the heart of every issue central to life for Philadelphia's disproportionately poor and urban communities of color, making discussion about sustainability a specific engagement with questions on the racial coefficients of urban life. Sustainability is one of the frameworks that can be used to map out the different ways in which black lives and white lives come to matter, as long as sustainability includes the vulnerabilities that mean black urbanites are more likely to die from guns than their white counterparts. Any definition of sustainability that would bracket out such discussions for other conversations (that would relegate it to separate and separable discursive and political spheres) actually reproduces a kind of parochialization of black subjectivity that is the very stuff disqualified citizenship is made of.

When "Black Lves Matter" was becoming a national slogan, *The Green Hour* was spending its time linking Tai Chi and the prison industrial complex to underfunded public education, the under-representation of black kids in STEM fields, and the mental/psychological value of personal goal-setting. This focus should not be read as simplistically "apolitical" and quietist. Instead, it speaks to the aforementioned Kingdom-wide assumption that "the political" is not nearly as expansive a basket as is necessary to hold the high stakes of our contemporary moment. Members of the Kingdom paid a lot of attention to the murders of Garner, Brown, and others but they were not surprised by them. If anything, they recognized those deaths as both quintessential examples of the devaluation of black life and as mounting evidence of just how historical disobedience to Yah's laws continues to impact the experiences of his chosen people. The "sins of the fathers" (as described in the Torah) are visited on their offspring. African American problems today were prophesied in the Bible and predicated on the disobedience of their ancient ancestors. This does not mean that the Hebrew Israelites are happy to see these deaths, gaining some sick satisfaction out of its instantiation of their historical reading. Instead, they are simply resigned to the justice and just-ness of divine punishment—a punishment that can only stop when Yah's chosen people choose to finally obey his commands as articulated in the Torah.

Besides disavowing a narrowly cast definition of their work as political, the Israelites also adamantly deny any identification with the term "religion." Saints are clear about the fact that they follow "the Torah and the prophesies of Yah," but for them their spiritual subjectivity must not be definitionally and institutionally compartmentalized. If politics is not a rich enough rubric to capture their sociocultural efforts, religion is cast as similarly inadequate—something that, as noted earlier, "holds one back" (their interpretation of the Latin root, *religio-*) from Yah as opposed to bringing one closer to his divine precepts and plans. For the saints who produce *The Green Hour*, the show is meant to treat questions of health literacy and environmentalism seriously in ways that allow their discussions of climate change, or the need for environmentally engaged citizens to actively work on clean-air policies, or the promotion of urban bee-keeping (given the importance of bees to our food supply) to serve as examples of what worshipping Yah should look like today. During Jackson's first visit to the radio studio to watch them record and broadcast an episode of the radio show, one of the producers gave him a quinoa salad that she had made for the entire crew. She also discussed her idea of potentially opening a vegan restaurant in Philadelphia like the one they had tried to open in Los Angeles.

The choice to emigrate from the United States in the 1960s, commit themselves to veganism (the diet prescribed by Adam and Eve), and invest in environmentalism (a contemporary manifestation of man's charge as guardians of Yah's creation in the Garden of Eden), are acts interpreted as the fulfillment of their literalist readings of sacred texts.

188 CITIZENS AS STEWARDS

To visit saints in southern Israel is to be struck by how much they emphasize the safety of their everyday lives in their *kfar* (village). Saints do not lock their doors at night. They have no fear of physical violence when they walk along Dimona's cement sidewalks in the middle of the night. And they offer this all up in contradistinction to the urban violence that they left behind in 1960s America—and that they continue to see streamed into their homes in Israel through CNN and Fox News. In that context, police shooting young black people is just another bit of bloody evidence about the fact that Yah's people need to leave the dangers of a foreign land and return to their homeland, contemporary Israel. "You'll never be free," one saint offered on the show in August 2014, "in the land of your captors."

The Green Hour provided hour-long opportunities for leaders in the Hebrew Israelite community to talk to their audience about the community's holistic approach to health and planetary stewardship. Via the airwaves, community healers like Rofah Aheedahlyah and international spokespeople like Nasik Immanuel Ben Yehuda attempted to bring their model of veganism and preventative health-care to Africa and the African diaspora, including South America and the West Indies. For members of the Kingdom, to frame their teachings as "politics" felt like a trivialization of their larger mission, which was redemption of the entire planet.

There have been ongoing debates about the links between politics and religion in African American life. Is religion, as Marx would put it, an opiate for the black masses, depoliticizing them and distracting them from the battles they need to wage? Does it in any of its denominational registers channel political action into more accommodationist, as opposed to radical, permutations, which is how some would read the difference between Christianity and Islam in 1960s black America? Or does religion provide more of a kind of divine justification and moral high ground for the versions of political resistance that came out of catholic socialisms of various forms and the kinds of "Liberation Theology" found in Latin America and beyond? Indeed, there are no simple answers to these questions. If anything, the anthropological response might be to triangulate between and among the specific tenets of the religion in question, the cultural and historical contexts of specific believers/practitioners, and the larger political struggles defining the moment.

For Hebrew Israelites, focusing only on Michael Brown, Eric Garner, Tamir Rice, Walter Scott, Sam DuBose, and so on . . . is almost akin to making a fetish out of them. The vulnerabilities of black life in America are about more than just an unnecessary death at the hands of over-zealous police officers. To focus on these deaths alone frames them as exceptions rather than the rule. French philosopher Jean Baudrillard's notion that some media events serve only to hide more deep-seated structural concerns and inequalities fits squarely with concerns about the bright light of sensationalist hype.[11] For many Hebrew Israelites the victims were already dead in the sense that all black people choosing to ignore that they are the chosen people of Yah are dead. Continuing to run afoul of the very clear and explicit mandates laid out in Yah's sacred text makes them vulnerable to punishment.

As an added wrinkle, there was a third denial in addition to their dis-avowal of politics and religion: race. When they left America in the late 1960s, the Hebrew Israelites framed their project in exclusively racial terms: black versus white, Jacob versus Esau, Israelites versus Edomites, chosen people versus imposters. Racial authenticity was their quintessen-tial organizing principle for belonging. The logic of inclusion was strictly genetic and patrilineal. Being an "Israelite" was presumptively and un-deniably predicated on being "black," and there was an unapologetically racialist underpinning to their entire mission. After forty-five years in Israel and continuous revelations from Ben Ammi about the true nature of their leadership role on the planet, they had become clear in the early 2000s about the fact that their former focus on race was also a kind of misplaced preoccupation. It was not that they were anti-black. Indeed, their entire project placed the Garden of Eden squarely in Africa and defined a large swath of Africa as peopled by descendants of Jacob. Race was not completely irrelevant. It was just that race had formerly been such an obsession, they claimed, that it did not allow them to accept their more universalist goal, which they began to make more explicit almost half a century after arriving in Israel. They were as committed to their Palestinian friends as they were to their Israeli military compatriots (their high school graduates started serving in the Israeli military as soon as the community received permanent residency status in 2003).

Some of this explains why discussions of race/racism in *The Green Hour* were structured the way they were. Clearly, WURD was an unabashedly black talk radio station, but this was an articulated notion of blackness that spent less time speaking its name than trying to get people to unlearn and recalibrate expectations about what black listeners were doing with their everyday lives. There was no way to ignore racial injustices in America. But if your job was to reclaim the world for Yah, starting with the promised land of Israel, then the point was less about being preoccupied with small scale tweaks to a racist criminal justice system than it is was to trying to completely reconfigure what blackness—indeed, humanity—meant in a much more all-encompassing way.

This was the version of the Hebrew Israelite community one heard on that weekly Philadelphia radio show. And the focus on divine redemption is what Jackson encountered through ongoing ethnographic research with the community in its varied physical and virtual manifestations. But this was a community that very self-consciously policed its own public image, watching and listening closely for how others characterized it, especially ethnographers. Moreover, they had the resources to turn the ethnographic/observational eye, with all of its critical potential, back on the social scientist in ways that hinted at some of the issues that also haunted, in interestingly analogous ways, discussions about racism, policing, and new media.

Thinking about the Hebrew Israelites and the positions they take in debates about history and culture, racism and the state, provides us with a powerful way to understand what redemption can look like even for a group that considers politics, religion, and race to be less than helpful categories or constructs. Part of the point is to say that a discussion about "televised redemption" has high stakes: life and death. Indeed the AHIJ proffer and circulate—through shows like *The Green Hour*—a narrative about the planet's condition and its relevance for human health, which argues for a notion of global citizenship as planetary stewardship. Told through the specific narrative of Philadelphia-rooted environmental activism, their (religious) ethos questions common assumptions about how environments should be understood and negotiated. Moreover, it helps us think about what to make of a media moment when footage of everything is available online—when Scott-Heron's witnessing "of pigs shooting down brothers on the instant replay" is realized. Police shootings reinforce a collective cynicism that reads the state as reified and ruthlessly racist. Black Hebrew Israelite philosophies free blacks from having to react to every soul-crushing reminder of their own abjection and vulnerability. Importantly they give them something to do other than be cynical and angry. It is also important to note the difference between redemption and, say, resistance or even revolution. This is a notion of stewardly citizenship that both outstrips the nation-state and also appears to sidestep the entire question of political revolution in the short term. Indeed, the convergence between political and existential moves in this instance need not necessarily make the revolution (televised or not) more or less realizable. Instead, the entire question of resistance (or revolution) is displaced by ongoing commitments to the seeds that might be planted in the hearts and minds of open-minded interlocutors, one radio hour at a time.

The story of *The Green Hour* radio show is one small manifestation of the AHIJ's multifaceted attempt to mobilize mass media as a tool for engaging various publics and for challenging conventional assumptions about black life and humanity. The weekly broadcast, which is also archived and accessible online, links discussions of environmental sustainability, nutritional health, and personal growth to questions of urban vulnerability by staging a series of conversations between those topics in ways that presuppose their relevance for a mostly black and urban listening audience. At the same time, they are also making an explicit case that such concerns represent a more holistic context within which claims about black political and existential resistance must be understood. Ultimately, their particular calculation for how to put those varied thematics into critical and constructive dialogue is constantly revised or challenged by other Israelite/black Jewish communities—or by black religionists from other formal traditions. And that is actually yet another reason why the show and its AHIJ co-producers represent an important node in a chain of connections (through time and space), demonstrating the sparks that fly when Africana subjects link religio-spiritual concerns with the power of mass mediation.

Conclusion

"Black Lives Matter" became a hashtagged online distillation of all the anger, angst, and activism that accompanied highly covered police shootings of African Americans in 2014 and 2015. For several months after white Ferguson, Missouri, police officer Darren Wilson shot and killed an unarmed black eighteen-year-old named Michael Brown on a hot summer day in August 2014, cities across the nation were aflame with public demonstrations against the continuing racial inequities of America's criminal justice system. In November of that year, after a grand jury declared that there was not enough evidence to indict Wilson for Brown's death, many skeptical and angry protesters began to mobilize their social networks, online and off, in outrage over that decision—and over a history of racism that has diminished the value of black lives.

Many of the Christians, Muslims, and Jews/Israelites who constitute the U.S.-based communities that we have studied in this book would be quite familiar with the vernacular adage that for some whites "justice" means "just us." Political philosopher Charles Mills invokes the same claim when he provocatively argues that American and European politics can be reduced to a sometimes implicit and sometimes explicit pact between and among white men to exclude people of color from full membership in the body politic.[1] Such a "racial contract" might be invisible to (or denied by) some of its ostensible signatories, but many African Americans take such racialized exclusions for granted.

This distrust surges through urban vernacular forms, most notably hip-hop, which has voiced this critique of social injustice in America for decades, most infamously with songs such as NWA's "Fuck the Police" and Ice-T's "Cop Killer." Soon after the grand jury announced that it would not indict Wilson for Brown's death, hip-hop artist Nas took to Twitter to cite rapper KRS-One's canonical 1989 formulation of black America's deep-seated cynicism toward the policing of black bodies:

"You were put here to protect us, but who protects us from you?" It was re-Tweeted thousands of times.

If only there were video footage of the Wilson-Brown altercation, some protesters lamented. At least then we would have definitive proof of guilt and innocence. The hope was that images of injustice would have rhetorical force that could change hearts and minds, painting sharp contrasts between victims and perpetrators. Indeed, that was precisely what news reports on television and front-page photographs in local newspapers had done during the ugliest attacks on civil rights activists in the 1960s. And as if some patron saint of snuff films saw fit to answer those prayers, multiple videos emerged. In fact so many camera phone videos were televised during this time period that the American public lost track of the body count of unarmed black men shot by police officers.

Their airing provided an opportunity for public adjudication of criminal justice excesses, and while African Americans believed that these images would lead directly to reform, what they learned was that the value and humanity of blacks remain contingent. Rather than being seen as smoking guns, the videos were interpreted through the haze of America's fraught racial history. The conclusion of several grand juries and justice committees was that the dead must have been up to no good. And they knew this because in the absence of further proof, blacks cannot be considered the moral equal of whites—at least that is what centuries of racism have taught us. The only deaths that spurred profound reform were the killing of nine black Christians in the middle of their religious service.

On June 17th, 2015, a gunman entered the doors of the Emanuel African Methodist Episcopal Church in Charleston, South Carolina. After sitting in Bible study with the pastor and several other members, he stood up and opened fire. At the end of his rampage, nine people lay dead, their names added to the list of black Christian martyrs who believed against hope in the faithfulness of the scriptures and the promise of this country.[2]

Strikingly, the white twenty-one-year-old gunman's manifesto read like the pages of a nineteenth-century Klansmen's diary, replete with musings about taking back "his" country and why he chose the black church and this one in particular. For too long, the manifesto mused, the church had been the heart of black protest; it had rallied blacks to oppose white oppression. On these points Emanuel African Methodist Episcopal Church had indeed been an exemplar. Founded in 1816, it was the first AME church established in the South. It was home to slave revolt leader Denmark Vessey, and in 1822 the church was burned to the ground after plans of Vessey and his co-conspirators' revolt became known. Rebuilt in 1834, it continued to champion the cause of justice and serve the needs of those in the community. Through the long walk of redemption efforts, it was Emanuel where Martin Luther King, Jr., had come to rally support for the Civil Rights movement.

Unlike the circumstances surrounding all the other killings, in this case the innocence of the Emanuel Nine went unquestioned. They were not wearing hoodies, eating skittles, listening to (black) music, selling loosies, or running away from police. The fact that they were dedicated Christians, physically in their house of worship, connected them with centuries of black religious media created to redeem the race. The discursive work of this media filled in the missing details. There was little the public could do but concede that indeed the humanity of these religious worshippers was beyond challenge. The other killings by police generated very little structural change, and even produced the shaming riposte "All Lives Matter," "White Lives Matter," and "Police Lives Matter," which effectively whittled away the redemptive power of "Black Lives Matter." Religion, once again, became the difference that made the difference, and so, soon after the Emanuel Nine were laid to rest, the Confederate flag was removed from the South Carolina state house. On July 10, 2015, the American Civil War was finally over—or was it?

Coming on the heels of the shedding of so much innocent black blood, from Trayvon Martin (a black teen killed by a neighborhood vigilante in Florida) to the Emanuel Nine, the social unrest of 2014 and 2015 raised questions regarding the utility of individual effort apart from collective action as well as the power of media to motivate social change at the local level. Moral Mondays, Black Lives Matter, and Say Her Name, which focused on police violence directed at black women, point decidedly to the power of mediation to impact deep-seated structural inequalities. The Internet saw a veritable avalanche of video clips depicting more and more police shootings of unarmed black men. But there is an inherent ambiguity to visuality: Not only is the visual image rife with layers of nuanced and conflicting (and ideologically driven) meanings; it can also be read as inadequate for rendering the fullness of social life. Philosopher Gilbert Ryle and anthropologist Clifford Geertz agree that any film camera's rendition of the world is "thin" and inadequate, which is why Geertz championed the idea of "thick description" as ethnography's central methodological intervention. Good written ethnographies provide thick contextual information to help explain even fleeting moments observed by the anthropologist. Media does not allow for this depth and texture. There is far too much that the camera (like "the naked eye") does not or cannot capture—too much that lies just beyond its frame, too much that transpired before the camera was ever turned on.[3]

Given the thinness of televised "proof," religion is asked to do a lion's share of the work to deflect the racisms that overdetermine discourses about blackness. Contemporary global mediascapes continue to generate possibilities for social activism, but when it comes to black religious media, its focus is on the longue durée. This redemptive media lies in wait, slowly reshaping the dispositions of those with power such that when the moment arrives, the humanity of those victimized by a racialized state apparatus goes unquestioned.

As we have seen, Christian prosperity ministries attempt to associate blacks, both materially and ideologically, with mainstream, neoliberal white America in service to individual and socioracial transformation. Not all black televangelists preach a message of prosperity, and among those that do, there is variety in their approaches. Nevertheless, T. D. Jakes, Creflo Dollar, and other black Christian televangelists like them want their congregations to identify with the Protestant work ethic and the Horatio Alger story of self-uplift as a mechanism for producing the kinds of material successes that ostensibly help to shield them from the damages of social marginalization.[4] They read in/into scripture the importance of individualism, personal responsibility, and a host of other attributes that map onto mainstream American values to provide an ideological justification for disavowing and nullifying exclusively racialist logics of belonging and nonbelonging. Neoliberalism is sold in televangelism as a redemptive disposition in the sense that God rewards self-control with the gift of wealth, and it is a material wealth that is meant, at least in part, to also fill existential bank accounts. One might include in this roster of televangelists celebrity figures such as Oprah Winfrey, who champion a kind of commodity fetishism (the accumulation of middle-class stuff and symbolism) specifically for its would-be liberationist potential.

Far from simply falling prey to prosperity ministers, congregants struggle with whether or not the relationship among consumption, personal self-fulfillment, and financial and community empowerment is real or illusory. The black community's ongoing questions about neoliberal capitalism are always put in dialogue with the likes of James Cone's canonical articulation of black Liberation Theology.[5] One must be able to buy not just blue jeans and fancy cars but also at least some form of freedom. Yet the popularity and resonance of these voices of black liberation seem to fade in an era marked by mass-mediated spirituality dominated by a handful of popular and ostentatiously wealthy religious figures.

Just as "the talented tenth" was used by black Baptists at the turn of the twentieth century to define a particular ethic of goodness and moral character, prosperity ministries work similarly to reaffirm the fundamental goodness of blacks—for blacks and for others. What distinguishes Christian televangelism from Muslim or black Hebrew Israelite media is that it offers up a way to the promised land through the temptation-riddled byways of Mammon and unapologetic displays of accumulated wealth.

Early religious media icons like Reverend Ike promulgated a crass materialist impulse that was spurred by the selling of religious talismans like prayer clothes, healing waters, and so on, to enlarge his own coffers while simultaneously functioning as rhetorical fodder to reinforce the legitimacy of his financial gains and the accuracy of his spiritual teachings. Dressed exquisitely in the finest apparel and driving different colored Rolls Royces to match his various outfits, Ike preached possibility thinking: Believing strongly enough can bring social, material, and spiritual goals into existence. Late in his life, he suggested that his preaching was an effort to redeem black folks:

"Black people, many of the masses of colored people," Reverend Ike contended, "did not believe that they should be anything, do anything, or have anything. God forbid money; money was evil. . . . And then this Rev. Ike comes along, because, you see, the Bible says 'the love of money is the root of all evil.' This Rev. Ike comes along and gets right into people's faces on radio and television and in these big meetings and says, 'No.' It's not the love of money that's the root of all evil, it's the lack of money that's the root of all evil."[6]

Many contemporary televangelists, elaborating on Ike's earlier pronouncements, preach a variation of this gospel, repurposed to help followers "walk in their destiny." Embedded in all of these newfangled messages of prosperity is a critique of a limited, stifled, or hostage subjectivity. Contemporary discourses insist upon upward social mobility, toward greater wealth, ownership, and entrepreneurship. These discourses are fit for television in ways that Pastor Jeremiah Wright's decontextualized ramblings were ostensibly not. One caters to classic American ideals. The other unflinchingly critiques the system of American governance and capitalism as racist, classist, and fundamentally antithetical to black achievement.

Contemporary televangelists, even if ideologically aware and critical of the entrenchment of racial inequality in the United States, do not build successful, audience-driven television ministries by exploiting these details. Messages of upward mobility resonate with many blacks attempting to make their way in a post–Civil Rights, post–women's rights era. Legally codified barriers to financial achievement seem all but removed for many striving middle-class blacks, and televangelists preach narratives of unlimited possibility through varied combinations of right thinking, right living, Holy Spirit power, a hard work ethic, and a commitment to reinvesting earnings back into God's ministry ("sowing seeds"). When female televangelists pick up these narratives, they often add to them by encouraging female followers to triumph over past emotional and/or physical pain and to walk into even greater promise as women of God. In this respect, these media-based practices attempt to redeem blacks in a purposefully consumerist sense, which holds in tension the need for spiritual, physical, and emotional transformation. Money "buys" salvation not by indicating that one is already saved and chosen (in classic Protestant terms), but by showing that one has the power to prove oneself worthy of saving by obedience to God's purported financial mandates and expectations.

Though an investment in financial independence grounded their iconic and ubiquitous sidewalk sales of newspapers, bean pies, and other items, the Nation of Islam is most often remembered as a violent black radical religion whose leaders emphatically encouraged blacks to defend themselves against white violence. The Nation was not, however, the first to espouse such self-defense. As we have seen, well before the twentieth century, many prominent African Americans, including David Walker and Frederick Douglass, penned rationales for why blacks had the right to take up arms against the state and its oppressive operatives. And some of these calls for active black self-protection were cased in decidedly religious registers. For instance, Nat Turner claimed to have received his justification for armed and violent revolt against white people in 1831 directly from God. In the 1950s and 60s, when media by and about the Nation could be juxtaposed with images of white violence toward largely peaceful civil rights protesters, white Americans began to take notice of the Nation's specific rhetoric and organizing principles. As more and more Americans purchased televisions and newspapers, the Nation's oft-cited description of whites as blue-eyed devils seemed less the rantings of a lunatic fringe and more like a potentially persuasive pitch for black racial superiority aimed at poor "slum" dwellers seething over their societal marginalization. What television in the 1950s did to highlight white-on-black violence (in Selma and Cicero and Birmingham) provided a powerful foreshadowing of what cell phones captured in the 2010s vis-à-vis police violence. This media provided the evidence necessary to help alter, or potentially alter, dispositions toward race and the state in ways that sent people into the streets.

The power of the Nation's message was that it challenged the state's monopoly on violence by asserting that blacks embodied goodness. Black spiritual equality meant that blacks had a divine right to physically defend themselves against state-endorsed violence. The Nation's ontological narrative of racial origin and Godly salvation was necessary in order for Muslims to begin to rebuild their identities and sense of purpose outside the oppressive racial frameworks that dominated and continue to dominate how Americans express their sense of belonging—a belonging that is always in some mode of flux. As one of Rouse's Sunni Muslim interlocutors, a man in his late fifties, related back in 1990, "I cut my teeth on the Nation of Islam." For him, the teachings of the Honorable Elijah Muhammad freed him from self-hate such that he was able to embrace what he saw as the more mature truths to be found in "orthodox" Islam.

The contemporary African American Muslim community has been able to use its unique approach to racial justice during the civil rights era as proof of Islam's fungibility, expansiveness, and progressive possibilities. Being read by others as always already feminist and progressive, African American women in particular have a unique position within the *ummah*. They are able to speak against the types of discourses that Lila Abu-Lughod writes about in *Do Muslim Women Need Saving?* that render Muslim women, without exception, victims of male patriarchy. Unfortunately, at the same time, many African American Muslims have found that they are not taken seriously by immigrant Muslims of different races and ethnicities. In response, African American Muslims have used media to prove their religious bona fides and their authority as scholars and practitioners of the faith—both to other Americans and to other Muslims.

Audience presumptions that all African American Muslims are relatively recent converts and therefore less knowledgeable about the faith, or that they practice some wildly unorthodox form of Islam, mean that media producers must employ signifying strategies that mark the speaker simultaneously as religiously orthodox and as African American. Embracing Islam as the spiritual instantiation of black political progressivism means that how African Americans read the Qur'an and hadith, and interpret its value for other believers, is informed by a kind of discursive synthesis that includes elements of socialism and "black power" added to a base of American individualism and multiculturalism. Engaging Muslim media, it is difficult to know if one is hearing/reading/seeing a religious discussion framed politically or a political discussion framed religiously. This follows a long tradition of blurred, even unintelligible, distinctions between "the secular" and "the religious" within African American Christianity, Judaism, and Islam.

While mass-mediated representations of Islam for non-Muslims are important, the vast majority of African American Muslim media, including documentaries, journals, books, hip-hop songs, and blogs, is used to generate an internal dialogue about how to properly interpret and practice the faith. Intertextual signifiers that allude to diverse historical, religious, and political narratives are used to make claims about what religious dispositions and political subjectivities are in keeping with religious orthopraxy. Everything from representations of how to live one's life, including advice on how to cope with marriage difficulties, to analyses of President Obama's presidency are tied symbolically or explicitly to traditional forms of Islamic reasoning.

Within this media, religion trumps race as the defining identity. At the same time, however, race cannot be ignored. What we find is that racial discourses wend their way through African American Muslim media, picking up threads of still-unfinished conversations about exclusions and slights big and small, historical and contemporary, institutional and representational. In other words, while there are no particular demands on African American Muslim media when it comes to how one should represent or be disposed toward blackness, race and racism are rarely more than one step removed from any explicit topic at hand. Cooking advice pivots on the specificities of soul food, fashion focuses on the particularities of the black female body, gendered *ayat* and hadith link to black masculinities, hip-hop links to urban empowerment and discourses traceable to the Nation of Islam—all with a simmering recognition of how race and racism explain black denigration.

Liberation, as defined by African American Muslim communities, requires seeing past the discourses and commonsense renderings of the world nourished by American and European imperialism. Confusing a racial identity with a religious essence means that one misses the point of being Muslim. Stripping race of its power, or essentially freeing a Muslim from a sense that he or she needs to react to racialized sleights, is a transformation that comes with conversion or, if born into the faith, further education. Cultivating this disposition toward seeing beyond race is nurtured by the community, not surprisingly, through African American media and specifically African American Muslim media. Importantly, refusing to frame commentary in explicitly racial terms becomes part of a blogger's or rapper's proof of religious commitment. But while race is still signified in Muslim media and is treated as politically meaningful, it must simultaneously be disavowed by anyone who truly understands Islam.

Representing religious authority differs for women and men. For Muslim women, iconographically signifying knowledge of Islam often entails the use of *hijab*. In keeping with this signifying aesthetic, the cover image for *Azizah* magazine always includes the photo of a woman wearing a headscarf. The cover model is usually a powerful Muslima whose story is featured between articles about eating, fashion, and Qur'anic exegesis. For African American men, on the other hand, a beard, *kufi*, and *shalwar kameez* (traditional South Asian garb of various kinds) signify commitment, but do not necessarily give them the full authority and status to speak for the community. Black men who dress in Muslim-identified clothing are thought to be underemployed, politically radical, and/or poor interpreters of the faith. A Muslim brother in a three-piece business suit and well-groomed beard, or no beard, on the other hand, often commands more respect. Employing the proper gendered signifiers in the media is only the first step toward being taken seriously. The authority to speak about faith and politics is earned based on a complex algorithm that includes internal consistency of message and life choices, accuracy of religious information, racial sincerity, creativity, intelligence, and aesthetics.

It is important not to overstate the gender differences, but generally men tend to assert themselves in ongoing public debates either directly or obliquely while women tend to narrate their religious beliefs and practices by embedding those pronouncements within personal stories. Neither of these descriptions fits perfectly, but a person's gender influences what he or she says and is are allowed to say, as well as affecting how he or she is allowed to say it in the context of an ever-evolving African American Muslim community—a community that mobilizes media-making as constitutive of its religious identity and proselytizing mission.

The question of what is being redeemed, and to what ultimate end, can become quite complex when examining the media production of black religious communities, especially when the community consists of Hebrew Israelites, a group with an origin story that is imagined to differ rather profoundly from standard histories of Northern Africa, the Middle East, or the United States. Hebrew Israelites intentionally rupture normative narratives of black exclusion to produce a deeply empowering and unconventional kind of liberation. Any engagement with African American investments in "Hebrewism" must be predicated on an appreciation of its variously pitched racial commitments to a reconfiguration of community and political possibility. This "Hebrewism" is defined in contradistinction to rather unflattering characterizations of "religion" and the superficiality of strictly religious practices. Israelites specifically call their belief in African Americans' genealogical connections to ancient Hebrews (and the behavioral imperatives that flow from that fact) a "lifestyle," not a religion. Indeed, the very naming of their project as religious (the reduction of their goals to the institutionalizations of religious denominations) would be deemed inadequate and even offensive to many Hebrew Israelites. Moreover, they also contend that Christianity, Islam, and Judaism (which they distinguish from Israelite identity) are all responsible for the violent conflicts in the region. This distinction between their "cultural practices" and others' "religious" ones is meant to disparage the kind of compartmentalization of spiritual commitments that most organized religions are assumed to exemplify.

The African Hebrew Israelites' ability to sustain a five-continent, transnational community of believers is an important element in the history of diasporic longings and the power of new media technologies, both of which help to keep the far-flung nodes of their global network together. Sustaining religious communities through historically, politically, and religiously elaborated storytelling would be impossible without mass media technology—technology quite specifically put in service of the reclamation of Africana identity, humanity, and citizenship. So, even as one focuses analytical energy on unpacking black Hebrews' larger cosmological universe, one is forced to address the group's sophisticated use of media as a sociopolitical and organizing tool. For instance, their Ministry of (Divine) Information" (MOI) in Southern Israel is a full-fledged production facility and media archive consisting of thousands of hours of footage, produced by the community itself or recorded from cable broadcasts. The archive also contains hundreds of documentaries, fictional films, and recorded news programs that speak to many aspects of the Hebrew Israelites' social and spiritual claims. The MOI's accumulation and housing of this material in a village compound in southern Israel serves as a model for archiving and disseminating media in their satellite communities around the world, as well as being a model for how to deploy mass media (specifically film, television, and the Internet) to make sense of (and circulate) their beliefs. They effectively forge a political (even when explicitly disavowed in such terms) and transnational brand of spiritualized racial subjectivity that is in critical and convergent conversation with the forms of televisual spirituality that black Christians and Muslims deploy.

And all of this media work is in service to the idea that their central goal is to challenge a grand lie, a global conspiracy that begins with the discursive and geopolitical construction of the "Middle East" and is physically realized in construction of the Suez Canal, which tries to breathe life, they argue, into the claim that Israel is not a part of the African continent. The reason why authentic black Hebrews/Jews seem so unthinkable to so many people, saints argue, is an outgrowth of such conspiratorial fictions that make Jewishness normatively white and that disconnect Israel from the continent of Africa, even though it "rests squarely on Africa's tectonic plate," as Sar Ahmadiel, the community's Minister of Information, says time and again.

The notion of "soul citizenship" (as Fran Markowitz, Sara Helman and Dafna Shir-Vertesh lay out their discussion of "Black Hebrews" and the Israeli state) is a potentially useful way to talk about how African Americans have dealt with the fact of being excluded from the body-politic in ways that pivot on existential and immaterial responses as much as traditional political agitation and activism.[7] It is the kind of subject position that might be necessary in the context of the distinction Devon Carbado makes between American citizenship, a technical and mostly bureaucratic category that is incredibly politicized vis-à-vis immigration issues but less so vis-à-vis non-Latino/a black subjects, and American identity, which pivots on a recognition that being fully American means understanding the racial logic that produces a hierarchy of citizenship and learning to treat citizens differently based on race—and increasingly religion (the latter, only accelerated after 9/11).

Final Reflections

Race and religion have been central themes in anthropology since its founding as a discipline, but the decidedly contemporary nature of electronic mediation is relatively new to formal anthropological debates. A discussion about how race, religion, and media can be constructively theorized together can help us to think about how "value" is produced both within the field of anthropology and in the field-sites within which anthropologists conduct research. The idea of "value" is built upon the appreciation of difference, but it is impossible, as David Graeber reminds us, without an equally fundamental sameness to ground the comparison/hierarchy.[8] Race and religion (like, say, economics and art) are examples of how we create not just wealth, markets or masterpieces, but human beings themselves, in their interconnected manifestations. This is a point that Graeber also hammers home in his work, especially *Toward an Anthropological Theory of Value*, even if he does not spend much time on race as a specific form of sociocultural valuation. Race and religion say a lot about the kinds of humans we imagine ourselves to be, the kinds we produce and reproduce, even as we maintain that a certain version of enlightened secular modernity is predicated on the transcendence of seemingly shoddy and atavistic forms of sociality such as religious community and racial affinity, forms inescapably constituted through the circulation of electronic media technology.

The stories of black Christians, Muslims, and Israelites tell us—in ways that are sometimes quite similar and at other times irreconcilably discrepant—how the systematically marginalized make normative claims about a fuller and more inclusive humanity than others have been willing to concede. And such claims are increasingly circulating in and through forms of electronic mass mediation that impact both the speaking subjects themselves and the modes of communicative possibility that such stories require and reconfigure.

NOTES

INTRODUCTION

1   *Plessy v. Ferguson*, 163 US 537 (1896).

2   Ibid., and Bernstein, "*Plessy v. Ferguson.*"

3   Genovese, *Roll, Jordan, Roll*, 214.

4   Douglass, *The Narrative of the Life of Frederick Douglass*; Washington, *Up From Slavery*; Du Bois, *The Souls of Black Folk*; Locke, *The Negro*; Klotman and Cutler, *Struggles for Representation*; Gates, *The Slave Narratives*.

5   West, "The New Cultural Politics of Difference."

6   Hall, "What Is This 'Black' in Black Popular Culture?"

7   Frankenberg, "Local Whitenesses, Localizing Whiteness, Whiteness," 5.

8   Bonilla-Silva, *Racism without Racists*.

9   Wade, *A Troublesome Inheritance*.

10 Walker, *David Walker's Appeal*.

11 Jones, *The Known World*.

12 Douglas, *Purity and Danger*.

13 Walker, *David Walker's Appeal*; *Muhammad Speaks*.

14 While Mississippi did not fly the Confederate flag, its state flag did contain an image of the Confederate flag, and voters in 2015 fought to keep their flag. Backlashes against antiracism continue to be responsible for the temporized pacing of reform.

15 Clarke and Thomas, *Globalization and Race*, 188–205.

16 Malcolm X's famous poetic typology, house versus field negro, resonated with an existing tension between black reformers, often referred to as the "black bourgeoisie" and/or "assimilationists" and "black radicals"/"revolutionaries" (sometimes glossed as "separatists" or "supremacists"). Of course, the "peculiar institution" has long been a euphemism for chattel slavery in the United States.

17 Transcript of speech delivered by Malcolm X at Michigan State University on January 23, 1963. The speech was filmed and an excerpt of that film is embedded in the Al Qaeda video referenced in the text.

18 Jackson, *Real Black*.

19 "Al Qaeda Leader on Obama's Victory.".

20 Film director Quentin Tarantino deploys the same house negro/field negro dichotomy in *Django Unchained* (2012). The Samuel L. Jackson character, "Stephen," identifies with his sociopathic master "Monsieur" based on the favors Stephen

receives for his loyalty and fierce control over the field slaves. For Tarantino, this dichotomous trope is explanation enough for why Stephen wants Django dead.

21 Legal scholar Jack M. Balkin in *Constitutional Redemption: Political Faith in an Unjust World* asks similar questions about how historical narratives impact how we interpret the Constitution. He argues that the indeterminacy of how we read the founding documents is related to the numerous interpretations of the stories we associate with legal reformation: "There are stories of icons (the Minutemen, the Pioneers, Rosa Parks), of events (the Revolution, the Civil War, the New Deal), of persons (Abraham Lincoln, Susan B. Anthony, Martin Luther King), of achievements (the Voting Rights Act, Social Security, the "Winning" of the West)" (4).

22 A "birther" was someone who did not believe that Barack Obama was born in the United States and was therefore an illegitimate president.

23 Notably an American citizenship that Devon Carbado distinguishes from full American identity. See Carbado and Gulati, *Acting White?*.

24 One example, it seems, of the kind of "embedded concept"—in this instance, religiously inflected calls for secularist reform—that can be compared across time and space, between and among different social groups.

25 Asad, *Formations of the Secular*, 146.

26 Institutional racism challenged the United States' sense of itself in ways that mirror how the Dreyfus Affair in the late nineteenth and early twentieth century challenged France's sense of its own political rationality. The media also played a role in impassioning the mob either with anti-Semitic fervor or anticorruption fervor in ways that speak to the role of media in either inflaming or pushing back against racial instinct in the United States.

27 Burkett, *Black Redemption*.

28 Ibid., 8.

29 Frederick, *Between Sundays*.

30 Du Bois, *The Talented Tenth*.

31 Williams, *Enough*.

32 Lewis, *La Vida*.

33 Alexander, *The New Jim Crow*; Cohen, *The Boundaries of Blackness*.

34 It may be the case that Obama was illegible even to himself given that he refused to lean on any iconic figures for his authority. Instead, he relied on the fact that he was elected by a majority of citizens and his sense that people are reasonable. All other presidents have relied on the traditional authority of white men. Obama had no such authority, and he suffered during his presidency as a result.

35 In the summer of 2013, on television Cornel West called President Obama "a global George Zimmerman." Zimmerman, a white man, was acquitted of killing an unarmed black teenager. Spradley, "Cornel West: 'Obama is a Global George Zimmerman.'"

36 For instance, in Gordon, *Bad Faith and Antiblack Racism* and also *Existentia Africana*.

37 Bourdieu, *Outline of a Theory of Practice*, 72–95.

38 De Certeau, "Reading as Poaching," in *The Practice of Everyday Life*.

39 Rouse, "If She's a Vegetable, We'll Be Her Garden."

40 Clegg, "The Knowledge of Self and Others," 42.

41 McLuhan, "The Medium is the Message," in *Understanding Media: The Extensions of Man*, 23–35, 63–67.

42 McLuhan et al.

43 Tapper, *In the Blood*.

44 Walker, *David Walker's Appeal*.

CHAPTER 1. BLACK CRISTIAN REDEMPTION

1 King, *Why We Can't Wait*, ix. To illustrate the urgent need for direct action, King invokes the imagery of these two young people's lives to expose poverty that still plagued African Americans in the rural South and in the urban North one hundred years after the signing of the Emancipation Proclamation. The entrenchment of poverty meant that blacks were still not free. The Civil Rights struggle was intended to bring about social, economic, and political freedom. Epigraphs from Evans, *The Burden of Black Religion*, 5, and Jackson, *Islam and the Blackamerican*, 31.

2 King, *Why We Can't Wait*, 90.

3 Amos 5:24, New International Version.

4 Alexander, *The New Jim Crow*.

5 Weber, *The Protestant Ethic and the Spirit of Capitalism*.

6 Lincoln and Mamiya, *The Black Church in the African American Experience*.

7 Baer and Singer, *African American Religion*.

8 McRoberts, *Streets of Glory*.

9 Equiano, *The Interesting Narrative of the Life of Olaudah Equiano*; Jacobs, *Incidents in the Life of a Slave Girl*; Douglass, *Narrative of the Life of Frederick Douglass*.

10 Conflicts within white Methodist and Baptist organizations over the legitimacy of slavery existed throughout the nineteenth century. In 1844 the Methodist Episcopal Church split over the issue with the establishment of the Methodist Episcopal Church, South. The following year, northern and southern Baptists split with the establishment of the Southern Baptist Convention.

11 Senna, *The Black Press and the Struggle for Civil Rights*, 16.

12 Ibid.

13 Ibid., 37.

14 Du Bois, *The Souls of Black Folk*. See discussion of "double consciousness," DuBois's historic articulation of blacks wrestling with being both African and American.

15 E. Franklin Frazier coined the term "nation within a nation" to describe the many tentacles of the black church that worked to secure rights and opportunities for blacks, long denied them by the state and other civic and social organizations:

education, social outlet, political power, burial rights, bank loans for building homes and businesses, along with spiritual sustenance. See Frazier, *The Negro Church*.

16 *New Orleans Times*, July 31, 1866; *Daily Picayune*, July 31, 1866

17 See Giddings, *Ida: A Sword among Lions*.

18 Martin, *Preaching on Wax*.

19 Ibid., 42.

20 Ibid., 43.

21 Ibid., 61.

22 Ibid., 155.

23 Ibid.

24 McGuire, *At the Dark End of the Street*.

25 Savage, *Broadcasting Freedom*.

26 Similarly, in his biography on Robert F. Williams, Timothy Tyson explores the ways in which Williams's articulation of "armed self-reliance" offered a counter-narrative to the nonviolent message of the Christian-led Civil Rights movement. After fleeing the United States for Cuba in the 1960s, Williams's show, "Radio Free Dixie," continued to be broadcast from coast to coast and as far away as China. In the examples presented by both Savage and Tyson, radio in the early part of the twentieth century proves central in narrating and constructing a progressive black movement. Tyson, *Radio Free Dixie*.

27 Torres, *Black, White, and in Color*, 26.

28 Marsh, *God's Long Summer*.

29 Torres, *Black, White, and in Color*, 6.

30 Acham, *Revolution Televised*, 28.

31 Ibid.; Torres, *Black, White, and in Color*.

32 See Luker, *The Social Gospel*, 30–56.

33 Dupont, *Mississippi Praying*, 9.

34 Ibid., 16.

35 Ibid., 17.

36 King, "Letter from Birmingham City Jail," in *Why We Can't Wait*, 77–100.

37 Voskuil, "The Power of the Air," 85–86. Voskuil cites Murch, *Cooperation without Compromise*, 78–79.

38 Dochuk, *From Bible Belt to Sunbelt*, 99.

39 Lynerd, *Republican Theology*, 160.

40 Walton, *Watch This!*, 73.

41 Frederick, Interview with Rev. Frederick Eikerenkoetter on May 5, 2005, Bal Harbour, Florida.

42 Frederick, *Between Sundays*; Harrison, *Righteous Riches*; Mitchem, *Name It and Claim It?*; Lee, *T. D. Jakes*; Billingsley, *It's a New Day*; Walton, *Watch This!*; Tucker-Worgs, *The Black Megachurch*; Mumford, *Exploring Prosperity Preaching*; Moultrie, "Between the Horny and Holy." A special edition of *Pneuma*, edited by Jona-

than Walton, addresses the questions of religion, media, and Afro-Protestantism. Walton, "Will the Revolution be Televised?"

43 Walton, *Watch This!*, 15.

CHAPTER 2. RACIAL REDEMPTION

1 Clegg, "Public Enemy," in *An Original Man*, 88–108.
2 Much of the contemporary condemnation is directed at Louis Farrakhan, who revived the Nation of Islam in 1978 after it transitioned to Sunni Islam in 1975. This chapter does not focus on Farrakhan's Nation of Islam.
3 Members were forbidden to carry firearms.
4 Marable, *Living Black History*, 154.
5 King, "Letter from Birmingham City Jail," in *Why We Can't Wait*.
6 Charles L. Zelden, *Thurgood Marshall: Race, Rights, and the Struggle for a More Perfect Union*, 115. His words about the Nation of Islam were delivered in a speech at Princeton University, October 1959. Nasser and Malcolm X publicly supported one another around Islamic and Pan Africanist causes.
7 Ibid.
8 The idea that Christians were accommodating and Muslims were hardline was more a perception than a fact. The house negro versus field negro distinction did similar work, which was to name how differently each group was positioned with respect to power and tools for resisting that power. Many converts to the Nation did not have the opportunities open to Thurgood Marshall, who had access to an excellent education.
9 Rouse, "African American Muslims."
10 Wells-Barnett, "How Enfranchisement Stops Lynching." In 1944 Gunnar Myrdal, with the help of his research associate Ralphe Bunche, described it similarly as "the Negro problem." Myrdal, *An American Dilemma*.
11 Wells-Barnett, "How Enfranchisement Stops Lynching."
12 Ibid., 43, 45.
13 Silverstein, "Language Structure and Linguistic Ideology"; Woolard, "Introduction: Language Ideology as a Field of Inquiry," 47.
14 Shaw, *Pygmalion*.
15 Alim and Smitherman, *Articulate while Black*.
16 Woolard, Introduction, 8.
17 Lehmann, *The Promised Land*; Wilkerson, *The Warmth of Other Suns*.
18 Muhammad, "Prophet Fard Muhammad Is Our Deliverer by Prophecy of the Bible and Quran," and "A Warning to the Black Man of America." "No longer are we in bondage of ignorance of that which we originally possessed. The dead are rising, the sick are being healed, yea, the blind are seeing, the deaf are hearing and the prisoners are being freed; because our SAVIOUR is in the midst of us and is doing great things."
19 Muqaddin, *City of Muslims*.

20 Kristeva, *Powers of Horror*, 128.

21 Ibid., 206. "A language of abjection of which the writer is both subject and victim, witness and topple. Toppling into what? Into nothing more than the effervescence of passion and language we call style, where any ideology, thesis, interpretation, mania, collectivity, threat, or hope become drowned."

22 With respect to Elijah Muhammad's influence on social dispositions and feelings about the self, "We now have a yardstick by which to measure our actions" is how Sister Evelyn X describes this "Divine Guidance" in the Nation of Islam's newspaper *Muhammad Speaks* (Published in a section entitled, "What Islam Has Done for Me," the article is entitled "Islam Provides New Direction for Black People," May 17, 1968, p. 25).

23 Genovese, *Roll, Jordan, Roll*.

24 Bacon, "The History of *Freedom's Journal*," 4.

25 Walker, *David Walker's Appeal*.

26 "'Muslims' Riot: Cultist Killed, Policeman Shot." *Los Angeles Times*, April 28, 1926.

27 Bacon, "The History of *Freedom's Journal*," 4. *Freedom's Journal* (1827–1829) was published by two free-born African Americans, Pastor Samuel Cornish and Bowdoin College graduate John B. Russwurm, both of New York City.

28 *Freedom's Journal* was in keeping with the times. The first periodical dedicated to labor issues began in 1927, *Journeyman Mechanic's Advocate*, and the first paper dealing with Native American issues began in 1928, *Cherokee Phoenix*.

29 Green, *Selling the Race*.

30 Bacon, "The History of *Freedom's Journal*," 5

31 Russworm ultimately decided that citizenship and equality were not possible for blacks in the United States and eventually moved to Liberia, where he taught and continued to publish.

32 Walker, *David Walker's Appeal*, 1.

33 "Comparing our miserable [founding] fathers, with the learned philosophers of Greece, [Mr. Jefferson] says: '[A]mong the Romans, their slaves were often their rarest artists. They excelled too, in science, insomuch as to be usually employed as tutors to their master's children; Epictetus, Terence and Phaedrus, were slaves,— but they were of the race of whites. It is not their *condition* then, but *nature*, which has produced the distinction.'" (Walker, *David Walker's Appeal*, 15).

34 Walker, *David Walker's Appeal*, 75; "To my no ordinary astonishment, [a] Reverend gentleman got up and told us (coloured people) that slaves must be obedient to their masters—must do their duty to their masters or be whipped . . . to hear such preaching from a minister of my Master, whose very gospel is that of peace and not of blood and whips . . . Perhaps they will laugh at or make light of this; but I tell you Americans! that unless you speedily alter your course, *you* and your *Country are gone! ! ! ! !*" (Walker, *Walker's Appeal*, 39).

35 Ibid.

36 Garrison resolution presented before the Massachusetts Anti-Slavery Society in 1843. See Merrill, *Against Wind and Tide*, 205. "Agreement from hell," is taken

from the Bible when the prophet Isaiah argues against political compromise. Balkin, *Constitutional Redemption*, 5.

37 Balkin, *Constitutional Redemption: Political Faith in an Unjust World*, 6.

38 Genovese, *Roll, Jordan, Roll*, 27.

39 Isaiah Berlin used the terms positive versus negative liberty to capture the relationship between constraints and freedom, described by scholars from the Enlightenment (Hobbes) to the present, including Saba Mahmood in her work on Muslim women in Egypt. Berlin, "Two Concepts of Liberty," in *Four Essays on Liberty*.

40 In many ways, the Nation of Islam replicated the mission and strategy for racial uplift of Marcus Garvey's United Negro Improvement Association, whose motto was "One God! One Aim! One Destiny!"

41 Fauset, *Black Gods of the Metropolis*.

42 *The Hate that Hate Produced* (1959), transcribed in Special Agent in Charge New York to Director of the FBI.

43 Ibid., 20.

44 Bakhtin, "Discourses in the Novel," in *The Dialogic Imagination*, 271.

45 Silverstein, "The Uses and Utility of Ideology: A Commentary," 129.

46 Foucault, *Power/Knowledge: Selected Interviews and Other Writings: 1972–1977*.

47 Omi and Winant, *Racial Formations in the United States*.

48 Kelley, "Playing for Keeps."

49 Arendt, *The Origins of Totalitarianism*.

50 Bakhtin, "Discourses in the Novel," 353–54.

51 Hill, *The Marcus Garvey and Universal Negro Improvement Association Papers*.

52 "'Muslims' Riot: Cultist Killed, Policeman Shot."

53 Lévi-Strauss, "Linguistics and Anthropology," in *Structural Anthropology*.

54 "'Muslims' Riot: Cultist Killed," 2.

55 "Muslim Leader Accuses Police of Murder."

56 Lévi-Strauss, "Linguistics and Anthropology," 67–80.

57 *City of Muslims*, minutes 7:09–7:19.

58 Weber, *The Sociology of Religion*; Giddens, *Central Problems in Social Theory*.

59 Marable, *Malcolm X*, 274.

60 *Muhammad Speaks*, March 5, 1965, 3.

61 Clegg, *An Original Man*; Haley, *The Autobiography of Malcolm X*; Marable, *Malcolm X*; Curtis, *Black Muslim Religion in the Nation of Islam*.

62 Evanzz, *The Messenger*.

63 Marable, *Manning Marable on Malcolm X*.

64 *Muhammad Speaks*, May 20, 1966, 7.

65 Ibid., August 15, 1969.

66 Ibid.

67 "Again West Learns Aid or No Aid Egypt Runs Egypt," 2.

68 In the wake of the criticism, in 1959 Malcolm X started a paper called *Messenger Magazine*. The magazine quickly failed for reasons that are unclear, but subse-

quently *Muhammad Speaks*, a new version of the *Final Call to Islam* was published.

69 *City of Muslims* was produced by Bait-Cal (Black Awareness in Television California), which also operated Muslim News Magazine Television Network, which streams online.

70 We focus on *City of Muslims* because Carolyn Rouse conducted fieldwork in Los Angeles in the 1990s and taught math a Sister Clara Muhammad School, which is profiled in the film. She also spent time with a number of the subjects in the film.

71 Muqqaddin, *City of Muslims*; quotation slightly edited for clarity. The tone at the end has the quality of a wink. Ali is speaking to a black female reporter with a headscarf.

72 ITV Sport Channel, "Muhammad Ali Interview."

73 Quote taken from *PBS Religion and Ethics Newsweekly* show, March 28, 2003, Bob Abernethy.

74 "African-American Muslims' Views on Iraq War."

75 Ibid.

76 Taha, "Muslims in Oakland Protest Showing of *She's Gotta Have It*."

CHAPTER 3. DIVINE REDEMPTION

1 Ben-Israel, *Physical Immortality*.

2 Of course, Liberia abuts Sierra Leone, which predates it as an emigrationist concoction from the Americas. Another big emigrationist project coming out of the Americas includes the 2,500 or so Rastafari who relocated to Shashame in Ethiopia in 1960. Far fewer of that number have stayed on since then. Bob Marley's song "Exodus" continues to be a symbolic rallying cry for Rastafari to this day.

3 Robinson, *Quitting America*.

4 Cullen, *Color*.

5 For a discussion about the group's use of the term "saint" for its members, see Jackson, *Thin Description*.

6 Patterson, *Slavery and Social Death*. Also, contemporary members of Ben Ammi's Hebrew Israelite group call one another "saints" as a term of endearment and community.

7 "Euro-gentile" is a term coined by Ben Ammi and members of his community as an evocative alternative to "European."

8 Wallace, "Revitalization Movements."

9 There are other, competing theories about the term's etymological roots.

10 Of course, a different interpretation of the Bible's implications would argue that blacks have been brainwashed into accepting Christianity's lies uncritically.

11 Goldenberg, *The Curse of Ham*.

12 Coon, *The Origin of Races*; Baker, *From Savage to Negro*.

13 For more on Clay, see Cobb, *Picture Freedom*.

14 Sahlins, *What Kinship Is—and Is Not*, 68.

15 Ibid.

16 Ibid., 69.

17 Nance, "Mystery of the Moorish Science Temple."

18 Gavriel and HaGadol, *The Impregnable People*, 46.

19 Ibid. Jewtown was the four square-block area bordered on the east by Clinton Street and on the west by Newberry Street, between Roosevelt Road to the north and South Fourteenth Street.

20 As discussed in Landing, *Black Judaism*.

21 Ibid.

22 Brotz called the Israelite community a version of "radical Protestantism." See Brotz, *The Black Jews of Harlem*.

23 Thompson, "Are Black Americans Welcome in Africa?," 48.

24 Ibid.

25 Jackson, *Thin Description*; Parfitt, *Black Jews in Africa and the Americas*.

26 Tudor Parfitt, Ruth Landes, and Israel Gerber might be put in such a camp. Jackson, *Thin Description*, talks about this position.

27 For more of a discussion of these distinctive Hebrew Israelite investments in Africa, see Jackson, *Real Black*.

28 They would also have a complicated relationship to the Israel/Palestine conflict.

29 For more discussion about the airline ticket schemes and other illegal efforts to keep themselves housed in Israel, see Jackson *Thin Description*.

30 Some of these are run out of the MOI proper, and some by individual saints.

CHAPTER 4. REIMAGINED POSSIBILITIES

1 Pseudonyms are used for the names of people and church communities.

2 For a discussion of prosperity gospels and religious media in black religious communities, see Lee, *T. D. Jakes*; Harrison, *Righteous Riches*; Billingsley, *It's a New Day*; Walton, *Watch This!*; Tucker-Worgs, *The Black Megachurch*; and Mumford, *Exploring Prosperity Preaching*.

3 Selected works exploring the global dimensions of the movement include Anderson and Hollenweger, *Pentecostals after a Century*; Dempster, Klaus, and Peterson, *The Globalization of Pentecostalism*; Coleman, *The Globalisation of Charismatic Christianity*; Robbins, "The Globalization of Pentecostal and Charismatic Christianity"; Miller and Yamamori, *Global Pentecostalism*; Noll, *The New Shape of World Christianity*; Asamoah-Gyadu, *Contemporary Pentecostal Christianity*; and Anderson, *To the Ends of the Earth*.

4 Walton, *Watch This!*.

5 For further discussion of the "religious dandy," see Frederick, *Colored Television*, 38. The religious dandy is a take on art historian Richard Powell's discussion of the black dandy of the nineteenth and early twentieth centuries. These were men who, despite their local economic standing, dressed up often with outrageously colorful suits and posh shoes in order to disrupt social expectations of their low status. In

tandem, black religious dandies have disrupted not only social expectations based on race, but also long-standing religious expectations that valorize poverty.

6 Hull, Scott, and Smith, *All the Women Are White, All the Blacks Are Men, but Some of Us Are Brave.*

7 Payne, "Men Led, but Women Organized."

8 Gilkes, "The Politics of 'Silence.'"

9 Higginbotham, *Righteous Discontent.*

10 Ibid., 196.

11 McGuire, *At the Dark End of the Street*, 80.

12 Acham, *Revolution Televised*, 29.

13 Torres, *Black, White, and in Color*, 11.

14 Since the heyday of *The Cosby Show*, Bill Cosby has experienced a monumental fall from grace after several women accused him of sexual assault over the course of his storied career. Their accusations stand in direct contrast to the family man image portrayed by his character Heathcliff Huxtable in the show and suggest behavior far removed from the conservative narrative of personal responsibility he has preached to African Americans.

15 Emerson and Smith, *Divided by Faith*, 21.

16 Einstein, *Brands of Faith*; Hendershot, *Shaking the World for Jesus.*

17 Coleman, "Transgressing the Self," 421.

18 The genre of such testimonies with their emphasis upon what is "real" dominates contemporary television. Although Bynum no longer draws the attention she garnered in the heyday of Shonda's transformation, new television reality shows offer viewers an opportunity to watch in real time the "rags to riches" stories of television ministers who choose to put their lives on display. Reality television, with a focus on individual shortcomings and an attention to redemption in its religious versions, has a marked presence in primetime television. *Preachers of LA, Preachers of Detroit,* and *Preach!* are all versions of this attempt to capture a market for the narrative of religious success through failure and triumph. Yet these forms of media, unlike the televangelist shows, trade in a particular form of made-for-television drama often expressed through interpersonal conflict. Televangelists like Jakes, Bynum, and Meyer, however, narrate their lives as success stories, often including personal failures and extraordinary rebounds.

19 Frankl, *Televangelism*, 129.

20 Harrison, *Righteous Riches*, 27.

21 Walton, "Tax-Exempt? Lifestyles of the Rich and Religious."

22 See Didymus, "Creflo Dollar Responds to Critics Over $65 Million Jet."

23 Harrison, *Righteous Riches*, 156.

CHAPTER 5. RACE, ISLAM, AND LONGINGS FOR INCLUSION

1 Fischer, *The Halal Frontier.*

2 Moll, *Fashioning Faith.*

3 Mandaville, *Transnational Muslim Politics.*

4 Karim, *American Muslim Women*, 29.

5 Farole, "Race Matters."

6 Ibid.

7 See Grewal, *Islam Is a Foreign Country*.

8 Ibid.

9 Appadurai, "Disjuncture and Difference in the Global Cultural Economy.".

10 Ibid., 296.

11 Anthony Appiah takes up these same questions later in *Cosmopolitanism*.

12 Appadurai, "Disjuncture and Difference in the Global Cultural Economy."

13 Umm Adam, "My America Part 3."

14 Tom Boellstorff, *Coming of Age in Second Life*.

15 Ibid., 145.

16 On Tariq Nelson's blog many people wrote favorable responses.

17 Muslimah Media Watch's list missed a number, of websites and some of the websites on the list had already been removed by the time we tried to access them in June 2009. Therefore, an exact number was difficult to determine.

18 The gender and age demographic of Muslim bloggers mirrors that of bloggers generally. See Lawson-Borders and Kirk, "Blogs in Campaign Communication."

19 Usman, "The Shaykh 'n Bake Shame Grenade."

20 Harding, *The Book of Jerry Falwell*.

21 Umm Adam, "It's So Hard to Say Goodbye to Yesterday."

22 Umm Adam, "My America Part 3."

23 Comment by Outcast, "My America Part 3: A Tale of Two Worlds," *Soliloquies of a Stranger*, January 30, 2010, http://ummadam.wordpress.com.

24 See Alim and Geneva Smitherman. *Articulate while Black*; Bourdieu, *Distinction*; Goffman, *The Presentation of Self in Everyday Life*.

25 Lee, "Rise and Fall of the Salafi Movement."

26 Ibid.

27 Appadurai, "Disjuncture and Difference in the Global Cultural Economy."

28 The Prophet Muhammad's last sermon delivered: 632 A.C., 9th day of Dhul al Hijjah, 10 A. H. in the 'Uranah valley of Mount Arafat. Found in Al-Bukhari, Hadith 1623, 1626, 6361; also Sahih of Imam Muslim, Hadith 98; also Imam al-Tirmidhi, Hadith 1628, 2046, 2085; also Imam Ahmed bin Hanbal, Masnud, Hadith 19774.

29 Artist: Native Deen, Album: *The Remedy*, "My Voice My Faith," 2011.

30 Olsson, *The Black Power Mixtape 1967–1975*.

31 Hijrah refers to the journey made in 622 C.E. by the Prophet Muhammad from Mecca, where he and his followers were being persecuted, to Medina. With his followers in Medina, he established the religion as simultaneously a faith and a social and legal framework for maintaining peace.

32 Rueb, "Seeking the Real in a Desert City Known for Artifice."

33 *Re: Constructions: Reflections on Humanity and Media after Tragedy* was a journal website developed in response to the events of September 11, 2001, where Muslims made some of us questioned what in the world we (meaning capitalist consumers)

had created (meaning a world that thinks that the image we project of ourselves through media is real).

34 Žižzek, "Welcome to the Desert of the Real." The article was later incorporated into his book, *Welcome to the Desert of the Real.*

35 Kathiravelu, *Migrant Dubai.*

36 Hannerz, "Scenarios for Peripheral Cultures."

37 Mahmood, *Politics of Piety*, 148.

38 Charles Hirschkind similarly focuses on the use of cassette tapes to cultivate faith dispositions in *The Ethical Soundscape.*

39 Appadurai, "Discussion: Fieldwork in the Era of Globalization."

40 Jackson, *Islam and the Blackamerican.*

41 Ismail, "Flying Rickshaw," 84.

42 Lukose, "Empty Citizenship."

43 Hannerz, *Transnational Connections: Culture, People, Places* (New York: Routledge, 1996), 88.

44 Oldfield, "Citizenship and Community."

45 Rosaldo, "Cultural Citizenship and Educational Democracy."

46 Soysal, *Limits of Citizenship.*

47 Markowitz, Helman, and Shir-Vertesh, "Soul Citizenship."

48 D'Alpoim Guedes et al. "Is Poverty in Our Genes?"; Saletan, "Liberal Creationism."

49 Ismail, "If Malcolm X Had Lived to 85, What Would He Say?"

CHAPTER 6. CITIZENS AS STEWARDS

1 Levin, *Modernity and the Hegemony of Vision.*

2 Scott-Heron, *The Revolution Will Not Be Televised.*

3 Washington, *Medical Apartheid.*

4 Smedley, Stith, and Nelson, *Institute of Medicine (U.S.), Committee on Understanding and Eliminating Racial and Ethnic Disparities in Health Care.*

5 Boellstorff, *Coming of Age in Second Life.*

6 Miller and Slater, *The Internet.*

7 Bessire and Fisher, *Radiofields*; Di Leonardo, "Grown Folks Radio."

8 Horowitz, *The Universal Sense.*

9 Someone from the Strawberry Mansion Civic Association was interviewed and tasked with narrating a version of the recreational history of African Americans in South Philadelphia. Indeed, one of the things they do is take people on tours of that history, highlighting both the need for more outdoor recreation for people of color and the value of disseminating information about important black outdoor spaces that do not usually get publicized by mainstream media outlets.

10 *The Green Hour*, WURD Philadelphia, September 21, 2014.

11 Baudrillard, "The Implosion of Meaning in the Media and the Implosion of the Social in the Masses."

CONCLUSION

1 Mills, *The Racial Contract*.
2 Those shot included the pastor, Reverend Clementa Pinckney, a forty-one-year old South Carolina state senator, Reverend Sharonda Coleman-Singleton (45), Cynthia Hurd (54), Tywanza Sanders (26), Ethel Lance (70), Susie Jackson (87), Depayne Middleton Docton (49), Reverend Daniel Simmons (74), and Myra Thompson (59).
3 Jackson, *Thin Description*.
4 Weber, *The Protestant Ethic and the Spirit of Capitalism*; Alger, *Ragged Dick*.
5 Cone, *A Black Theology of Liberation*.
6 Frederick, *Colored Television*, 41.
7 Markowitz, Helman, and Shir-Vertesh, "Soul Citizenship."
8 Graeber, *Toward an Anthropological Theory of Value*.

BIBLIOGRAPHY

CASES CITED
Plessy v. Ferguson, 163 US 537 (1896).

MAGAZINES
Azizah
Freedom's Journal
Muhammad Speaks
Muslim Journal

PRIMARY AND SECONDARY SOURCES
Abu-Lughod, Lila. *Do Muslim Women Need Saving?* Cambridge: Harvard University Press, 2015.

Acham, Christine. *Revolution Televised: Prime Time and the Struggle for Black Power.* Minneapolis: University of Minnesota Press, 2004.

"African-American Muslims' Views on Iraq War." *Religion & Ethics Newsweekly PBS*, March 28, 2003. www.pbs.org.

"Again West Learns Aid or No Aid Egypt Runs Egypt." *Muhammad Speaks*, March 5, 1965.

Alexander, Michelle. *The New Jim Crow: Mass Incarceration in the Age of Colorblindness.* New York: New Press, 2012.

Alger, Horatio. *Ragged Dick: Or, Street Life in New York with the Boot-Blacks.* New York: Penguin, 1985.

Alim, H. Samy, and Geneva Smitherman. *Articulate while Black: Barack Obama, Language, and Race in the U.S.* New York: Oxford University Press, 2012.

"Al Qaeda Leader on Obama's Victory." Youtube Video. Uploaded November 19, 2008. www.youtube.com.

Anderson, Allen. *To the Ends of the Earth: Pentecostalism and the Transformation of World Christianity.* New York: Oxford University Press, 2013.

Anderson, Allen, and Walter J. Hollenweger, eds. *Pentecostals after a Century: Global Perspectives on a Movement in Transition.* Sheffield, UK: Sheffield Academic Press, 1999.

Appadurai, Arjun. "Disjuncture and Difference in the Global Cultural Economy." *Theory, Culture & Society* 7 (1990): 295–310.

———. "Discussion: Fieldwork in the Era of Globalization." *Anthropology and Humanism* 22, no. 1 (1997): 115–18.

Appiah, Anthony. *Cosmopolitanism: Ethics in a World of Strangers*. New York: W. W. Norton, 2007.

Arendt, Hannah. *The Origins of Totalitarianism*. New York: Harcourt Brace Jovanovich, 1973.

Asad, Talal. *Formations of the Secular: Christianity, Islam, Modernity*. Palo Alto, CA: Stanford University Press, 2003.

Asamoah-Gyadu, J. Kwabena. *Contemporary Pentecostal Christianity: Interpretations from an African Context*. Eugene, OR: Wipf & Stock, 2013.

Bacon, Jacqueline. "The History of *Freedom's Journal*: A Study in Empowerment and Community." *Journal of African American History* 88, no. 1 (Winter 2003): 1–20.

Baer, Hans, and Merrill Singer. *African American Religion: Varieties of Protest and Accommodation*, 2nd ed. Knoxville: University of Tennessee Press, 2002.

Baker, Lee D. *From Savage to Negro: Anthropology and the Construction of Race, 1896–1954*. Berkeley: University of California Press, 1998.

Bakhtin, M. M. "Discourses in the Novel." In *The Dialogic Imagination: Four Essays*, translated by Caryl Emerson and Michael Holquist, edited by Michael Holquist, 269–422. Austin: University of Texas Press, 1981.

Balkin, Jack M. *Constitutional Redemption: Political Faith in an Unjust World*. Cambridge, MA: Harvard University Press, 2011.

Baudrillard, Jean. "The Implosion of Meaning in the Media and the Implosion of the Social in the Masses." In *The Myths of Information: Technology and Postindustrial Culture*, edited by Kathleen Woodward, 137–50. Madison, WI: Coda Press, 1980.

Ben-Israel, Ben Ammi. *Physical Immortality*. Dimona, Israel: Communicators Press, 2013.

Bernstein, Barton J. "*Plessy v. Ferguson*: Conservative Sociological Jurisprudence." *Journal of Negro History* (1963): 196–205.

Berlin, Isaiah. *Four Essays on Liberty*. London: Oxford University Press, 2002.

Bessire, Lucas, and Daniel Fisher. *Radiofields: Anthropology and Wireless Sound in the 21st Century*. New York: New York University Press, 2012.

Billingsley, Scott. *It's a New Day: Race and Gender in the Modern Charismatic Movement*. Tuscaloosa: University of Alabama Press, 2008.

Boellstorff, Tom. *Coming of Age in Second Life: An Anthropologist Explores the Virtually Human*. Princeton, N.J.: Princeton University Press, 2008.

Bonilla-Silva, Eduardo. *Racism without Racists: Color-Blind Racism and the Persistence of Racial Inequality in America*. Lanham, MD: Rowman & Littlefield, 2013.

Bourdieu, Pierre. *Outline of a Theory of Practice*. Cambridge: Cambridge University Press, 1977.

———. *Distinction: A Social Critique of the Judgment of Taste*. London: Routledge, 1984.

Brotz, Howard. *The Black Jews of Harlem: Negro Nationalism and the Dilemmas of Negro Leadership*. Glencoe, IL: Free Press of Glencoe, 1964.

Burkett, Randall K. *Black Redemption: Churchmen Speak for the Garvey Movement*. Philadelphia: Temple University Press, 1978.

Carbado, Devon W., and Mitu Gulati. *Acting White?: Rethinking Race in Post-Racial America*. Oxford: Oxford University Press, 2013.

Clegg, Claude Andrew, III. *An Original Man: The Life and Times of Elijah Muhammad*. New York: St. Martin's Press, 1998.

Cobb, Jasmine Nichole. *Picture Freedom: Remaking Black Visuality in the Early Nineteenth Century*. New York: New York University Press, 2015.

Cohen, Cathy J. *The Boundaries of Blackness: AIDS and the Breakdown of Black Politics*. Chicago: University of Chicago Press, 1999.

Coleman, Simon. *Globalization of Charismatic Christianity: Spreading the Gospel of Prosperity*. New York: Cambridge University Press, 2000.

Coleman, Simon "Transgressing the Self: Making Charismatic Saints." *Critical Inquiry* 35, no.3 (Spring 2009): 417–39.

Cone, James H. *A Black Theology of Liberation*. New York: Orbis Books, 2010.

Coon, Carleton S. *The Origin of Races*. New York: Knopf, 1962.

Cullen, Countee. *Color*. New York: Arno Press, 1969.

Curtis, Edward E. *Black Muslim Religion in the Nation of Islam, 1960–1975*. Durham: University of North Carolina Press, 2006.

D'Alpoim Guedes, Jade, Theodore C. Bestor, David Carrasco, Rowan Flad, Ethan Fosse, Michael Herzfeld, Carl C. Lamberg-Karlovsky, et al. "Is Poverty in Our Genes? A Critique of Ashraf and Galor, 'The 'Out of Africa' Hypothesis, Human Genetic Diversity, and Comparative Economic Development.'" *Current Anthropology* 54, no. 1 (February 1, 2013): 71–79.

De Certeau, Michel. *The Practice of Everyday Life*, translated by Steven Rendall. Berkeley: University of California Press, 1984.

Dempster, Murray W., Byron Klaus, and Douglas Peterson, eds. *The Globalization of Pentecostalism: A Religion Made to Travel*. Oxford: Regnum Books International, 1999.

Didymus, Johnthomas. "Creflo Dollar Responds to Critics Over $65 Million Jet: Wait Until I Need a Billion Dollar Jet to Spread the Gospel to Mars." Inquisitr.com, April 26, 2015.

Di Leonardo, Micaela. "Grown Folks Radio: U.S. Election Politics and a 'Hidden' Black Counter Public." *American Ethnologist* 39, no. 4 (2012): 661–72.

Dochuk, Darren. *From Bible Belt to Sunbelt: Plain-Folk Religion, Grassroots Politics, and the Rise of Evangelical Conservatism*. New York: W.W. Norton, 2011.

Douglas, Mary. *Purity and Danger*. London: Routledge, 1966.

Douglass, Frederick. *Narrative of the Life of Frederick Douglass, an American Slave, Written by Himself*, edited by Benjamin Quarles. Cambridge: Belknap Press, 1960.

Du Bois, W. E. B. *The Souls of Black Folk*. Oxford: Oxford University Press, 1903.

———. *The Talented Tenth*. New York: James Pott, 1903.

Dupont, Carolyn Renée. *Mississippi Praying: Southern Evangelicals and the Civil Rights Movement, 1945–1975*. New York: New York University Press, 2013.

Einstein, Mara. *Brands of Faith: Marketing Religion in a Commercial Age*. New York: Routledge, 2008.

Emerson, Michael O., and Christian Smith. *Divided by Faith: Evangelical Religion and the Problem of Race in America*. Oxford: Oxford University Press, 2000.

Equiano, Olaudah. *The Interesting Narrative of the Life of Olaudah Equiano, Or, Gustavus Vassa, the African*. New York: Broadview Press, 2001.

Evans, Curtis J. *The Burden of Black Religion*. New York: Oxford University Press, 2008.

Evanzz, Karl. *The Messenger: The Rise and Fall of Elijah Muhammad*. New York: Pantheon, 1999.

Farole, Safia. "Race Matters: Colorblind Racism in the Ummah." *Muslimmatters*, February 21, 2011. http://muslimmatters.org.

Fauset, Arthur Huff. *Black Gods of the Metropolis: Negro Religious Cults of the Urban North*. Philadelphia: University of Pennsylvania Press, 1944.

Fischer, Johan. *The Halal Frontier: Muslim Consumers in a Globalized Market*. New York: Palgrave Macmillian, 2011.

"Flogging, Stoning and Illicit Sex: A Look at Hadd Punishments for Adultery and Fornication in Qur'an, Hadith and Islamic Jurisprudence." *Azizah* 3, no. 2 (Fall 2003): 14.

Foucault, Michel. *Power/Knowledge: Selected Interviews and Other Writings: 1972–1977*. Edited by Colin Cordon. New York: Pantheon Books, 1980.

Frankenberg, Ruth. "Local Whitenesses, Localizing Whiteness, Whiteness." In *Essays in Social and Cultural Criticism*, edited by Ruth Frankenberg, 1–33. Durham, NC: Duke University Press, 1997.

Frankl, Razelle. *Televangelism: The Marketing of Popular Religion*. Carbondale: Southern Illinois University Press, 1987.

Frazier, E. Franklin. *The Negro Church*. New York: Schocken Books, 1964.

Frederick, Marla. *Between Sundays: Black Women and Everyday Struggles of Faith*. Berkeley: University of California Press, 2003.

———. *Colored Television: American Religion Gone Global*. Stanford, CA: Stanford University Press, 2016.

Gavriel, Israel, and Odehyah B. HaGadol. *The Impregnable People*. Dimona, Israel: Communicators Press, 1992.

Gates, Henry Louis. *The Slave Narratives*. New York: Signet, 2002.

Genovese, Eugene D. *Roll, Jordan, Roll: The World the Slaves Made*. New York: Vintage, 1976.

Giddens, Anthony. *Central Problems in Social Theory: Action, Structure and Contradiction in Social Analysis*. Berkeley: University of California Press, 1986.

Giddings, Paula. *Ida: A Sword among Lions: Ida B. Wells and the Campaign against Lynching*. New York: Amistad, 2008.

Gilkes, Cheryl T. "The Politics of 'Silence': Dual-Sex Political Systems and Women's Traditions of Conflict in African-American Religion." In *African-American Christianity*, edited byPaul E. Johnson, 80–110. Berkeley: University of California Press, 1994.

Goffman, Erving. *The Presentation of Self in Everyday Life*. New York: Anchor, 1959.

Goldenberg, David. *The Curse of Ham: Race and Slavery in Early Judaism, Christianity, and Islam*. Princeton, NJ: Princeton University Press, 2005.

Gordon, Lewis R. *Bad Faith and Antiblack Racism*. Atlantic Highlands, NJ: Humanities Press, 1995.

———. *Existentia Africana: Understanding Africana Existential Thought*. New York: Routledge, 2000.

Graeber, David. *Toward an Anthropological Theory of Value: The False Coin of Our Own Dreams*. New York: Palgrave Macmillan, 2001.

Green, Adam. *Selling the Race: Culture, Community, and Black Chicago, 1940–1955*. Chicago: University of Chicago Press, 2009.

Grewal, Zareena. *Islam Is a Foreign Country: American Muslims and the Global Crisis of Authority*. New York: New York University Press, 2013.

Haley, Alex. *The Autobiography of Malcolm X: As Told to Alex Haley*. New York: Ballantine, 1965.

Hall, Stuart. "What Is This 'Black' in Black Popular Culture?" In *Stuart Hall: Critical Dialogues in Cultural Studies*, edited by David Morley and Kuan-Hsing Chen, 465–75. London: Routledge, 1999.

Hannerz, Ulf. *Transnational Connections: Culture, People, Places*. New York: Routledge, 1996.

———. "Scenarios for Peripheral Cultures." In *Culture, Globalization and the World-System: Contemporary Conditions for the Representation of Identity*, edited byAnthony D. King, 107–28. Minneapolis: University of Minnesota Press, 1997.

Harding, Susan Friend. *The Book of Jerry Falwell: Fundamentalist Language and Politics*. Princeton, NJ: Princeton University Press, 2000.

Harrison, Milmon. *Righteous Riches: The Word of Faith Movement in Contemporary African American Religion*. New York: Oxford University Press, 2005.

Hendershot, Heather. *Shaking the World for Jesus: Media and Conservative Evangelical Culture*. Chicago: University of Chicago Press, 2010.

Higginbotham, Evelyn Brooks. *Righteous Discontent: The Women's Movement in the Black Baptist Church*. Cambridge, MA: Harvard University Press, 1993.

Hill, Robert A., ed. *The Marcus Garvey and Universal Negro Improvement Association Papers*. Berkeley: University of California Press, 2014.

Hirschkind, Charles. *The Ethical Soundscape: Cassette Sermons and Islamic Counterpublics*. New York: Columbia University Press, 2009.

Horowitz, Seth S. *The Universal Sense: How Hearing Shapes the Mind*. New York: Bloomsbury, 2012.

Hull, Gloria T., Patricia Bell Scott, and Barbara Smith. *All the Women Are White, All the Blacks Are Men, but Some of Us Are Brave: Black Women's Studies*. Old Westbury, NY: Feminist Press, 1982.

Ismail, Maryam. "Flying Rickshaw." *Time Out Dubai* 7, no. 47 (November 22, 2007): 84.

———. "If Malcolm X Had Lived to 85, What Would He Say?" *The National UAE*, May 28, 2010.

ITV Sport Channel. "Muhammad Ali Interview with Ian Wooldridge, 1969." YouTube video. www.youtube.com.

Jackson, John L., Jr. *Real Black: Adventures in Racial Sincerity*. Chicago: University of Chicago Press, 2005.

———. "Gentrification, Globalization, and Georaciality." In *Globalization and Race: Transformations in the Cultural Production of Blackness*, edited by Kamari Maxine Clark and Deborah A. Thomas, 188–205. Durham, NC: Duke University Press, 2006.

———. *Thin Description: Ethnography and the African Hebrew Israelites of Jerusalem*. Cambridge, MA: Harvard University Press, 2013.

Jackson, Sherman. *Islam and the Blackamerican: Looking toward the Third Resurrection*. New York: Oxford University Press, 2005.

Jacobs, Harriet Ann. *Incidents in the Life of a Slave Girl*, edited by Lydia Maria Child. New York: Harcourt Brace Jovanovich, 1973.

Jones, Edward P. *The Known World*. New York: Penerbit Serambi, 2003.

Karim, Jamillah. *American Muslim Women: Negotiating Race, Class, and Gender within the Ummah*. New York: New York University Press, 2008.

Kathiravelu, Laavanya. *Migrant Dubai: Building a Global City*. London: Palgrave Macmillan, 2015.

Kelley, Robin D. G. "Playing for Keeps: Pleasure and Profit on the Postindustrial Playground." In *The House that Race Built*, edited by Wahneema Lubiano, 195–231. New York: Random House, 1997.

King, Martin Luther, Jr. *Why We Can't Wait*. New York: Penguin, 2000 (1963).

Klotman, Phyllis R., and Janet K. Cutler. *Struggles for Representation: African American Documentary Film and Video*. Bloomington: Indiana University Press, 1999.

Knoll, Mark A. *The New Shape of World Christianity: How American Experience Reflects Global Faith*. Downers Grove, IL: InterVarsity Press Academic, 2009.

Kristeva, Julia. *Powers of Horror: An Essay on Abjection*, translated by Leon S. Roudiez. New York: Columbia University Press, 1982.

Landing, James E. *Black Judaism: Story of an American Movement*. Durham, NC: Carolina Academic Press, 2002.

Lawson-Borders, Gracie, and Rita Kirk. "Blogs in Campaign Communication." *American Behavioral Scientist* 49 (2005): 548–59.

Lee, Shayne. *T. D. Jakes: America's New Preacher*. New York: New York University Press, 2005.

Lee, Umar. "Rise and Fall of the Salafi Movement." *Umar Lee: Ahk Love the Correctifier AKA the St. Louis Stranger*, blog, January 28, 2014. umarlee.wordpress.com.

Lehmann, Nicholas. *The Promised Land: The Great Migration and How It Changed America*. New York: Vintage, 1992.

Lévi-Strauss, Claude. "Linguistics and Anthropology." In *Structural Anthropology*, translated by Claire Jacobson and Brooke Grundfest Schoepf, vol. 1, 67–80. New York: Basic Books, 1963.

Levin, David Michael, ed. *Modernity and the Hegemony of Vision*. Berkeley: University of California Press, 1993.

Lewis, Oscar. *La Vida: A Puerto Rican Family in the Culture of Poverty—San Juan and New York*. New York: Random House, 1966.

Lincoln, C. Eric, and Lawrence Mamiya. *The Black Church in the African American Experience*. Durham, NC: Duke University Press, 1990.

Locke, Alain, ed. *The Negro: Voices of the Harlem Renaissance*. New York: Albert & Charles Boni, 1925.

Luker, Ralph E. *The Social Gospel in Black and White: American Racial Reform, 1885–1912*. Chapel Hill: University of North Carolina Press, 1992.

Lukose, Ritty. "Empty Citizenship: Protesting Politics in the Era of Globalization." *Cultural Anthropology* 20, no. 4 (2005): 506–33.

Lynerd, Benjamin T. *Republican Theology: The Civil Religion of American Evangelicals*. New York: Oxford University Press, 2014.

Mahmood, Saba. *Politics of Piety: The Islamic Revival and the Feminist Subject*. Princeton, NJ: Princeton University Press, 2011.

Mandaville, Peter G. *Transnational Muslim Politics: Reimagining the Umma*. New York: Routledge, 2003.

Marable, Manning. *Living Black History: How Reimagining the African-American Past Can Remake America's Racial Future*. New York: Basic Books, 2011.

———. *Malcolm X: A Life of Reinvention*. New York: Viking, 2011.

———. *Manning Marable on Malcolm X: His Message & Meaning*. Westfield, NJ: Zuccotti Park Press, 2012.

Markowitz, Fran, Sara Helman, and Dafna Shir-Vertesh. "Soul Citizenship: The Black Hebrews and the State of Israel." *American Anthropologist* 105, no. 2 (2003): 303–12.

Marsh, Charles. *God's Long Summer: Stories of Faith and Civil Rights*. Princeton, NJ: Princeton University Press, 1997.

Martin, Lerone A. *Preaching on Wax: The Phonograph and the Shaping of Modern African American Religion*. New York: New York University Press, 2014.

McGuire, Danielle. *At the Dark End of the Street: Black Women, Rape, and Resistance—A New History of the Civil Rights Movement from Rosa Parks to the Rise of Black Power*. New York: Alfred A. Knopf, 2010.

McLuhan, Marshall. *Understanding Media: The Extensions of Man*. New York: Signet, 1964.

McLuhan, Marshall, Terrence Gordon, Elena Lamberti, and Dominique Scheffel-Dunand. *The Gutenberg Galaxy: The Making of Typographic Man*. Toronto: University of Toronto Press, 2011.

McRoberts, Omar. *Streets of Glory: Church and Community in a Black Urban Neighborhood*. Chicago: University of Chicago Press, 2005.

Merrill, Walter M. *Against Wind and Tide: A Biography of William Lloyd Garrison*. Cambridge, MA: Harvard University Press, 1963.

Miller, Daniel E. and Don Slater. *The Internet: An Ethnographic Approach*. New York: Berg, 2000.

Miller, Donald E. and Tetsunao Yamamori. *Global Pentecostalism: The New Face of Christian Social Engagement*. Berkeley: University of California Press, 2007.

Mills, Charles Wade. *The Racial Contract*. Ithaca, NY: Cornell University Press, 1997.

Mitchem, Stephanie. *Name It and Claim It?: Prosperity Preaching in the Black Church*. Cleveland: Pilgrim Press, 2007.

Moll, Yasmin. *Fashioning Faith*, produced by Yasmin Moll. Watertown, MA: Documentary Educational Resources, 2009.

Moultrie, Monique. "Between the Horny and Holy: Womanist Sexual Ethics and the Cultural Productions of *No More Sheets*." PhD diss.,Vanderbilt University, 2010.

Muhammad, Elijah. "A Warning to the Black Man of America." *Final Call to Islam*, August 18, 1934.

———. "Prophet Fard Muhammad is Our Deliverer by Prophecy of the Bible and Quran." *Final Call to Islam*, August 18, 1934.

———. "Mr. Muhammad Speaks." *Pittsburgh Courier*, 1956–1975.

———. "The Messenger of Allah Speaks on the Importance of the Muhammad Speaks Newspaper, 1964." *Nation of Islam's Women Committed to Preserving the Truth*. www.noiwc.org.

Mumford, Debra. *Exploring Prosperity Preaching: Biblical Health, Wealth, and Wisdom*. Valley Forge, PA: Judson Press, 2012.

"Muslim Leader Accuses Police of Murder." *Los Angeles Times*, May 5, 1962.

"'Muslims' Riot: Cultist Killed, Policeman Shot." *Los Angeles Times*, April 23, 1962.

Muqaddin, Samir, dir. *City of Muslims*. Los Angeles, CA: Muslim News Media, 2007.

Murch, James DeForest. *Cooperation without Compromise: A History of the National Association of Evangelicals*. Grand Rapids, MI: Eerdmans, 1956.

Myrdal, Gunnar. *An American Dilemma: The Negro Problem and Modern Democracy*. Piscataway, NJ: Transaction, 1995.

Nance, Susan. "Mystery of the Moorish Science Temple: Southern Blacks and American Alter Spirituality in 1920s Chicago." *Religion and American Culture* 12, no. 2 (2002): 123–66.

Native Deen. "My Faith My Voice." Youtube Video. Uploaded September 23, 2010. www.youtube.com.

Oldfield, Adrian. "Citizenship and Community: Civic Republicanism and the Modern World." In *The Citizenship Debates*, edited by Gershon Shafir. Minneapolis: University of Minnesota Press, 1998.

Olsson, Göran Hugo. *The Black Power Mixtape 1967–1975*, produced by Annika Rogell, Joslyn Barnes and Danny Glover. New York: Louverture Films, 2001.

Omi, Michael, and Howard Winant. *Racial Formations in the United States: From the 1960s to the 1990s*. London: Routledge, 1994.

Parfitt, Tudor. *Black Jews in Africa and the Americas*. Cambridge, MA: Harvard University Press, 2013.

Patterson, Orlando. *Slavery and Social Death: A Comparative Study*. Cambridge, MA: Harvard University Press, 1985.

Payne, Charles. "Men Led, but Women Organized: Movement Participation of Women in the Mississippi Delta." In *Women in the Civil Rights Movement: Trailblazers and Torchbearers 1941–1965*, edited by Vicki L. Crawford, Jacqueline Anne Rouse, and Barbara Woods, 1–11. Bloomington: Indiana University Press, 1993.

Robbins, Joel. "The Globalization of Pentecostal and Charismatic Christianity." *Annual Review of Anthropology* 33 (2004): 117–43.

Robinson, Randall. *Quitting America: The Departure of a Black Man from His Native Land*. New York: Dutton, 2004.

Rouse, Carolyn. "Paradigms and Politics: Shaping Health Care Access for Sickle Cell Patients through the Discursive Regimes of Biomedicine." *Culture, Medicine and Psychiatry* 28, no. 3 (2004): 369–99.

———. "If She's a Vegetable, We'll Be Her Garden: Embodiment, Transcendence, and Citations of Competing Metaphors in the Case of a Dying Child." *American Ethnologist* 31, no. 4: 514–529 (2004).

———. "African American Muslims." In *The Handbook of American Islam*, edited by Yvonne Haddad and Jane I. Smith, 87–99. New York: Oxford University Press, 2014.

Rueb, Emily. "Seeking the Real in a Desert City Known for Artifice." *New York Times*, May 18, 2007.

Sahlins, Marshall. *What Kinship Is—and Is Not*. Chicago: University of Chicago Press, 2013.

Saletan, William. "Liberal Creationism." *Slate Magazine*, November 2007.

Savage, Barbara Dianne. *Broadcasting Freedom: Radio, War, and the Politics of Race, 1938–1948*. Chapel Hill: University of North Carolina Press, 1999.

Scott-Heron, Gil. *The Revolution Will Not Be Televised*. New York: Flying Dutchman Records, 1970.

Senna, Carl. *The Black Press and the Struggle for Civil Rights*. New York: Franklin Watts, 1994.

Shaw, George Bernard. *Pygmalion*. New York: Simon and Schuster, 2012.

Silverstein, Michael. "Language Structure and Linguistic Ideology." In *The Elements: A Parasession on Linguistic Units and Levels*, edited by Paul R. Clyne, William F. Hanks, and Carol L. Hofbauer, 193–247. Chicago: Chicago Linguistic Society, 1979.

Silverstein, Michael. "The Uses and Utility of Ideology." In *Language Ideologies: Practice and Theory*, edited by Bambi B. Schieffelin, Kathryn A. Woolard, Paul V. Kroskrity, 123–145. New York: Oxford University Press, 1998.

Smedley, Brian, Adrienne Stith, and Alan Nelson, eds. *Institute of Medicine (U.S.), Committee on Understanding and Eliminating Racial and Ethnic Disparities in Health Care: Unequal Treatment Confronting Racial and Ethnic Disparities in Health Care*. Washington, DC: National Academy Press, 2002.

Soysal, Yasemin Nuhoğlu. *Limits of Citizenship: Migrants and Postnational Membership in Europe*. Chicago: University of Chicago Press, 1994.

"Special Agent in Charge New York to Director of the FBI, July 16, 1959." United States Government Office Memorandum. Columbia University Archives, 105-7809. www.columbia.edu.

Spradley, Jermaine. "Cornel West: 'Obama Is a Global George Zimmerman." *Huffing-ton Post*, July 22, 2013, www.huffingtonpost.com.

Strain, Christopher Barry. *Pure Fire: Self-Defense as Activism in the Civil Rights Era.* Athens: University of Georgia Press, 2005.

Taha, A. W. "Muslims in Oakland Protest Showing of *She's Gotta Have It." Muslim Journal* (1986).

Tapper, Melbourne. *In the Blood: Sickle Cell Disease and the Politics of Race.* Philadelphia: University of Pennsylvania Press, 1999.

Tarantino, Quentin, dir. *Django Unchained.* Hollywood, CA: The Weinstein Company/ Columbia Pictures, 2012.

Thompson, Era Bell. "Are Black Americans Welcome in Africa?" *Ebony*, January 1969, 48.

Torres, Sasha. *Black, White, and in Color: Television and Black Civil Rights.* Princeton, NJ: Princeton University Press, 2003.

Tucker-Worgs, Tamelyn. *The Black Megachurch: Theology, Gender, and the Politics of Public Engagement.* Waco, TX: Baylor University Press, 2011.

Tyson, Timothy. *Radio Free Dixie: Robert F. Williams and the Roots of Black Power.* Chapel Hill: University of North Carolina Press, 2001.

Umm, Adam. "It's So Hard to Say Goodbye to Yesterday." *Soliloquies of a Stranger*, blog, April 14, 2007. http://ummadam.wordpress.com.

———. "My America Part 3: A Tale of Two Worlds." *Soliloquies of a Stranger*, blog, January 30, 2010, http://ummadam.wordpress.com.

Usman, Omar. "The Shaykh 'n Bake Shame Grenade— A Muslim Internet Phenomenon." *Muslimmatters*, August 26, 2013.

Voskuil, Dennis N. "The Power of the Air: Evangelicals and the Rise of Religious Broadcasting." In *American Evangelicals and the Mass Media: Perspectives on the Relationship between American Evangelicals and the Mass Media*, edited by Quentin J. Schultze, 69–95. Grand Rapids, MI: Academic Books, 1990.

Wade, Nicholas. *A Troublesome Inheritance: Genes, Race, and Human History.* New York: Penguin Books, 2014.

Walker, David. "David Walker's Appeal." In *David Walker's Appeal, in Four Articles: Together with a Preamble to the Coloured Citizens of the World, but in Particular, and Very Expressly, to Those of the United States of America*, edited by Sean Wilentz. Revised ed. New York: Hill and Wang, 1995.

Wallace, Anthony. "Revitalization Movements." *American Anthropologist* 58, no. 2 (1956): 264–81.

Walton, Jonathan L. "Tax-Exempt? Lifestyles of the Rich and Religious." *Christian Century*, January 29, 2008.

———. *Watch This!: The Ethics and Aesthetics of Black Televangelism.* New York: New York University Press, 2009.

———. "Will the Revolution be Televised? Preachers, Profits and the 'Post-Racial' Prophetic!" *Pneuma* 33, no. 2 (2011): 175–79.

Washington, Booker T. *Up from Slavery.* Boston: Dover, 1995.

Washington, Harriet A. *Medical Apartheid: The Dark History of Medical Experimentation on Black Americans from Colonial Times to the Present.* New York: Doubleday Books, 2006.

Weber, Max. *The Protestant Ethic and the Spirit of Capitalism*, translated by Talcott Parsons. New York: Routledge, 1992.

———. *The Sociology of Religion.* Boston: Beacon Press, 1993.

Wells-Barnett, Ida B. "How Enfranchisement Stops Lynching." *Original Rights Magazine* 1, no. 4 (1910): 42–53.

West, Cornel. "The New Cultural Politics of Difference." In *The Cornel West Reader*, 119–139. New York: Basic Books, 1999.

Wilkerson, Isabel. *The Warmth of Other Suns: The Epic Story of America's Great Migration.* New York: Vintage, 2011.

Williams, Juan. "Thurgood Marshall—American Revolutionary." *University of Arkansas at Little Rock Law Review* 25 (2003): 443–58.

———. *Enough: The Phony Leaders, Dead-End Movements, and Culture of Failure That Are Undermining Black America—and What We Can Do About It.* New York: Crown Books, 2006.

Woolard, Kathryn Ann. "Introduction: Language Ideology as a Field of Inquiry." In *Language Ideologies: Practice and Theory*, edited by Bambi B. Schieffelin, Kathryn Ann Woolard, and Paul V. Kroskrity, 3–51. New York: Oxford University Press, 1998.

Zelden, Charles L. *Thurgood Marshall: Race, Rights, and the Struggle for a More Perfect Union.* New York: Routledge, 2013.

Žižek, Slavoj. *Welcome to the Desert of the Real.* New York: Verso Books, 2002.

INDEX

Note: page numbers followed by "f" and "n" refer to figures and endnotes, respectively.

Carolyn Moxley Rouse is an anthropologist and author of *Engaged Surrender: African American Women* and *Islam and Uncertain Suffering: Racial Health Care Disparities and Sickle Cell Disease*. Her work explores the intersection of race and inequality.

John L. Jackson, Jr., is Richard Perry University Professor and Dean of the School of Social Policy & Practice at the University of Pennsylvania. He has written several books, including *Thin Description: Ethnography and the African Hebrew Israelites of Jerusalem* and, with Cora Daniels, *Impolite Conversations: On Race, Politics, Sex, Money and Religion*. He is also an ethnographic filmmaker.

Marla F. Frederick is Professor of African and African American Studies and the Study of Religion at Harvard University. An anthropologist whose research focuses on race, religion, and social institutions, she is the author of *Between Sundays: Black Women and Everyday Struggles of Faith* and *Colored Television: American Religion Gone Global*.

CPSIA information can be obtained
at www.ICGtesting.com
Printed in the USA
BVOW08s0218021116
466688BV00001B/20/P